Praise for INFORMative Assessment . . .

INFORMing yourself about formative assessment is one of the most important journeys you can take as a teacher, and I can't think of any better guides for your learning adventure than Jeane Joyner and Mari Muri. Their guidebook is easy to read, with the kind of practical guidance and common-sense advice that can only come from years of experience and study. Enjoy the trip!

—Cathy Seeley, author of *Faster Isn't Smarter: Messages About Math, Teaching, and Learning in the 21st Century*; past president, National Council of Teachers of Mathematics; senior fellow, Charles A. Dana Center, The University of Texas at Austin

Many talk about formative assessment and much research touts its importance, but few have been able to translate the tenets of meaningful formative assessment as effectively as Mari and Jeane do in this wonderfully written and most helpful book. Using a slew of practical examples, classroom vignettes, and student work, the authors bring the powerful ideas of continuously assessing student understanding to life in very accessible ways.

—Steve Leinwand, principal research analyst, American Institutes for Research

Understanding the use and impact of assessments is challenging for many. *INFORMative Assessment* captures the elusive nature and importance of varied assessments beautifully, including the link to curriculum and instruction and the critical role of formative assessment. As schools and school districts transition to the Common Core State Standards and their related assessments, this amazing resource will become an important "use every day" reference!

—Francis (Skip) Fennell, L. Stanley Bowlsbey Professor of Education and Graduate and Professional Studies, McDaniel College, Westminster, Maryland; project director, Elementary Mathematics Specialists and Teacher Leaders Project; past president, National Council of Teachers of Mathematics

In clear, practical terms, the authors show what formative assessment really is and how to implement it in your classroom. The readable style, the examples of student work, and the opportunities for reflection make the use of formative assessment feel doable as well as essential for improving student understanding of mathematics.

—Nancy Teague, grades 4–6 mathematics specialist, Greensboro Day School, North Carolina

(continued)

Continued Praise for **INFORMative Assessment** . . .

Each chapter in *INFORMative Assessment* is a professional development handbook packed with strategies to assist teachers with the tools needed to improve instruction; it's an ideal resource for a district workshop or a college mathematics methods class.

—Audrey Jackson, board of directors (2005–2008), National Council of Teachers of Mathematics; director of professional development, St. Louis Public Schools, St. Louis, Missouri

INFORMative Assessment is a powerful resource for helping districts and teachers move from covering curriculum in their approach to teaching, learning, and assessment to clearly defining learning targets and assessments that inform instruction.

—Sally Alubicki, director of teaching and assessment, West Hartford Public Schools, West Hartford, Connecticut

Getting directly to the heart of the matter, *INFORMative Assessment* illustrates beautifully how to use assessment as a tool to impact instruction rather than as a tool to label and rank.

—Catherine Twomey Fosnot, founding director, Mathematics in the City; coauthor, *Young Mathematicians at Work*; author, *Contexts for Learning Mathematics*

This resource helps teachers use formative assessment to better understand student thinking and plan appropriate instruction; it's an ideal match for today's emphasis on assessment.

—Barbara J. Reys, president, Association of Mathematics Teacher Educators; Distinguished Professor, University of Missouri-Columbia

INFORMative Assessment makes the process of assessment, and the reasons it is critical to student achievement, very clear. It is a wonderful resource for the classroom teacher, as well as teacher leaders looking to build capacity.

—Gail Englert, mathematics department chair, W. H. Ruffner Academy, Norfolk Public Schools, Norfolk, Virginia

Teachers need the support and information that *INFORMative Assessment* so carefully and thoroughly presents, and they need it *right now*.

—Miriam A. Leiva, founding president, TODOS: Mathematics for ALL; Distinguished Professor of Mathematics Emerita, University of NC Charlotte

Good teaching is not following a script; *INFORMative Assessment* takes teachers on a thoughtful, reflective journey to making instruction decisions based on what their students know and still need to learn.

—Kathy Richardson, program director, Math Perspectives; developer, Assessing Math Concepts/AMC Anywhere formative assessments

INFORMative Assessment

[Formative Assessment to Improve **MATH ACHIEVEMENT**]

GRADES K–6

➤ **Jeane M. Joyner**

➤ **Mari Muri**

Foreword by Mary Lindquist

Math Solutions
Sausalito, California, USA

Math Solutions
One Harbor Drive, Suite 101
Sausalito, California, USA 94965
www.mathsolutions.com

Library of Congress Cataloging-in-Publication Data
Joyner, Jeane M.
  INFORMative assessment : formative assessment to improve math achievement, grades K–6 / Jeane M. Joyner, Mari Muri.
    p. cm.
  Summary: "Teachers can change classroom practices so that the information they gather through formative assessment
    strategies (good questions; written, oral, and self-assessments; mathematically rich tasks) supports their instructional
    decisions and leads to greater student learning and long-term success"-- Provided by publisher.
  Includes bibliographical references and index.
  ISBN 978-1-935099-19-2 (alk. paper)
  1.   Mathematics—Study and teaching (Elementary) I. Muri, Mari. II. Title.
  QA135.6.J69 2011
  372.7—dc22   2011001450

Editor: Jamie Ann Cross
Production: Melissa L. Inglis-Elliott
Cover design: Wanda Espana/Wee Design
Interior design: Susan Barclay/Barclay Design
Photo Credits: Tery Gunter; Bill Lovin, Marinegrafics; Margaret Jeane Malone; Katherine Mawhinney
Composition: MPS Limited, a Macmillan Company

Printed in the United States of America on acid-free paper
15 14 13 12   ML   2 3 4 5

A Message from Math Solutions

We at Math Solutions believe that teaching math well calls for increasing our understanding of the math we teach, seeking deeper insights into how students learn mathematics, and refining our lessons to best promote students' learning.

Math Solutions shares classroom-tested lessons and teaching expertise from our faculty of professional development consultants as well as from other respected math educators. Our publications are part of the nationwide effort we've made since 1984 that now includes

- more than five hundred face-to-face professional development programs each year for teachers and administrators in districts across the country;
- professional development books that span all math topics taught in kindergarten through high school;
- videos for teachers and for parents that show math lessons taught in actual classrooms;
- on-site visits to schools to help refine teaching strategies and assess student learning; and
- free online support, including grade-level lessons, book reviews, inservice information, and district feedback, all in our Math Solutions Online Newsletter.

For information about all of the products and services we have available, please visit our website at *www.mathsolutions.com.* You can also contact us to discuss math professional development needs by calling (800) 868-9092 or by sending an email to *info@mathsolutions.com.*

We're always eager for your feedback and interested in learning about your particular needs. We look forward to hearing from you.

We are grateful to our husbands
who patiently supported us through the many hours of creating this book
and to our grandchildren
who are daily reminders of the importance of good teachers.

Contents

Reflections

Contents: An INFORMative Assessment Journey Perspective

Where We've Been . . . Where We're Going

Moving from . . .	Chapter	Moving toward . . .
Teaching primarily page-by-page from a textbook and covering everything in equal segments	Chapter 2	Using diagnostic assessments to determine what topics need more or less time and which students need extra assistance or additional challenges
Planning lessons based on general goals and the next topic in the textbook	Chapter 3	Clearly defining learning targets with criteria for their achievement and communicating these to students
Relying primarily on multiple-choice tests to measure achievement	Chapter 4 Chapter 5	Employing a variety of assessment strategies—personal conversations, constructed response and open-ended questions—to identify achievement of learning targets
Assessing at the end of the week or the end of a unit and using the results primarily to assign grades	Chapter 4 Chapter 5 Chapter 6	Assessing daily throughout instruction to uncover student thinking and make decisions about instruction
Providing whole-class instruction with students working individually on the same tasks	Chapter 6	Having students work on tasks chosen to address identified strengths and needs with the whole class, alone, with partners, and in flexible groups

(continued)

Contents: An INFORMative Assessment Journey Perspective

Moving from . . .	Chapter	Moving toward . . .
Expecting students to know how to improve their work	Chapter 7	Creating an environment that promotes reflection, self-assessment, and responsibility with rubrics, models, and class discussions that explain quality work
Showing and telling students the most efficient way to solve problems or to compute	Chapter 6 Chapter 7 Chapter 8	Encouraging students to share solution strategies and facilitating class discussions that move students to efficient algorithms
Calling on students who have raised their hands and accepting their answers	Chapter 6 Chapter 7 Chapter 8	Calling on a variety of students daily and asking them to justify their answers
Asking questions that are primarily recall or require yes-or-no responses	Chapter 8	Asking questions to engage students in the task or discussion and questions that probe students' thinking
Scoring student responses as *right* or *wrong* and giving feedback primarily in the form of grades	Chapter 9	Scoring student work for both the process and the answer and providing actionable feedback to inform the student on how to improve
Defining successful teaching as having a large percentage of the class score well on tests	Chapters 1–10	Defining successful teaching as having students who reason mathematically, exhibit perseverance in solving problems, communicate their ideas, and develop long-term knowledge and skills in using mathematics

Foreword

The play on the term *formative assessment*, reflected in the words of this resource's title, *INFORMative Assessment*, was the first indication that I would learn from this book. I yearned to be back in the classroom with the insights, ideas, and inspiration gained from reading it.

Formative assessment has come to the forefront of mathematics teaching and learning in recent years. There have been attempts to initiate formative assessment, often named differently, through the years of my career. One of the first elementary school mathematics projects in which I was involved called it *continuous assessment*:

> Continuous assessment of each child's progress is an integral part of DMP [Developing Mathematical Processes]. Only with a continuing evaluation of the children's progress can you build an instructional program that evolves from the children's experience and avoids being overly repetitious while guarding against teaching content for which the children are unprepared. (Romberg et al. 1974, 117)

Even with the push for more emphasis on formative assessment, the pressures of high-stakes testing have focused teachers on making their students "ready" for these summative tests. Although accountability is important and it is not a question of either formative or summative testing, strategic formative assessment allows for teachers to make the decisions needed for students to succeed on the summative assessments.

> When the cook tastes the soup, it's formative evaluation, and when the guest tastes the soup, it's summative evaluation. (Stake 2004, 17)

This book is certainly not a cookbook filled with recipes, but a book that helps the cook (the teacher) to develop the processes of how to decide whether the soup tastes good (whether the students are learning the mathematics expected). All good chefs have basic recipes, remedies for potential disasters, alternate paths, and standards of acceptance and of excellence. This book helps teachers develop the analogous tools for helping children learn mathematics.

"When the cook tastes the soup, it's formative evaluation, and when the guest tastes the soup, it's summative evaluation."
—*Standards-Based and Responsive Evaluation* (Stake 2004, 17)

Jeane M. Joyner and Mari Muri are the master chefs of the classroom. They have been there, both as teachers and teacher leaders. Their practical wisdom, understanding of the complicated profession of teaching, and background in both formative and summative assessment pervades the book. They well understand how much change teachers can make and what type of change is important to them.

As you take this journey with Jeane and Mari, you will build on your own strengths. Take the risks that challenge you, make the children part of this journey, and decide how far you will go at first. Remain cognizant of the fact that the longer you go, the easier the journey will become. The journey will be rewarding, especially since your students will be with you.

—MARY LINDQUIST
FULLER E. CALLAWAY PROFESSOR OF MATHEMATICS EDUCATION,
EMERITUS, COLUMBUS STATE UNIVERSITY
PAST PRESIDENT, NATIONAL COUNCIL OF TEACHERS OF MATHEMATICS

Acknowledgments

This book is about determining what students know and can do, their understandings and their misunderstandings. It is about teachers changing classroom practices so that the information gained through formative assessment strategies supports instructional decisions and leads to greater student learning. The book is based on the premise that teachers do "touch the future" and have the power to make a difference in the lives of all of their students.

Coauthoring this book about formative assessment has been a continuing professional development opportunity for the two of us. As we worked, we spent many hours in conversations about teaching, learning, and our beliefs about formative assessment. Our reflections became an important part of shaping what we wrote. We hope that you will have similar rich experiences with colleagues as you read the book. We have included pages to encourage you to also pause and think about your beliefs related to the content of each chapter.

We have organized the book around the idea of a journey. Changing classroom practices is similar to the journey an apprentice undertakes to become a master. Each experience offers challenges but also opportunities for success and greater expertise. According to Bill Gates, "the Gates Foundation has learned that two questions can predict how much [students] learn: 'Does your teacher use class time well?' and, 'When you're confused, does your teacher help you get straightened out?'" (Tough 2010). We believe that students in classrooms where teachers embrace INFORMative assessment are likely to answer both questions with "yes."

Like all educators, we have benefited from the studies of numerous researchers and authors whose wisdom helped to shape our thinking. Teachers, whose creativity and commitment to excellence make them our valued colleagues, contributed ideas that supplemented our own classroom experiences. Some of the content is drawn from handouts and guides we created as mathematics and classroom assessment consultants at the North Carolina Department of Public Instruction and the Connecticut Department of Education.

The majority of the student work and classroom examples are from teachers with whom we have worked. We have tried to be consistent in using pseudonyms for these colleagues and their students as we share their stories. Teachers in the Team and Partners for Mathematics Learning Projects generously provided classroom experiences and samples of student work from their schools across North Carolina. We thank each of them, especially Tery Gunter, Kayonna Pitchford, Nancy Teague, Gail Cotton, Lisa Davis, Rendy King, Judy Rucker, Susan Riddle, Ana Floyd, Rene Lemons-Matney, Wendy Rich, and Lisa Williamson. They will recognize themselves and their students' thinking in every chapter.

We also thank colleagues in Connecticut: Kit Bishop, principal, Daisy Ingraham School in Westbrook; Christine Newman, math specialist for West Hartford Schools; and Mary Santilli, math specialist for Trumbull Schools. Without their help and the help of their students and teachers, our book would have been incomplete.

Our appreciation goes to the students, their parents, and the teachers who permitted us to include their pictures in the book. The photographs were taken by Bill Lovin of Marinegrafics, Margaret Jeane Malone, Katherine Mawhinney, and Tery Gunter. Meghin Griffith and Julie Malone helped gather all of the permissions.

We are grateful to Mary Lindquist for her guidance and willingness to read and reread multiple drafts of each chapter. To Jamie Cross and Melissa Inglis-Elliott we say thank you for guiding us through each step, helping us craft a manuscript that brings a clear message, and designing a book that is a pleasure to read.

Finally, we thank our families—husbands who encouraged us, daughters and sons-in-law who answered every call for help, and grandchildren who continually gave us hugs to keep us inspired.

—Jeane M. Joyner and Mari Muri

Section I

What Is INFORMative Assessment?

Beginning an Assessment Journey

What we believe affects how we teach, and how we teach affects what and how our students learn. In this chapter you will examine your own beliefs and actions as an introduction to INFORMative assessment. The chapter tackles the question "What is INFORMative assessment?" and gives you a road map for starting to think about formative assessment in your classroom. The chapter concludes with an overview of the rest of the resource.

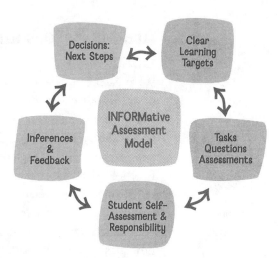

Overview
Are My Beliefs and Actions Congruent?
What Is INFORMative Assessment?
How Do I Use This Resource?
>   The Model
>   The Chapters
>   The Reflections

INFORMing My Practice

In the day-to-day pressures of making lesson plans, reviewing student work, and completing the myriad of paperwork associated with teaching, we rarely have time to stop and reflect on *why* we are doing *what* we are doing. Take a moment to think about where you are right now in your beliefs related to assessment.

Are My Beliefs and Actions Congruent?

What each of us believes should determine how we do things in our classrooms; after all, what we say and do will always impact our students. Identify three or four things that you feel strongly about related to teaching and learning and complete the chart in "Reflection 1–1: INFORMing My Practice: My Beliefs" (see page 11). First, record your beliefs. What do you feel strongly about related to assessment? Next, write down how your actions "play out" in your classroom. Describe your assessment practices that reflect your beliefs. Do your actions match what you believe? And finally, reflect on how these actions impact your students. Do this before continuing to read; below is an example to get you started:

> "Although assessment is done for a variety of reasons, its main goal is to advance students' learning and inform teachers as they make instructional decisions."
> —*Assessment Standards for School Mathematics* (NCTM 1995, 13)

Reflection 1–1

INFORMing My Practice: My Beliefs

Page 11

REPRODUCIBLE

My beliefs . . .	are reflected in my classroom actions . . .	and impact my students in this way . . .
Students should be tested on what I have taught.	I plan lessons to prepare students for my tests.	My students do well on my tests.

Look at your reflection chart as a whole. Is there a match between what you believe and what is happening in your classroom? When we say we believe something but our day-to-day actions model something different, no matter how good our intentions, our actions are what most often shape our classrooms.

Our Beliefs vs. Our Actions

Have you ever heard anyone say something like . . .

"I believe in having students share their ideas. We just don't have time for extended conversations because we have so much content to cover."

Or

"I believe in hands-on activities to help students make sense of mathematics, but there is not time for exploratory lessons. I model the manipulatives rather than have students use them."

Or

"Open-ended questions do give more information about what students know, but the benchmark and end-of-grade tests are multiple choice. I need to use those kinds of assessments so students are comfortable with that assessment format."

All teachers want what is best for their students; no teacher wants to make decisions that impede student learning. In an ideal world, teachers collaborate with each other to plan lessons and assessments, discuss student work, and have strong support from parents and school leaders. Learning goals are clear and resources are plentiful. Students and teachers have a vision of the mathematics that students are learning and what accomplishment looks like. In these situations, we feel empowered and students are likely to flourish.

In reality, however, many teachers work more in isolation, with little time for planning and collaboration with colleagues. We may feel alone in articulating specific learning targets and establishing what student performance will look like when the goals are accomplished. Because we feel the pressures of district initiatives and state tests, we may believe we must use similar measures throughout the year to "prepare" students for the high-stakes assessments. In these situations teachers often make instructional decisions without a clear understanding of the logic or the misunderstandings behind student answers. The results of such a system are instructional decisions that may not support student learning.

What Is INFORMative Assessment?

Formative assessment is not a one-time event. It is not the product or end result of a set of well-defined steps. Rather, formative assessment is a process that we believe is better identified as INFORMative assessment when it is a collection of strategies that engage teachers and students in becoming partners to support students' learning. INFORMative assessment is used to make instructional decisions that guide improvement rather than summarize performance. As teachers, we continually sharpen our abilities to unpack student thinking and provide feedback that encourages students to take greater responsibility for their own learning.

Assessment Tip ✓

INFORMative assessment is not the end of a lesson but the beginning of better instruction.

The word assessment comes from Medieval Latin *assessus*, "to sit beside." Webster gives one definition of formative as "capable of alteration by growth and development." Putting these two ideas together, it is easy to create a mental image of a teacher moving throughout the classroom, stopping by individuals' desks, and talking with students about the mathematics they are doing. Rather than the teacher spending the majority of the time telling, the teacher is spending more time listening. Students tell about how they solved a problem and talk about what they are not sure of. Their written work and their conversations become assessments that INFORM us of their learning. Together, teacher and students evaluate the students' progress toward a particular learning target. We use information from conversations and student work to give feedback to students and decide about the next activity that will help students move away from a misconception or "not knowing" to becoming competent and confident in the mathematics.

Assessment comes from a root word meaning "to sit beside."

At first glance it is easy to understand why many educators feel that classroom assessment is "low stakes." After all, classroom tasks are not "secure," and the scoring is not necessarily uniform. The results of classroom assessments are used—or not used—in many different ways. As teachers we have different levels of expertise in asking questions and choosing tasks. Our decisions are always influenced by our content knowledge and the disposition of the class. Classroom assessments are usually viewed as "low stakes" in comparison with "high-stakes" assessments such as tests that are used as factors in awarding scholarships or end-of-grade tests used for decisions about promotion or retention. However, it is a serious error in judgment not to recognize the

What are most likely to improve the quality of mathematics education for all students are the thoughtful shifts that teachers make during daily lessons to understand students' thinking, and using that knowledge to make decisions.

power and potential of formative assessment. What is most likely to improve the quality of mathematics education for all students are the thoughtful shifts that we make during daily lessons as we become better at understanding our students' thinking, and using that knowledge to make decisions. INFORMative assessment at work is the interaction between teacher and students. We are "informed" about what students understand and thus are able to better plan opportunities for further learning.

Throughout this book we emphasize the links between teaching and learning, investigating the "what" of formative assessment and describing "how to." Sometimes formative

INFORMative Assessment: Six Key Questions

- Whom are we assessing?
  Our students.

- What are we assessing?
  Our students' knowledge and skills, their thinking and reasoning, their dispositions; the processes they use and their abilities to apply what they are learning.

- Why are we assessing?
  To better plan instruction and to monitor our students' progress.

- When do we assess?
  Daily—along with instruction as well as during specific, planned assessments.

- Where do we assess?
  Wherever we are interacting with and observing students.

- How are we assessing?
  In traditional and alternative ways such as through conversations and observations, along with samples of students' work.

assessment is referred to as ongoing classroom assessment. We refer to all assessment that guides instructional decisions and helps us monitor student progress as INFORMative assessment. On the previous page is a list of key questions to help clarify formative assessment as an INFORMative process. We will be revisiting and exploring these questions throughout the book.

Changing classroom practices so that teaching and learning become seamless can be thought of as a journey toward creating an environment in which INFORMative assessment is a routine and powerful tool for promoting student success. For each of us that journey—toward the goal of better understanding student thinking—can take many paths. Just as students in the same classroom learning a new mathematics concept bring different backgrounds to their tasks, we come to ideas of INFORMative assessment with different experiences, levels of expertise, and administrative support.

> Formative assessment gives *all* teachers tools for helping *all* students learn more mathematics.

Part of that journey is doing what we just did—examining our beliefs and actions. The next step is deciding to implement strategies and practices that better support student learning. The power of well-implemented INFORMative assessment is that it gives *all* teachers tools to help students learn more mathematics than they have in the past and to achieve at higher levels.

How Do I Use This Resource?

This book is a collaborative reading journey. Together we will investigate ways to gather information about students' thinking, reasoning, and understanding in order to provide feedback to students, to help them take greater responsibility for their own learning, and to guide our instructional decisions. Along the way we will explore numerous assessment ideas and discuss how to implement them. By the end of this book we hope you will have a foundational understanding of formative assessment as an INFORMative process.

The Model

Although different assessment models and diagrams appear in resources such as the *Assessment Standards for School Mathematics* (NCTM 1995), we prefer the INFORMative Assessment Model for Teaching and Learning

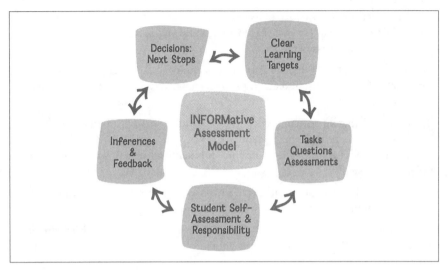

FIGURE 1–1. INFORMative Assessment Model for Teaching and Learning

(see Figure 1–1) because it not only demonstrates important aspects of formative assessment, it also includes "student self-assessment and responsibility" as a critical component. While the arrows in the model indicate important relationships, notice that arrows could connect each of the cells in the model with every other cell. Chapters 2 through 9 provide more information about the components of the model.

The Chapters
Following is a brief overview of each chapter.

Chapter 2: This chapter is about the tough decisions teachers make in planning instruction and monitoring students' progress. These decisions about "what's next" impact what students learn.

Chapter 3: Quality instruction begins when teachers clarify the learning targets and identify criteria for successful accomplishment of the mathematics. This chapter identifies four major categories of learning targets.

Chapter 4: This chapter identifies critical strategies for using oral assessments to elicit evidence of learning—interviews, class discussions, and observations. Documentation strategies highlight ways to create anecdotal records.

Chapter 5: Identifying evidence of learning in written work is the focus of this chapter. We explore ways to gather information through forced-choice and constructed response assessments.

Chapter 6: In Chapter 6 there are five questions to consider when choosing mathematically rich tasks for teaching and learning. We identify important ways to use tasks to support learning.

Chapter 7: Creating an environment to support student responsibility and self-assessment is a critical component of INFORMative assessment. This chapter suggests strategies for motivating students and identifies structures that promote student responsibility.

Chapter 8: Teachers use questions for many purposes. This chapter provides guidance for framing classroom conversations and creating good questions.

Chapter 9: This chapter highlights the importance of our inferences about students' understandings. We discuss ways to provide feedback and develop interventions and differentiate instruction.

Chapter 10: Continuing the implementation of INFORMative assessment means focusing our energies for long-term success. This chapter provides opportunities for personal reflections and setting goals.

The Reflections

Throughout the book we have included many opportunities for you to reflect on your own teaching and learning. At the end of each chapter there is also an "INFORMing My Practice" section with a reflection about the chapter and a place for you to record your use of INFORMative assessment—the changes in your thinking, your questions, your frustrations. And, most importantly, your successes!

INFORMing My Practice

Earlier in this chapter (see page 4) you completed the chart in "Reflection 1–1: INFORMing My Practice: My Beliefs." Before beginning Chapter 2, take a moment to look once more at the chart. Is there anything else you want to include?

Reflection 1–1: INFORMing My Practice: My Beliefs

My beliefs . . .	are reflected in my classroom actions . . .	and impact my students in this way . . .

Section II

What Will I Assess?

Key Strategies for Making Tough Decisions About "What's Next?"

In this chapter, we identify and explore six types of decisions that teachers make each day. Because they directly impact what students learn, exploring these decisions is the next step in the INFORMative assessment journey. We highlight the decisions and illustrate the "Decisions" component of the Model for INFORMative Assessment for Teaching and Learning.

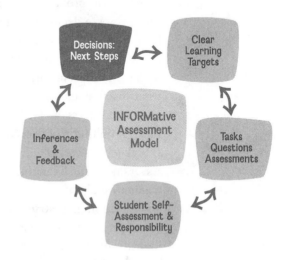

Overview

Six Decision-Making Strategies

Strategy 1: Make Decisions About What Students Already Know

Strategy 2: Make Decisions About to Teach

Strategy 3: Make Decisions as Students Respond to Instruction

Strategy 4: Make Decisions That Support Student Learning

Strategy 5: Make Decisions from Reflecting on Data

Strategy 6: Make Decisions About Evaluating Learning

INFORMing My Practice

Think for a moment about the multiple decisions you make related to your mathematics lessons. In planning, we must decide the specific mathematics concepts and procedures to be addressed in the lesson and what we want students to accomplish. We think about what problems to use and how to organize the class. We decide how to introduce the lesson and how to link the content with what students already know. We plan what to do as a whole group and what to have students work on independently. We decide what discussions are important for the class and what assignment to make for homework. In other words, we make a multitude of decisions each day.

Each stage of the Model for INFORMative Assessment for Teaching and Learning requires that teachers make decisions and provides a glimpse into the complexity of good teaching. Instruction begins with knowing what we are to teach (clear learning targets); we decide how we will teach the content and identify questions (instructional tasks and questions) that will support learning. We plan ways to encourage and promote student responsibility and support students' self-assessment (student self-assessment and responsibility). At every step in a teaching–learning process we infer what our students are learning and provide feedback to the class and to individual students (inferences and feedback). We base our decisions about the next lessons on what students say and write and do. Whether we move to different content or different delivery of the same content, we define our learning targets for the next lessons. (See Figure 2–1.) Arrows going in two directions remind us that teaching and learning do not necessarily flow in a linear way. At times there are back-and-forth interactions between the various stages. There could, for example, be arrows going back and forth from each component of the model to every other part. Interestingly, this model reflects an overall structure for planning large units of instruction as well as the oft-repeated ebb and flow of daily lessons.

> "All teachers are faced with a dizzying array of mathematics concepts and skills they are expected to teach to groups of students who come to their classrooms with differing levels of preparedness for learning."
>
> —*How Students Learn: Mathematics in the Classroom* (National Research Council 2005, 259)

Assessment Tip ☑

Think About the Assessment Principle

"Assessment should support the learning of important mathematics and furnish useful information to both teachers and students."

—*Principles and Standards for School Mathematics* (NCTM 2000, 372)

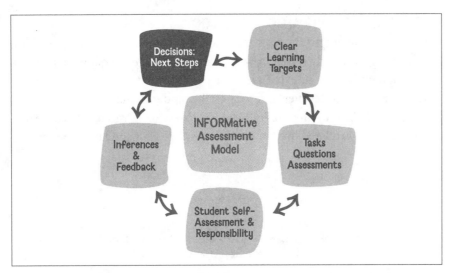

FIGURE 2-1. INFORMative Assessment Model for Teaching and Learning

Although states specify the goals for mathematics at each grade and districts or schools adopt curricular materials, teachers decide how each day's lessons will be implemented. Ultimately, it is the decisions we make about the implementation of lessons that affect what students learn.

It is these decisions that fuel the need for INFORMative assessment. Without information about the specifics of what students are thinking, what they can do, what they understand and misunderstand, and what they still need to learn, the assumption is that everyone needs to begin at square one. In this situation, deciding what to do tomorrow is easy—just move from one lesson to the next and do page 47 because it comes after page 46. Easy! The "what's next" decision is made.

INFORMative assessment is fueled by the need to make decisions about instruction.

As good teachers, however, we are not satisfied with such a rote approach to teaching. We choose to be in education because we believe that all children can learn; we believe we can make a difference in our students' lives. We look for better ways to make decisions about teaching and learning.

Six Decision-Making Strategies

While each of us might describe the decisions we make related to teaching and learning in slightly different ways, we have chosen to focus on six areas of decision making where INFORMative assessment assists in supporting both the role of the teacher and that of the student. These decisions occur at different points in the INFORMative Assessment model. Because the decisions are interrelated, we continue these discussions in later chapters.

The Six Strategies

1. Make decisions about what students already know (diagnostic assessments).

2. Make decisions about what to teach and how to organize the class (learning targets, good tasks, appropriate groups).

3. Make decisions as students respond to instruction (questioning and moment-to-moment decisions).

4. Make decisions that support student learning (the learning environment, student self-assessment).

5. Make decisions from reflecting on data (analyzing student work, inferences, interventions, and feedback).

6. Make decisions about evaluating learning (evidence, rubrics, portfolios, grades).

Strategy 1: Make Decisions About What Students Already Know

Determining what students already know in relation to what is to being taught next helps us identify starting points for instruction. Rather than assuming that all students need to begin at the beginning (and then likely re-teaching skills and concepts students have already mastered), these decisions help us make adjustments in the amount of time we spend on different learning targets. Through the use of INFORMative assessments, particular needs of individuals can be identified for additional help or preteaching. Misconceptions can also be identified early so that we do not, unintentionally, reinforce mistakes through practice. Overall, tools that help us gather information about what students know prior to instruction play a significant role in deciding what mathematics needs greater or lesser emphasis. Let's take a closer look at tools for guiding decisions about what students already know: diagnostic assessments and pretests, class discussions, KWL charts, concept maps, and conversations with individual students.

Tools for Guiding Decisions About What Students Already Know

1. Diagnostic assessments and pretests

2. Class discussions, KWL charts, and concept maps

3. Conversations with individual students

Use Diagnostic Assessments and Pretests

We frequently think of diagnostic tests as in-depth assessments sometimes administered by someone other than the classroom teacher and pretests as shorter, less formal assessments administered in the classroom. The distinction need not be an issue. Diagnostic assessments identify students who need challenges to broaden their understandings as well as those who need more assistance. Some districts name their diagnostic assessments Common Formative Assessments or Universal Assessment Probes. Pretests usually target the next unit of study to determine what students know and need to learn about the new content. All of these assessments are designed to give information prior to instruction. All are used throughout the school year. It is important to critically think about these assessments and how we use them to inform instruction.

Three Critical Considerations for Guiding the Use of Diagnostic Assessments

1. Diagnosis is valuable only if the information gathered is used purposefully.

2. Diagnostic assessments and pretests are starting points—teachers continually probe student thinking and monitor student responses to adjust instructional decisions.

3. Diagnostic assessments and pretests should be focused and specific to the immediate learning targets in order to provide the most useful information.

When North Carolina educators first implemented the state's K–2 assessment more than twenty years ago, many teachers commented that they were very frustrated because the more they learned about what individual students understood, the harder it was to plan their mathematics lessons. They recognized the students' broad range of prior knowledge and realized that frequently one lesson plan for the entire class was not sufficient.

This may happen (or has happened) to you, too. As you look at your students' work through the lens of understanding their thinking, you will notice more clearly the broad range of understandings, misconceptions, and reasoning of your students. You may find that students could be organized into more groups than you can easily manage. Or you may have more questions and decide that you need to talk with some of the students because you do not have a clue as to where their answers come from.

> Using formative assessment, teachers recognize that students have a broad range of prior knowledge and realize that frequently one lesson plan for the entire class is not sufficient.

Throughout the year, consider the use of pretests. Because the content of most pretests is narrowly focused, teachers can use the results to plan instructional groups as well as identify what students already understand and what they still need to learn.

For example, early in the school year the second-grade students had worked on subtraction. At midyear the teacher was planning a new unit of instruction and wanted to see how the students would solve subtraction problems, so she used the following problem in a diagnostic manner to gather information about students' strategies:

Second-Grade Problem

There were 73 markers in the bag. Makayla gave away 39 markers. How many are still in the bag?

The fifth-grade teacher, on the other hand, had focused on thinking through nonroutine problems in recent lessons and was interested in how the students would approach a new task, so she used a task involving mathematical reasoning:

Fifth-Grade Problem*

The Small Island Post Office carries only two stamps, 5¢ and 7¢ stamps. What are all of the amounts of postage that you could not make using only 5¢ and 7¢ stamps? Write a brief explanation to explain why you know your answer is correct.

*Adapted from the Hawaii Algebra Learning Project.

The students' responses are representative of the class as a whole. (See Figure 2–2 on the following page; see also Reflection 2–1.) Study the students' responses from one of these grades and think about what experiences these students might have had and how the students' solutions would influence your instructional plans. Respond to each of the questions in Reflection 2–1 before continuing.

The second-grade teacher made these comments when she shared the students' work with us:

> Most of my students displayed a good sense of number and a conceptual understanding of subtraction. I was pleasantly surprised that the students used such a variety of strategies, but I was dismayed that a number of students were confused when they used a traditional algorithm. They seemed to lack a true grasp of the procedure. I am planning to talk with several of the students individually. For the whole class, I want to use samples I saved from last year's class to do a review of different subtraction strategies.

If you examined the fifth-grade work samples, did you decide, as we did, that some students would benefit from more discussion about "unpacking problems" while others need to talk about clear and complete explanations? We also thought that having students share how they organized the *possible* and *impossible* sets of numbers would reinforce the value of making organized lists. Consider using the reflection questions to examine a set of work samples from your own students. Notice that the reflection questions prompt you to look for ways the student work can inform your plans.

Reflection 2–1

Focus on the Mathematics

Pages 42–45

Second-Grade Problem
There were 73 markers in the bag. Makayla gave away 39 markers. How many are still in the bag?

Olivia (Second Grade)

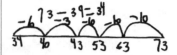

Ezra (Second Grade)

$73 - 39 = 34$

$70 - 30 = 40$
$3 - 9 = -6$
$40 - 6 = 34$

Fifth-Grade Problem*
The Small Island Post Office carries only two stamps, 5¢ and 7¢ stamps. What are all of the amounts of postage that you could not make using only 5¢ and 7¢ stamps? Write a brief explanation to explain why you know your answer is correct.

*Adapted from the Hawaii Algebra Learning Project.

Ella (Fifth Grade)

Can not make 1, 2, 3, 4, 6, 8, 9, 11, 13, 16, 18, 23

I wrote down some numbers and circled the ones that couldn't be made. Up until a number that I couldn't make, all of the numbers after that I realized I could make.

Tommy (Fifth Grade)

1, 2, 3, 4, 6, 8, 9, 11, 12, 13,
16, 17, 18, 19, 22, 23, 24,
26, 27, 29, 31, 32, 33
34, 36, 37, 38, 39, 41, 43,
44, 46, There are more but I can't write a 1000,000 answers

All the numbers that are not multiples of 5 or 7 are answers.

FIGURE 2-2. Teachers Use Examples from Second- and Fifth-Graders' Pretests to Assess Students' Strategies and Plan Instruction (see pages 43, 44, and 45 for more examples)

Creating a Pretest If you are not already using diagnostic assessments to plan, you might begin by administering a pretest for your next unit of instruction. The assessment does not need to be lengthy. Think about three or four things you want students to know and be able to do when you finish the unit. Your pretest can have several (two or three) questions for each of the learning targets. Use resources you already have in hand for good questions. Just remember that you are looking for students' understanding and use of mathematics concepts, facts, and procedures. The "scoring" will be for your planning—not to assign a grade.

Once you've administered the pretest and gathered the students' work, you will be able to gather information about individuals and the class as a whole. Writing notes as you study the students' pretests will save you from having to go through the set of papers multiple times.

> **Steps in Designing a Pretest**
>
> 1. Decide what students should *know* at the end of the unit.
> 2. Decide what students should *be able to do* at the end of the unit.
> 3. Identify 3–4 specific learning targets for the unit.
> 4. Choose 2–3 questions for each learning target.

> *Three Critical Steps for Gathering Information from a Diagnostic Assessment*
>
> 1. Make notes about individual strengths. Are there clear "outliers" from the majority of the students? Some students may need specific interventions that involve preteaching, coaching, or different tasks; other students may not need the planned instruction and appear to be ready for opportunities to delve more deeply into the mathematics content.
>
> 2. Identify groups of students who missed the same problems. This information may lead to temporary instructional groups, especially if the problems focus on a particular aspect of the mathematics planned for the next unit.
>
> 3. Notice if there are some problems that only a few students miss. This information may cause you to rethink how you will allocate time on that particular learning target or change the tasks you plan to use.

> **Assessment Tip**
>
> The same questions used in your instruction can be used for diagnostic assessments or in final evaluations. It is how a teacher uses the students' work that is different—to inform instructional decisions, to converse with students about their ideas, or to evaluate achievement when you are ready to move on.

With practice, you will be able to use diagnostic assessments to identify clusters of understandings and needs of your students so that as your unit of instruction proceeds, more students are engaged with content that is accessible yet challenging.

Use Class Discussions, KWL Charts, and Concept Maps

Class Discussions There are times when we decide to engage students in a class discussion or small-group activity as a pretest to determine what they already know. This assessment strategy works well in classroom environments where teachers are committed to engaging students robustly in their learning. Often younger students record their ideas on newsprint and older students use notebook-size paper or make charts. For example, Mrs. Basile planned for her fourth-grade students to use Venn diagrams to sort geometric figures; she wanted to know what they understood about Venn diagrams, so she drew intersecting circles on the board and asked students to explain what they knew about the diagrams. (See Figure 2–3.)

Question: What do you know about using Venn diagrams?

"Venn diagrams sort things. The left circle stands for a column, as well as the right. The middle means both. And, if something doesn't fit either columns, then it goes outside of them."

"There are two groups and the middle is where they go in both groups. The outside is they don't go into anything."

"There are usually several circles. These [sic] is a middle for each category is alike."

"It is a way to show more information, like USA and Canada. In the middle, percent of kids who ice skates"

"The left circle fits in the description about it and the right circle fits in the description about it. The middle circle fits in the 2 circles' description, so it goes in the middle."

"If the two columns were four-sided shapes and three-sided shapes it would show which shapes were more alike than others."

"They help you organize data. It puts things in categories. You can use it for any subject. You can give it your own labels."

FIGURE 2–3. Students' Comments About Venn Diagrams

Mrs. Basile realized from the class discussion that most of the students knew that Venn diagrams could be used to compare and contrast information. Several students stated that anything in the middle space fit into both categories. However, many students' comments were vague and required that she infer what they really understood. This prompted her to have each student create an example of a Venn diagram using labels of *things that we eat* and *things that are red* so that she could assess their understanding of how to use Venn diagrams rather than assess mathematical understandings that might be incomplete.

KWL Charts For many years language arts teachers have used KWL charts: *What I **know**, What I **want** to learn, What I **learned*** (Ogle 1986). Stated as questions, the first two columns of the chart have potential for rich class discussions that help us avoid repeating lessons that do not extend students' learning. We get useful information in planning how much time to allot for different learning targets and students have a heads-up to begin thinking about what they will be learning. Asking students to create their own charts and inviting them to share gives us information about what students know; collecting the charts will help us identify the range of students' knowledge about the topic. For example, one third-grade student created a KWL chart prior to a class discussion about multiplication. (See Figure 2–4.) The information on his chart showed that he was interested in learning about multiplication but had very little prior knowledge beyond some memorized facts.

What I Know	What I Want to Learn	What I Learned
When you add gops of numbers	To understand about it.	$9 \times 9 = 8$
It is fising		$3 \times 3 = 9$

FIGURE 2–4. A Third-Grade Student's KWL Chart About Multiplication

Concept Maps A concept map is a graphic organizer that shows the connections among big ideas and related information. As a class or in small groups, students create a display, such as a bulletin board or a large poster, that they can add to, expand, and update as their knowledge about the topic increases. The initial concept map display tells us what the students already know about particular learning targets, and subsequent additions allow us to monitor students' progress as instruction moves forward. Two third-grade students created a concept map about geometric shapes as a way to begin study on the topic. (See Figure 2–5.)

Have Conversations with Individual Students

Brief conversations sometimes confirm what we believe about students, and sometimes conversations bring big surprises. Without a doubt, conversations and interviews with students often provide the most information about an individual student's thinking. Having time to talk with every student is the problem. One strategy is to write each student's name on an index card and

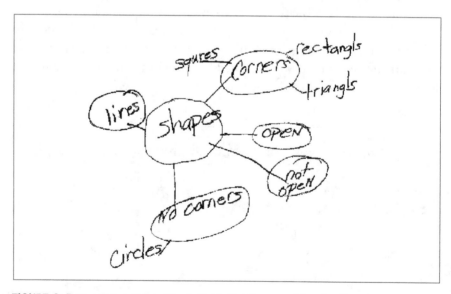

FIGURE 2–5. Two Third-Grade Students' Initial Concept Map for Geometric Shapes

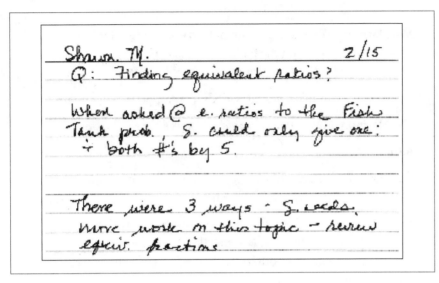

FIGURE 2–6. A Sixth-Grade Teacher's Index Card Notes for Student Conversations

note questions about the student's mathematics thinking you want to ask. (See Figure 2–6.)

Sometime during mathematics class, select an index card and stop beside the student's desk (or call the student over to a table). Initiate a three- or four-minute conversation about the questions. If you talk with a couple students each day, you will likely have had a private assessment conversation with each student in your class within two weeks. (See Chapter 4, page 97, for additional suggestions for keeping anecdotal assessment records.)

Following is a conversation between a second-grade teacher, Ms. Harmon, and John, a student just beginning second grade. John's first-grade teacher had stated that he was in her lower math group, able to complete his worksheets but usually made some mistakes. Ms. Harmon's personal goal was to talk with each of her second graders for five or ten minutes during the first week of school about mathematics. Ms. Harmon sat down beside John for a five-minute conversation about mathematics and made some amazing discoveries.

Ms. Harmon: (Points to a group of thirty-six loose interlocking cubes on the table.) *Just make a guess. How many cubes do you think there are?*

John: (Smiles, hesitates, and then responds.) *About thirty.*

Ms. Harmon: *All right. How could you figure out how many?*

John: *By counting them.*

Ms. Harmon: *You could count if you wanted to. Would you count and tell me how many?*

John: *One, two, three, four . . . twenty-one, twenty-two, twenty-three.* (Counts the same cubes multiple times and skips others. Only the first few cubes are counted aloud.)

Ms. Harmon: *Twenty-three. OK. Let me do this. Let me push these into sort of a line. This time, please count out loud so I can hear you.*

John: *One, two, three . . . twenty-six, twenty-seven, twenty-eight, ninety, ninety-one, ninety-two, ninety-three, ninety-four, ninety-five, ninety-six, ninety-eight, ninety-seven.* (When the cubes are in a line, John touches and counts each cube only once except for the final few cubes. He skips two cubes and recounts one.)

Ms. Harmon: *Do you know how to snap cubes into tens and ones?* (John nods and again smiles.) *If you snap them into tens and ones, how many do you think you will have?*

John: (Appears to be counting objects to himself and after a few moments answers.) *Eighty.*

Ms. Harmon: *Would you like to do it?* (John nods.) *OK, snap them into tens and ones for us.*

John:	(Counts to himself as he correctly makes three sticks of ten cubes and then counts the remaining ones.) *Three tens.*
Ms. Harmon:	*Three tens and how many ones?*
John:	(Recounts the loose cubes.) *Six ones.*
Ms. Harmon:	*Three tens and six ones. How many does that make?*
John:	(Looks at cubes on the table and then down at his fingers in his lap. He whispers to himself as he counts his fingers.) *Nine.*
Ms. Harmon:	*Three tens and six ones makes nine?* (John nods and smiles.) *Thanks for talking with me.*

Analysis of written diagnostic assessments or conversations with students such as this one illustrates how important it is to determine students' prior knowledge. Without interventions, John is likely to slip further and further behind as he moves through the second grade.

Take a moment to think about the previous conversation. Suppose you are John's second-grade teacher. Turn to "Reflection 2–2: Assessment in a Grade 2 Classroom: Conversation with John" (see page 46) and make notes from the conversation that would influence your decisions as John's mathematics teacher.

Reflection 2–2

Assessment in a Grade 2 Classroom: Conversation with John

Page 46

Strategy 2: Make Decisions About What to Teach

Teachers use the tasks and sequences for instruction provided in quality instructional materials to make decisions about what to teach and how to organize the classroom. However, students do not all learn at the same rate or in the same way; they bring different backgrounds to each lesson and often approach tasks in different ways. Some students grasp the underlying concepts of the mathematics and readily apply new ideas. Others struggle with the same mathematics and may not even be aware of their misconceptions or lack of understanding. Some students believe they can learn new mathematics content whenever their teacher introduces it. Others lack confidence in themselves as mathematics learners and fear that they will not be successful. Thus, our decisions about lessons involve individual differences and student motivations as well as mathematics content. The question is always "How do I meet the needs of each student within the context of teaching a full class of students?"

An uncomfortable reality in teaching is that no single set of curricular materials, approach, or intervention program can guarantee that all students will achieve at high levels. Sometimes, people not directly involved in education look at the Common Core State Standards, individual state goals for mathematics, district guidelines and pacing guides, and textbooks that describe lessons in detail, and believe that deciding what to teach is easy. We know the opposite is true: Teachers must make informed choices, including identifying specific content, process goals, and learning targets, to create daily lesson plans, meet students' needs, and engage students in the learning process.

"How do I meet the needs of each student within the context of teaching a full class of students?"

Learning targets include conceptual and factual content knowledge, skills and processes, reasoning and problem solving, applications and products, and attitudes and disposition. These learning targets often overlap and some are more long term than others. Teachers use clearly articulated process goals and learning targets to ask questions and make decisions about what to teach. The goal is to move mathematics instruction beyond simply procedural knowledge.

Reflection 2–3

Making Decisions About What to Teach: Guiding Questions

Page 47

REPRODUCIBLE

In "Reflection 2–3: Making Decisions About What to Teach: Guiding Questions" (see page 47), we designed questions for you to use repeatedly when planning units of instruction, including guiding conversations with colleagues in collegial planning or supporting your individual reflection. Given the many tasks that teachers are required to do, we intentionally focused on key questions. Note that this is not a form for daily lesson plans; rather, you might use it to organize your thinking about a new multiday or monthlong unit of instruction. In Chapter 4 we continue the discussion about deciding what to teach. Take a moment to think about your plans for next week. Answer the questions in Reflection 2–3 accordingly.

Questions for Guiding Decisions About What to Teach

- What do I want my students to understand and be able to do in relation to the mathematics in this unit?

- How will I know when they understand and can do these things? What do I expect as evidence of their learning?

- What tasks and instructional activities should I plan to engage all students to help them meet these expectations? (See more questions in Reflection 2–3.)

Strategy 3: Make Decisions as Students Respond to Instruction

In the classroom, we make hundreds of moment-to-moment decisions. We decide on whom to call, what questions to ask, when to probe an individual student's comments and when to move on. We decide if we need to provide more structure or if we need to change directions to provide a greater challenge. Not only do we make numerous decisions, we make many different kinds of decisions—some related to content and some related to classroom management. Thus, as a lesson progresses, the need for information about what students are thinking and how they arrive at their answers is critical.

> Formative assessment is likely to be most powerful during instruction because there is the opportunity for a constant feedback—INFORMative—loop.

It is during the process of instruction that formative assessment is likely to be most powerful because there is the opportunity for a constant feedback—INFORMative—loop. We assign tasks and pose questions; students respond; we make inferences about what students understand and decide what to do next. Sometimes the response is immediate feedback, a statement that helps us guide students toward a more productive path or an affirmation of a student's response. Other times the response is a question or a different task to see if any students thought about the problem in a different way.

In classroom assessment, not all information must be responded to immediately. Sometimes we file the information in our heads to address the issue later if we feel we need more details; other times the information may confirm plans that are already made or require a minor or even a major revision of plans. By having a clear picture of the learning targets and the intermediate steps along the way, we can keep the class moving forward even if we decide to gather more evidence about students' misconceptions or incomplete understandings. Likewise, if students have a clear picture of what they are trying to accomplish, they are more likely to explain how they are thinking about a problem or procedure.

During the process of instruction we do not have the luxury of time for reflection, for in-depth analysis of what students' statements reveal about their thinking, or for designing optimal feedback since we usually have only seconds to respond. Listening to students and responding appropriately are complex activities that occur repeatedly in every classroom; it is not practical to design one comprehensive set of statements to use in responding to students' comments since classroom discourse needs to be considered within the context of the problem or task at hand.

However, thinking about the typical mistakes and misconceptions of students as we plan lessons and units of instruction benefits all of us, novices and veterans alike. Strategies such as being alert to common errors and thinking about what they may represent and looking at student work and discussing possible next steps with colleagues allow us to be better prepared to respond to students "in the moment."

Discussions with colleagues about the wording of problems and the ways that students are likely to respond to them may be one of the most helpful strategies we can employ. Teachers' learning communities provide support as we try to improve our practice. Since student solution strategies and errors on particular content tend to be similar from year to year, discussions with colleagues help us be well prepared. Making a habit of thinking about tasks and problems through the lenses of the following four questions provides support for our moment-to-moment decisions.

> ### Assessment Tip ✓
>
> Remember that multiple sources of information about students' thinking are like having a photo album rather than a snapshot.

> ### Key Questions in Anticipating Students' Responses to Instruction
>
> 1. How might students solve the problem?
> 2. Are there other possible solutions or solution strategies?
> 3. What kinds of errors might the students make?
> 4. What thinking and reasoning do I hope students will exhibit?

Following is a list of problems drawn from kindergarten through the sixth grade. Choose one or more that would be appropriate for your students and revisit the four key questions above. We've provided "Reflection 2–4: Key Questions in Anticipating Students' Responses to Instruction" (see page 48) as a place to record your ideas.

Reflection 2–4

Key Questions in Anticipating Students' Responses to Instruction

Page 48

Problems from Grades K–6

1. *Eric has 18 stickers. He gave 2 stickers to his sister. How many stickers does Eric have now?*

2. *Hallie is 1 year younger than her brother Joey. She thinks that someday she can catch up to his age. Will Hallie's age catch up to Joey's age? _____ Explain. How old will Hallie be when Joey is 8 years old? _____*

3. *Kee and her brother are collecting cans. Kee has 4 cans and her brother has 6 cans. How many more cans does her brother have than Kee has?*

4. *The price of popsicles last summer was 60¢ each. Last summer Mrs. Wilson bought 1 popsicle for each of her 9 grandchildren. Now the same popsicles cost 75¢ each. How much more will popsicles cost this summer than last summer for all 9 children?*

5. *Ray has a colored pencil that is 14 cm long. Every time he sharpens the pencil it gets 1 cm shorter. If he sharpens it 6 times, how long will the pencil be?*

6. *Mr. Bright needs 5 new lightbulbs for his home. He can buy them separately for $1.25, or he can buy a package of 6 bulbs for $6.00. Which is the better buy? Why?*

7. *Jane's dad wanted to know how far she had walked their dog, Boots. Jane wasn't sure. "We walked about 60 steps every minute and we were gone for 12 minutes. I think my steps were about a yard long." About how far did Jane and Boots walk?*

8. *If 3 lbs. of potatoes costs $2.10, how much should 5 lbs. of potatoes cost?*

9. *Max surveyed his friends about the number of pets they have in their families. His survey results were 0, 3, 0, 4, 2, 38, 2, 0, 1. Explain why each measure of central tendency (mean, median, mode) may or may not be appropriate to describe the number of pets for these families.*

10. *Classify the following numbers as prime or composite: 2, 9, 10, 11, 17, 18, 23, 36, 51. How do you know?*

In the crush of preparing every day's lessons we rarely have time to ponder each problem using the four key questions. However, keeping these questions in mind as we plan will make our lessons more targeted for the goals we have set and the students we are teaching.

Strategy 4: Make Decisions That Support Student Learning

Making decisions that enhance student learning is always our goal, and formative assessment strategies offer support for these decisions. Black and Wiliam (2009) define assessment that is formative in this way:

> Practice in a classroom is formative to the extent that evidence about student achievement is elicited, interpreted, and used by teachers, learners, or their peers, to make decisions about the next steps in instruction that are likely to be better, or better founded, than the decisions they would have taken in the absence of the evidence that was elicited. (9)

Many times our students ask questions or make statements that should be red flags for further investigation of their understandings (and misunderstandings) of the mathematics. Sometimes a student has misconceptions that slip by for several years, as illustrated in this conversation between a sixth-grade student and his teacher:

Teacher: *How would you write $\frac{6}{12}$ as a decimal number?*

Student: *You write it as 0.6.*

Teacher: *How'd you get that?*

Student: *Well, $\frac{5}{10}$ is half and it is written as 0.5; and $\frac{6}{12}$ is half, so it should be written as 0.6.*

The evidence about this student's thinking from his statement points us toward finding out more about what he understands about decimal numbers and their relationship to fractions. Our task is to guide the student to appropriate notation that links to his conceptual understanding and also go beyond merely telling the student that 0.6 is an incorrect representation and should also be written as 0.5.

Like our students, we develop new habits through explicit practice. Turn to "Reflection 2–5: Making Decisions That Support Student Learning: What Might You Say or Do?" (see page 49). If you were these students' teacher, what would you infer about their thinking and what "in the moment" response might you make to a student or to the class? Complete the chart before continuing to read. We have filled in a response to the first student as an example.

In Chapter 9, we revisit the idea of making inferences about students' answers and our decisions about how to respond to them. Think about the importance of finding out if what students *say* is really what they *mean*. Are the students' statements "miscommunicated understanding" or "communicated misunderstanding" (Bright and Joyner 2004)?

Reflection 2–5

Making Decisions That Support Student Learning: What Might You Say or Do?

Page 49

Strategy 5: Make Decisions from Reflecting on Data

Every assignment that students complete generates data. When students respond in writing, their written work is "evidence" and scoring the work results in data. If students respond orally, data exist when teachers make annotations of students' answers and record a score related to the accuracy of the response. In the traditional sense, *data* are the measurements or statistics that are used to make decisions. However, in assessments to INFORM instruction, it is the responses, rather than the scores, that give students and teachers the most information about a student's understanding. Think about the difference in describing what the student knows and can do if you have access only to grades in a grade book versus having access to a portfolio containing the student's actual work or having opportunities to talk with the student.

Think about the difference in describing what students know and can do with access only to grades versus access to collections of students' actual work or opportunities to talk with students.

A New Approach to Scoring Student Work

Traditionally, teachers score a set of papers and record a grade in their grade books. But suppose we make a chart and categorize the answers according to certain criteria. For example, we might list students whose mistakes include making number fact errors, omitting explanations, completing only the first step of a multistep problem, or misunderstanding a problem; then we list those students who solve problems correctly. It takes only a little more time to make these notes, and now not only do we have multiple opportunities to reflect on student performance, but also we have data for creating targeted instruction. In Figure 2–7, we used a template to make three charts from the same set of student worksheets, including "naked number" exercises and four word problems that required students to explain their thinking.

Using this easy-to-prepare template to score your students' papers, you might tally the type of errors or the questions most missed by students, or, for even more information, specify the type of errors the students made. Notice that in the third chart, "Group students for instruction according to errors they made," you have the advantage of recording information about

Identify and tally types of errors students made

Number fact errors	Misunderstood	All correct
////	/	~~////~~ /
omitted explanation	**1st step only**	**correct; weak explain**
~~////~~ /	////	~~////~~

Tally number of students who missed each question.

1	2	3	4	5	6
	/		///		/
7	**8**	**9**	**10**	**11**	**12**
/		/ ~~////~~	///	///	///

Group students for instruction according to errors they made.

Number fact errors	*Misunderstood problem*	*All problems correct*
Eileen, Sara, Aaron, Meg	*Jameel*	*Juan, Katie, Lee, Tameka, Avery, Laura*
Omitted written explanation	***Worked only first of two steps***	***Problems correct; weak explanations***
Tommy, Erin, Sara, Meg, Jose, Carl	*Tommy, Carl, Jaime, Sara*	*Ken, Jorge, Marty, Cindy, Erin*

FIGURE 2–7. Representations of the Same Data Using Three Scoring Templates

individuals as well as groups; we also can determine which students may be ready for additional challenges. From this information you can decide what to revisit the next day in a class discussion; for example, you might notice that question 4 on the student worksheet involved subtraction across zeros and question 9 appeared to be the most difficult. The types and number of mistakes the students make can also influence the order in which you discuss the problems with the class. Additionally, when the reasons for a student's wrong answers are not obvious, you can make a list of questions to ask the student in a three-minute informal interview as the class is working the next day.

See "Reflection 2–6: A New Approach to Scoring Student Work" (page 50) for a blank template of the models shown in Figure 2–7 for use in your classroom.

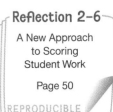

Reflection 2–6

A New Approach to Scoring Student Work

Page 50

REPRODUCIBLE

Benchmark Tests

In some districts, benchmark tests are considered cornerstones of the formative assessment program. These assessments are often tied to pacing guides and may be administered districtwide with each grading period. If teachers have the opportunity to score the tests themselves and see students' answers, they can use the data immediately to inform further instruction and plan interventions. If the central office scores the tests and returns the results to schools, teachers still may have the opportunity to provide guidance for instructional decisions. In some situations, however, teachers may receive only the number of items answered correctly and incorrectly and have no access to the test items themselves. As a result, teachers may have global information about their instructional program but not specific information about what individual students understand. Consider the following possible scenarios:

Case 1

When Ms. Warren's class completed the unit on time, students took a district-developed test. Even though Ms. Warren read through the test while the students were completing it, and knew from the centrally scored results that

(continued)

(continued from page 37)

two of her students each answered four of the six questions correctly, she could not tell what information each student knew and in what areas they needed more help. The district planned for the test to be part of a formative assessment system, but the test became a summative assessment since it did not give information to either the teacher or the students about what they still needed to learn.

Case 2

In another district with a centrally scored test, teachers receive a class roster listing each item number, the correct answer, and the answer choice marked by each student. Objective numbers indicate the content of the items. With this information the teachers study how the class as a whole responded to each question and how individual students scored. Bar graphs from the same data present a picture of content that does not need more review and what content needs further study. Unless teachers have a copy of the original test items, however, it is still difficult to plan specific interventions for individual students.

Benchmark tests are most effective when teachers have access to the actual assessments; it's essential to know the specific items students missed and the content of those items. For example, in one particular assessment, Kelly missed two questions, both related to calculating time across the noon hour, and Tyler also missed two questions. (See Figures 2–8, page 39, and 2–9, page 40.) By examining Tyler's work, his teacher determined that Tyler had difficulty converting hours to minutes. When teachers can examine actual student responses, they can group students according to what they know and what they still need to learn, and they can see what misconceptions need clarification. In Chapter 9, we explore the results of benchmark assessment.

1. Jay's mom baked a cake for his birthday. She put the cake into the oven at 4:23. It took 55 minutes to bake. At what time was the cake done baking? a. 5:18* b. 5:32 c. 4:78 d. 3:28	2. Jenna worked on her homework for 2 hours and 47 minutes. How much time, in minutes, did she spend on her homework? a. 49 b. 127 c. 147 d. 167*
3. Kylie's family wants dinner to be ready at 6:15. Kylie's mom knows the chicken needs to bake for 1 and a $\frac{1}{2}$ hours. At what time should she put the chicken in the oven? a. 4:15 b. 4:45* c. 5:00 d. 5:30	4. Which of the examples below is **not** another way to express 3 hours and 45 minutes? a. 1 hour and 65 minutes b. 2 hours and 105 minutes c. 225 minutes d. 345 minutes*
5. The high school football game started at 11:30 on Saturday morning. It lasted for 2 hours and 13 minutes. At what time did the game end? a. 12:43 b. 1:30 c. 1:43* d. 2:33	6. The girl scouts held a bake sale at their local grocery store for 4 hrs. and 30 min. They ended their sale at 3:20 in the afternoon when all their baked goods were sold. At what time did they begin their bake sale? a. 9:50 A.M. b. 10:50 A.M.* c. 11:20 A.M. d. 11:50 A.M.

FIGURE 2–8. Kelly's Assessment Items; the Asterisk Indicates the Correct Answer

Strategy 6: Make Decisions About Evaluating Learning

INFORMative assessment is even more important than evaluation in supporting learning and motivating students. It is information about what students are thinking that allows teachers to make a link between their teaching and students' learning.

The Grade Factor

In almost every school, teachers are required to evaluate students' work and give grades. Grades provide an evaluation of performance, but they are influenced by many factors. Some teachers use strict numerical averages in determining grades; others drop the lowest grade. Some teachers weight tests more heavily than daily grades, and others give checks rather than grades for homework. Despite the general public's belief that earning As in

1. Jay's mom baked a cake for his birthday. She put the cake into the oven at 4:23. It took 55 minutes to bake. At what time was the cake done baking? a. 5:18* b. 5:32 c. 4:78 d. 3:28	2. Jenna worked on her homework for 2 hours and 47 minutes. How much time, in minutes, did she spend on her homework? a. 49 b. 127 c. 147 d. 167*
3. Kylie's family wants dinner to be ready at 6:15. Kylie's mom knows the chicken needs to bake for 1 and a $\frac{1}{2}$ hours. At what time should she put the chicken in the oven? a. 4:15 b. 4:45* c. 5:00 d. 5:30	4. Which of the examples below is **not** another way to express 3 hours and 45 minutes? a. 1 hour and 65 minutes b. 2 hours and 105 minutes c. 225 minutes d. 345 minutes*
5. The high school football game started at 11:30 on Saturday morning. It lasted for 2 hours and 13 minutes. At what time did the game end? a. 12:43 b. 1:30 c. 1:43* d. 2:33	6. The girl scouts held a bake sale at their local grocery store for 4 hrs. and 30 min. They ended their sale at 3:20 in the afternoon when all their baked goods were sold. At what time did they begin their bake sale? a. 9:50 A.M. b. 10:50 A.M.* c. 11:20 A.M. d. 11:50 A.M.

FIGURE 2–9. Tyler's Assessment Items; the Asterisk Indicates the Correct Answer

one classroom represent the same accomplishment as earning As in another classroom, in some classes effort is rewarded equally with demonstrations of knowledge. In other classrooms grades reflect work measured against a performance standard. See Chapter 10 (page 281) for a more detailed discussion on grades.

Using Rubrics

Rubrics serve multiple purposes for teachers and students. In many schools, using rubrics to score student work is linked to assigning grades. Rubrics can be written to describe expectations for the accomplishment of learning targets and establish criteria for different levels of performance. Analytic rubrics can be used to describe performance for different aspects of tasks; holistic rubrics can be used to assign a value to student work. Teachers often use rubrics in an effort to bring consistency to evaluating student work.

Learn More About Decisions for Teaching and Learning

Assessment for Learning: Putting It into Practice
(Black, Harrison, Lee, Marshall, and Wiliam 2003)

Accessible Mathematics: 10 Instructional Shifts That Raise Student Achievement
(Leinwand 2009)

See Chapter 9 for more discussion about the use of rubrics and formative assessment.

INFORMing My Practice

Like all teachers, we make hundreds of decisions each day. It is not realistic to think that even the most dedicated teacher can add two more hours into his or her day to implement formative assessment strategies. Rather, each of us needs to begin with what we believe will help us do a better job of teaching our students and what we can envision trying. Think about the ideas in this chapter related to decision making. We've provided "Reflection 2–7: INFORMing My Practice: Making Tough Decisions About 'What's Next'" (see page 51) as a place for you to record your thinking.

Reflection 2–7

INFORMing My Practice: Making Tough Decisions About "What's Next?"

Page 51

Reflection 2–1: Focus on the Mathematics

Use the student work samples from either grade 2 or grade 5 to respond to these questions (see the following pages of this reflection). The second-grade students solved a computation in multiple ways. The fifth-grade work illustrates students' mathematical reasoning.

1. Are you surprised by the variety of strategies used by the students? Explain.

2. What number sense are students exhibiting? What do they understand?

3. What misconceptions can you identify? Are the mistakes conceptual or procedural?

4. Would you group students (and if yes, who would be in each group) or plan whole-class lessons and discussions?

5. What lessons would you plan to help all of the students become proficient?

(continued)

Reflection 2-1: Focus on the Mathematics
(continued)

Second-Grade Problem

There were 73 markers in the bag. Makayla gave away 39 markers. How many are still in the bag?

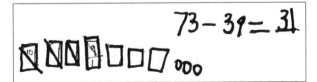

Zak

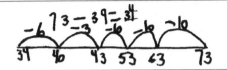

Olivia

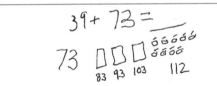

Debbie

Ezra
73 - 39 = 34
70 - 30 = 40
3 - 9 = -6
40 - 6 = 34

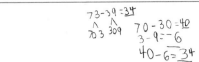

Ezra

Reilly

Chandler
73
- 39
46

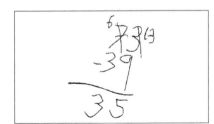

Deshaun

Amber

(continued)

Reflection 2-1: Focus on the Mathematics
(continued)

Fifth-Grade Problem*

The Small Island Post Office carries only two stamps, 5¢ and 7¢ stamps. What are all of the amounts of postage that you could not make using only 5¢ and 7¢ stamps? Write a brief explanation to explain why you know your answer is correct.

My awnser is correct because

all you had to do was find out the non-multiples of 5 and 7. Plus you had to 5+7 (12), I ranged my numbers 1-20. So the amounts of postage you can not make is 1,2,3,4,6,8,9, 11, 13, 16, 17 18, 19.

Holden

Can not make 1, 2, 3, 4, 6, 8, 9, 11, 13, 16, 18
23

I wrote down some numbers and circled the ones that couldn't be made. Up until a number that I couldn't make, all of the numbers after that I realized I could make.

Ella

$$+ \frac{5}{7} \over 12 \qquad \times \frac{5}{7} \over 35$$

$$- \frac{7}{5} \over 2$$

any numbers but these

Well it says to only use numbers 7 and 5 And if you multiply them, subtract them, and add them those are the only numbers you can use

Alex

(continued)

*Adapted from the Hawaii Algebra Learning Project.

1,2,3,4,6,8,9,11,13,16,18,23

My answer is correct
because I nocked out all
of the possibilities.

Lara

7,14,21,28,35,42, 49, 56,63
5,10,15,20,25, 30,35, 40,45,50

I know I'm right because 14 is below
five, so you can't do those, and I
also listed all the multiples
of 5 and 7 so those would not be an
answ if. You can really get to all
of the numbers except the numbers
above because you can just add
5 or 7 to another number you
made.

Ahmed

1, 2,3,4,6,8,9,11,12,13,
16,17,18,19,22,23,24,
26,27,29,31,32,33
34,36,37,38,39,41, 43,
44,46, There are more but I can't write a 1000,000 answers

All the numbers that are not multiples
of 5 or 7 are answers.

Tommy

Reflection 2-2: Assessment in a Grade 2 Classroom: Conversation with John

Suppose you are John's second-grade teacher. What notes might you make from the conversation on pages 28–29 that will influence your decisions as John's mathematics teacher?

1. What does John know?

2. What incomplete knowledge does he seem to demonstrate?

3. What other questions would you like to ask John?

4. What experiences and opportunities to learn might you plan for him?

5. What might you say to John that could help him understand what he needs to learn?

Reflection 2-3: Making Decisions About What to Teach: Guiding Questions

Use these guiding questions as a template for making decisions about what to teach when you begin new units of instruction.

Unit Goal: _____

1. What do I want my students to understand and be able to do related to the mathematics?

2. How will I know when they understand and can do these things; what do I expect as evidence of their learning?

3. What tasks and instructional activities should I plan to engage all students to help them learn these things?

4. What background knowledge do my students need to be successful with each aspect of the mathematics in the unit?

5. Does the class as a whole need to review any concepts, facts, or procedures as part of the lessons?

6. What are intermediate steps along the way that will help the students become proficient?

7. What are likely misconceptions that I need to watch for?

Reflection 2–4: Key Questions in Anticipating Students' Responses to Instruction

Choose one or more problems from page 33 that would be appropriate for your students and answer the four key questions.

Problem(s)

1. How might students solve the problem?

2. Are there other possible solutions or solution strategies?

3. What kinds of errors might the students make?

4. What thinking and reasoning do I hope students will exhibit?

Reflection 2-5: Making Decisions That Support Student Learning: What Might You Say or Do?

Problem

Kee and her brother are collecting cans. Kee has 4 cans and her brother has 6 cans. How many more cans does her brother have than Kee has?

Response:	And if the student . . .	What might you say or do?
Student 1 says $4 + 6 = 10$	often has difficulty understanding story problems.	Have student show number of cans for each child by using materials or drawing. Ask student to identify which child has more and tell how many more. Model for student how to write an equation that would reflect this conversation.
Student 2 draws ▨▨▨☐☐ and says, "two."	can solve most problems but has difficulty writing equations.	
Student 3 says $6 - 4 = 2$	solves problems correctly almost all of the time.	
Student 4 draws $4 +$ ////// and says, "ten."	insists that this is correct because the problem says "how many more."	
Student 5 draws ⦰ ⦰ ⦰ ⦰ ⦰ ○ and says, "one."	explains how to compare to find the answer but makes this error.	

Reflection 2-6: A New Approach to Scoring Student Work

Copy and use this template as you score a set of student work (see page 36 for an example).

Tally number of students who missed each question.

1	2	3	4	5	6
7	8	9	10	11	12

Identify and tally types of errors students made.

Group students for instruction according to errors they made.

Reflection 2-7: INFORMing My Practice: Making Tough Decisions About "What's Next?"

Think about the chapter you just read. Use this space to record your ideas related to the many decisions you make related to teaching mathematics.

Here is how my thinking about classroom decisions is changing as I reflect on INFORMative assessment:

Ideas I envision becoming a more important part of my practice:

Questions I have:

Frustrations/concerns I have:

Steps to Implementing Clear Learning Targets

Although there are many factors that contribute to students' success, in this chapter we focus on identifying specific learning targets. Being clear about learning targets is an important component of INFORMative assessment that leads to effective instruction and supports us in monitoring students' progress. Defining learning targets is often the first step in planning a unit of instruction.

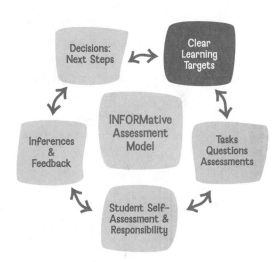

Overview

*O*nce there was a little seahorse that swam through the ocean to seek his fortune. He was very proud of himself and the mission he was undertaking. Soon he met a sponge.

"Psst, hey bud. Where are you going?" asked the sponge.

"I'm going to seek my fortune," replied the little seahorse very proudly.

"For two pieces of gold," said the sponge, "I will sell you these handy dandy flippers and your can zoom through the ocean twice as fast."

"Wow!" said the little seahorse as he paid his two pieces of gold. He put on the flippers and zoomed off into the ocean twice as fast.

Soon he met a clam. "Psst, hey bud. Where are you going?" asked the clam.

"I'm going to seek my fortune," said the little seahorse very proudly.

"For ten pieces of gold," said the sponge, "I will sell you this handy dandy scooter and your can zoom through the ocean five times as fast."

"Wow!" said the little seahorse as he paid his ten pieces of gold. He jumped on the scooter and zoomed off into the ocean five times as fast.

Soon he met a shark. "Psst, hey bud. Where are you going?" asked the shark.

"I'm going to seek my fortune," said the little seahorse very proudly.

Cunningly the shark said, "I know a great shortcut. I will carry you and you can get there twenty times as fast." He opened his mouth and pointed inside.

"Wow!" said the little seahorse as he jumped on the handy dandy scooter and zoomed off into the shark's mouth. There to be devoured.

The moral of the story is if you don't know where you are headed, you might end up someplace else and not even realize it. (Adapted from Mager 1962)

"Before their learning is assessed in a formal way, all students are informed about what they need to know, how they will be expected to demonstrate that knowledge, and what the consequences of assessment will be."

—*Assessment Standards for School Mathematics* (NCTM 1995, 17)

A major challenge at the beginning of a school year is figuring out where we are going. And like the flippers, the scooter, and the shark's supposed shortcut in this fable, we encounter many appealing resources.

From pacing guides and teacher's guides in textbooks to collections of activities and worksheets—and an Internet that provides more sites than anyone has time to thoughtfully pursue—the overwhelming abundance of options make it essential that we know where we're headed.

Knowing what is to be learned is the starting point for instructional planning and for determining what is to be assessed and how it will be measured. As our planning becomes focused, we continually break down large mathematics goals into multiple short-term learning targets. With specific mathematics targets in mind, we can choose tasks to match the content we want our students to learn.

> Knowing what is to be learned is the starting point for instructional planning. This knowledge is also the starting point for determining what is to be assessed and how it will be measured.

What Are Learning Targets?

To understand learning targets we first need to differentiate *goals* from *learning targets*. Many of the mathematics standards we are responsible for teaching are long-term goals. We explore, teach, and revisit learning goals (standards) throughout the school year or even over multiple years. Within each of these long-term learning goals there are likely to be multiple short-term learning *objectives*. Within these objectives are *learning targets* that we address in one or more lessons or a short unit of instruction. An example of a long-term learning goal (standard) is teaching students to use numbers to represent quantitative relationships. Several learning objectives contribute to this long-term goal, including understanding that there are a variety of representations for number relationships, using numbers and their properties to compute fluently and flexibly, and making reasonable estimates of measurements and quantities.

Mathematical goals—the content to be introduced, developed, and eventually mastered by students—remind us of where we are headed. Clear learning targets break down these goals, help us articulate the steps along the way, define what evidence of learning will look like, and identify what we want to assess on a day-to-day basis. (See Figure 3–1 on the following page.)

When we communicate learning targets to students in language that they understand, we all share a vision of what constitutes achievement. By clearly articulating learning targets, we are able to sequence problems and sets of tasks with purpose, guiding students along productive paths that allow them to succeed with larger mathematics goals.

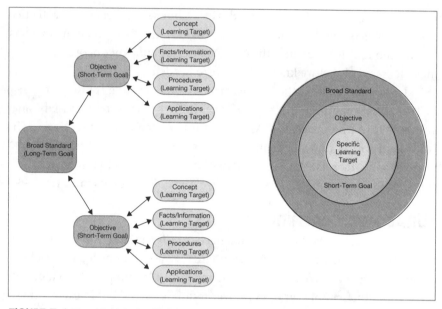

FIGURE 3–1. Two Models for Defining and Understanding Learning Targets Related to Short- and Long-Term Mathematical Goals

Navigating Definitions of Goals

Learning trajectories and continuums such as those developed through Cognitively Guided Instruction (Carpenter et al. 1999), the early childhood research by Clements and Sarama (2003), the number work of Richardson (2003), the early work of Driscoll and Confrey (1986), and other research related to rational number reasoning provide guidance in sequencing mathematics content. Standards, achievement goals, learning targets, learning progressions, objectives, grade-level expectations, and taxonomies may be defined differently by different authors and states' courses of study. As teachers, we recognize what is important to teach and what is important for students to learn. When we organize units of instruction, we identify learning targets and plan daily lessons, all of which focus on the unit's goals.

Step 1: Creating Learning Targets

Mathematical goals—the content to be introduced, developed, and eventually mastered by students—remind us of where we are headed. Clear learning targets help us articulate the steps along the way and define what evidence of learning will look like.

Categorizing Learning Targets by Knowledge Type

The first step in creating learning targets is to think about how we can categorize them. As classroom teachers, the way in which we are able to look at levels of thinking as we create lesson plans and assessments to address different learning targets is essential. We must be vigilant about the level of thinking we encourage our students to do. In part, we do this by the *verbs* we use in creating tasks and asking questions during class discussions, drawing on the work of Bloom (1956), Anderson and Krathwohl (2001), and their colleagues. Each step in the Bloom's Taxonomy pyramid builds on accomplishment of the types of thinking identified in lower level(s) of the pyramid. (See Figure 3–2.)

FIGURE 3–2. Bloom's Taxonomy Pyramid as Revised by Anderson and Krathwohl (2001), with Labels Changed from Nouns to Verbs

We use the verbs in the table below to represent levels of accomplishment and inform the design of our lessons and assessments.

Levels	Verbs Associated with Different Levels of Thinking
Creating	Compose, Create, Organize, Categorize, Design, Construct, Develop, Invent, Make, Perform, Plan, Model, Rewrite
Evaluating	Argue, Evaluate, Assess, Justify, Conclude, Critique, Decide, Generalize, Interpret, Judge, Prioritize, Prove, Rank
Analyzing	Analyze, Classify, Compare, Contrast, Relate, Prioritize, Differentiate, Discriminate, Separate, Deduce
Applying	Compute, Apply, Use, Solve, Change, Choose, Produce, Predict, Select, Show, Transfer
Understanding	Demonstrate, Convert, Discuss, Explain, Illustrate, Interpret, Predict, Restate, Summarize, Identify
Remembering	Count, Define, Describe, Identify, Label, List, Match, Name, Sequence, Tell, Write, Draw, Recall

Anderson and Krathwohl (2001) identify four types of knowledge: *factual, conceptual, procedural,* and *metacognitive.* Each is important as we break larger mathematics goals down into learning targets for our lessons.

> *Four Types of Knowledge for Helping to Create Learning Targets*
>
> 1. Factual Knowledge
> 2. Conceptual Knowledge
> 3. Procedural Knowledge
> 4. Metacognitive Knowledge

Factual Knowledge

Factual knowledge includes terms and vocabulary that have set meanings for a content area or discipline. A working factual knowledge of the specific meaning of mathematical vocabulary is an important learning target for students.

Mathematics vocabulary has specific meaning, even though the same words appear in everyday language. For example, what do you think of when someone says "table" or "similar" or "slope"? A table is a piece of furniture with a smooth, flat surface affixed to legs. Tables sometimes hold lamps or serve as places for people to eat. In mathematics, however, a *table* is an orderly arrangement of data, usually in rows and columns. And again, in everyday language, a person might say that all triangles are *similar* because triangles are closed figures made of three line segments. But mathematically speaking, *similar* figures are those with the same angle measures and proportional sides. And while someone walking on a nature trail may think of a *slope* as a gentle descending path, in mathematics, *slope* represents the degree of upward or downward slant.

> Factual knowledge includes terms and vocabulary that have set meanings for mathematics.

Order of operations is an example of factual knowledge that gives a fixed process for the order in which operations within expressions are carried out. Interestingly, order of operations may be thought of as part of the "good manners of mathematics." While Emily Post is likely to tell us that the fork goes to the left of the plate and the knife and spoon to the right, mathematicians agree that in solving an equation we first compute within parentheses, if they exist, then multiply or divide before adding or subtracting.

Another example of a factual knowledge learning target is the knowledge of number facts, such as $8 + 5 = 13$ and $6 \times 7 = 42$. Accurate, fluent, and flexible use of number facts is a goal for all students. If, however, students have not gained automaticity with facts, we want them at least to have conceptual knowledge of what the operations mean and to know strategies for figuring out the facts. We want our students to leave elementary school being able to say or write without hesitation that six multiplied by eight equals forty-eight and that forty-eight divided into six groups will have eight in each group.

Think of specific examples of factual learning targets for your grade level. Turn to "Reflection 3–1: Learning Targets to Illustrate Types of Knowledge" (see page 74) and complete the first section of the reflection. Use the same reflection page to record other examples after you read the appropriate sections that follow.

> **Reflection 3–1**
>
> Learning Targets to Illustrate Types of Knowledge
>
> Page 74

Conceptual Knowledge

Conceptual knowledge refers to the underlying big ideas of a discipline. In mathematics, it is the knowledge of the principles and generalizations, classifications, models, properties, structures, and theories.

An example of conceptual knowledge in mathematics is the understanding of the relationships within our place-value system. We use only ten digits in our base ten place-value system, and the order in which we combine these digits determines the value of each one. Quantities, both whole numbers and decimals, are related by powers of ten. As teachers, we recognize that there is a difference in the kind of knowledge that students display in being able to say that the three is in the tens place in the number 236 (factual knowledge) and that, when given 236 pencils, you could create twenty-three bags with ten pencils in each bag with some pencils left over (conceptual knowledge).

> *Conceptual knowledge refers to the underlying big ideas of a discipline.*

Another example of conceptual knowledge is the notion of *equivalence*. Equivalence is the understanding that if numbers or objects have the same value, they are equivalent. An early childhood example of equivalence is when a child recognizes that two red interlocking cubes plus one yellow interlocking cube are equivalent in number to three blue interlocking cubes. The differences in color do not influence the equivalence of the numbers in the groups of cubes. Similarly, three green pattern blocks (equilateral triangles) cover the same area as one red pattern block (trapezoid). When students begin to name numbers in different ways, they demonstrate an understanding that twenty-four has the same value as twenty plus four, or three groups of eight, or two tens and four ones, or twelve plus twelve, or thirty minus six. Three feet are equivalent to one yard and both are equivalent to thirty-six inches. Fifty percent is equivalent to five tenths and both are equivalent to one-half.

> "Procedural rules should never be learned in the absence of a concept."
>
> — *Teaching Student-Centered Mathematics: Grades K–3* (Van de Walle and Lovin 2006a, 8)

Conceptual knowledge of multiplication includes an understanding that repeated addition of the same digit and the comparable multiplication facts have the same value ($2 + 2 + 2 + 2 + 2 = 10$ or $5 \times 2 = 10$). Other examples relate to knowledge of properties of multiplication. Each of these properties illustrates that the order of numbers makes no difference in the resulting product. The order of the factors such as 4×3 or 3×4 is the *commutative property*. How factors are grouped, such as $3 \times (4 \times 5)$ or $(3 \times 4) \times 5$, is called the *associative property*. The *distributive property* is breaking apart numbers to multiply them in a different configuration, such as $6 \times 23 = 6 \times (20 + 3) = (6 \times 20) + (6 \times 3)$. When students understand these properties, they have flexibility as to how they can compute.

Conceptual knowledge in all areas of mathematics supports the development of flexible thinking and the use of multiple procedures. Consider a typical problem for second- and third-grade students: *Mike buys an apple for 74¢ and gives the clerk a dollar. How much money should he receive as change?* Students who have a conceptual understanding of the relationship between addition and subtraction or who understand the values of coins are able to avoid the messy subtraction of one hundred minus seventy-four. Their knowledge of the relationship between operations allows them to "count up" ($1 + 10 + 10 + 5$) to determine that Mike would get twenty-six cents in change. Those who quickly recognize that a quarter has a value of twenty-five cents and four quarters make a dollar are likely to recognize that the change is one quarter and one penny.

Return to "Reflection 3–1: Learning Targets to Illustrate Types of Knowledge" (see page 74) and add examples of learning targets that focus on conceptual knowledge.

Reflection 3–1

Learning Targets to Illustrate Types of Knowledge

Page 74

Procedural Knowledge

Procedural knowledge refers to the rules, algorithms, skills, and methodologies of a discipline. In mathematics, procedural knowledge is the application of a procedure such as an algorithm for addition of multidigit numbers or the process for determining the arithmetic mean of a set of data. The signs for operations $(+, -, \times, \div)$ indicate procedures that apply whether working with whole numbers, decimals, fractions, or algebraic expressions.

Some tasks require students to analyze situations as part of solving the problem and apply an organized way to determine the answer. For example, third-grade students are likely to draw pictures to determine how many different single-scoop ice-cream cones could be assembled with chocolate, vanilla, or strawberry ice cream and sugar or cinnamon cones. By sixth grade this procedural problem becomes an example of applying a procedure: *With three kinds of ice cream and two kinds of cones, how many different single-scoop cones can you make?*

Procedural knowledge includes more than just the ability to apply correctly a formula or procedure. It involves, for example, knowing what dimensions are needed to determine the volume of a rectangular prism and the appropriate formula for applying those numbers. Procedural knowledge involves being able to recognize the mathematics involved in situations and use the necessary strategies or algorithms to solve the problem. Bisecting an angle, constructing a similar figure, and using a measuring instrument correctly are additional examples. Given a thermometer, students know how to read the current temperature and determine how cold it was in the morning if the temperature has dropped 8 degrees.

Continue to complete "Reflection 3–1: Learning Targets to Illustrate Types of Knowledge" (see page 74) and add examples of learning targets that focus on procedural knowledge.

> Procedural knowledge involves being able to recognize the mathematics involved in situations and use the necessary strategies or algorithms to solve the problem.

Metacognitive Knowledge

Metacognitive knowledge is "thinking about one's own thinking." It is a reflection about what you understand and what you are uncertain about.

It is knowing that you understand different strategies for solving problems. Metacognitive knowledge is self-awareness of both thoughts and dispositions; it is knowing what we need to learn and what we need to do to remember new ideas and skills.

Learning targets related to thoughts, attitudes, and dispositions are often overlooked because they are difficult to develop and to assess. However, curiosity, open-mindedness, perseverance, and responsibility are important to student success. "Habits of mind" that include judging answers for reasonableness and looking for connections are part of intellectual prowess. If we wish to help students become better at self-assessment and to take greater responsibility for their own learning, we need to create an environment in which reflective thinking is modeled and metacognitive knowledge is valued.

> Metacognitive knowledge is "thinking about one's own thinking."

Take time to complete the chart in "Reflection 3–1: Learning Targets to Illustrate Types of Knowledge" (see page 74) and respond to the question that follows.

Reflection 3-1

Learning Targets to Illustrate Types of Knowledge

Page 74

Sample Place-Value Learning Targets Based on Knowledge Types

In order to link our planning to the different types of knowledge—factual, conceptual, procedural, and metacognitive—we begin by identifying clear unit learning targets and objectives and develop lesson plans with specific learning targets. While we do not identify *applications* as a type of knowledge, we require students to use applications to think about what they know (metacognition) and to strategically integrate their understandings to use mathematics productively. (See Figure 3–3.)

Intersecting Knowledge Types with Cognitive Processes

Part of the work of Anderson and Krathwohl (2001) in revising Bloom's Taxonomy (see Figure 3–2, page 57) was the creation of a Taxonomy Table to illustrate the intersection of the Knowledge Dimensions and the Cognitive Process Dimensions. We use a similar Taxonomy Table to classify four mathematical tasks, using symbols to indicate the intersection of knowledge types and cognitive processes. (See Figure 3–4, page 64) As we make tough decisions about how to use our time, recognizing how types of knowledge and cognitive processes relate

> "We suggest that teachers need a framework to make sense of objectives and organize them so that they are clearly understood and fairly easy to implement. This framework may help teachers plan and deliver appropriate instruction and assignments that are aligned with the objectives."
>
> —*A Taxonomy for Learning, Teaching, and Assessing* (Anderson and Krathwohl 2001, xxii)

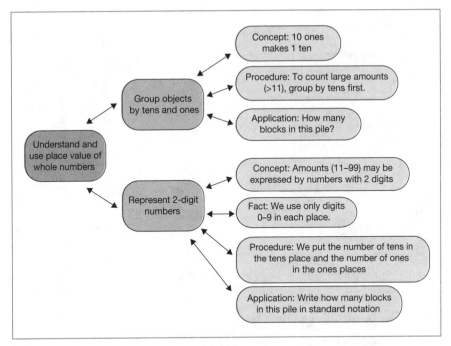

FIGURE 3-3. Place-Value Learning Targets: Linking Planning to Knowledge

ensures that we address the learning targets specified by our states and districts at appropriate performance levels. The Taxonomy Table is also a helpful tool for creating or choosing assessment tasks.

In Chapter 2 (page 33) we listed ten mathematical problems and asked you to think about how students would respond and what you might say or do in light of their different responses (Reflection 2–4). We revisit these problems in "Reflection 3–2: Classifying Problems: Intersection of Knowledge Types with Cognitive Processes" (see pages 75–76). Consider how each of the problems might be classified and fitted into a cell in the chart. This reflection would be a valuable exercise for you and your colleagues to complete separately and then compare your categorizations. Since different kinds of knowledge and different processes are often linked in contextual problems—authentic tasks— you and your colleagues may differ on exactly how items would be categorized in the chart. What is important is not the exact placement of an item into one cell, but our understanding of how types of knowledge and cognitive processes

Reflection 3-2

Classifying Problems: Intersection of Knowledge Types with Cognitive Processes

Pages 75–76

Cognitive Processes

Types of Knowledge	Remember List Memorize Name Describe Recall	Understand Classify Compare Interpret Explain Give Examples	Apply Carry Out Use Implement Calculate Illustrate Demonstrate	Analyze Organize Differentiate Construct/Deconstruct Compare/Contrast	Evaluate Judge Derive Hypothesize Validate Estimate	Create Generate Devise Design Invent Synthesize
Factual	●					
Conceptual			▲		♥	
Procedural						
Metacognitive		■				

(Adapted from Anderson and Krathwohl 2001, 28.)

● $4 \times 6 = 24$

▲ $7 + 3 \times 4 - 2 = 17$

♥ Students used three different nonstandard units to measure the diagonals of their desks. Sam concluded that the desks were different sizes because students reported that the diagonals were different lengths. Make an argument for why Sam is correct or incorrect.

■ I know that if the numerator is half of the denominator, the fraction is equivalent to one-half. This means that seven-twelfths is more than one-half.

FIGURE 3–4. Taxonomy Table: Intersection of Knowledge Types with Cognitive Processes

interact and how this can be beneficial in creating learning targets. Complete Reflection 3–2 before continuing to read.

What did you think about as you were deciding how you would classify the problems? Following are some of our thoughts for Problems 1, 2, 6, 8, 9, and 10.

Problem 1 is a familiar structure for problems for first- and second-grade students. Although the computation is easy (18 – 2), the context increases the difficulty for some students. Because the task is to solve a story problem, students must realize that they need to subtract. Did you classify this problem as Understand/Factual knowledge?

Problem 2 has simple numbers; however, we realize that students need to activate their conceptual knowledge to solve the task. They must understand that no matter how old the two children get, the relationship of their ages remains the same. Would you agree that this task could be classified as Understand/Conceptual knowledge?

To solve Problem 6, students must analyze the cost of the bulbs purchased either separately or in the package and compare the costs to make a decision. The numbers and context in this example are simple. Did you categorize this problem as Analyze paired with Procedural knowledge? The same analysis might appear more complex if the setting were different and the numbers less friendly.

The task of determining the cost of potatoes in Problem 8 is in some ways similar to Problem 6, but more straightforward. While there are several ways to determine the answer, students could merely carry out the two steps—calculate the cost of one pound and then multiply to find the cost of five pounds. The difference in this Apply/Procedural knowledge task and the Analyze/Procedure lightbulb task in Problem 6 is that the student does not need to compare any costs in making a decision.

In Problem 9, Max wanted to know how many pets most of his friends' families have. His survey generated data that he could use to figure this out, including the information that one of his friends has an aquarium. There are a number of ways that the data can be interpreted; therefore, in order to respond to this task, students need an understanding of measures of central tendency—how these measures are similar and how they are different. Students must judge if one measure is more appropriate for the context and make a case for that decision. You might have classified Problem 9 in the chart

Problem 1
Eric has 18 stickers. He gave 2 stickers to his sister. How many stickers does Eric have now?

Problem 2
Hallie is 1 year younger than her brother Joey. She thinks that someday she can catch up to his age. Will Hallie's age catch up to Joey's age? _____ Explain. How old will Hallie be when Joey is 8 years old? _____

Problem 6
Mr. Bright needs 5 new lightbulbs for his home. He can buy them separately for $1.25, or he can buy a package of 6 bulbs for $6.00. Which is the better buy? Why?

Problem 8
If 3 lbs. of potatoes costs $2.10, how much should 5 lbs. of potatoes cost?

Problem 9
Max surveyed his friends about the number of pets they have in their families. His survey results were 0, 3, 0, 4, 2, 38, 2, 0, 1. Explain why each measure of central tendency (mean, median, mode) may or may not be appropriate to describe the number of pets for these families.

as Evaluate/Conceptual; notice, however, that in the process of answering the question, students are likely to apply their procedural knowledge.

Problem 9 also provides a good example of how situating mathematics knowledge in a context influences the cognitive processes students must employ. If the task is simply to identify the mean, median, or mode of eight numbers, students are recalling definitions and simple procedures. But the addition of a context requires students to analyze and evaluate situations and make judgments. Our colleague Mike Gallagher suggests this example:

> I could imagine a scenario where the data had outliers, but the more appropriate measure was the average—for example, there are ten people on an elevator that can hold two thousand pounds. An eleventh person who weighs one hundred pounds wants to get on. Would you rather know the mean or the median weight of the first ten people?

Problem 10
Classify the following numbers as prime or composite: 2, 9, 10, 11, 17, 18, 23, 36, 51. How do you know?

The last problem, Problem 10, might be classified as Understand/Procedural knowledge. If the numbers were very large, students would need to apply an algorithm to determine if some numbers are prime.

Think About: Are Meaningful Contexts a Must?

There is a trend in some educational circles to equate quality instruction only with lessons that have meaningful contexts. In part, this may be a reaction to so-called mindless drill and practice in which students' misconceptions and errors are not specifically identified and addressed. However, there are times when learning targets taught without a context *can be powerful* if students focus on relationships in mathematics as they are learning. Suppose the learning target is to apply strategies for mentally multiplying two-digit numbers. Rather than a story situation—*Kyle wants to make 25 packages with 34 cartoon-character cards in each package. How many cards does he need?*—the problem is presented instead as 25×34. Students focus on developing strategies for finding the answer in different ways. They share how they thought about the problem, suggest alternative approaches, and hear thinking that is sometimes congruent and sometimes divergent from their own. Can you think of three different ways you might multiply these numbers mentally? If the task is presented in a context, the temptation is to focus on the story rather than on different ways to apply mathematical reasoning. Notice that it is during the discussion of the students' thinking about the mathematics that learning is taking place. It is also during discussions that students reveal their understanding of number relationships and use of properties.

Step 2: Communicating Learning Targets to Students

We not only need to have a clear understanding of what the learning targets are for our classes, but we also must be able to "unpack" those targets with language that is student-friendly so that students also have a clear vision of what accomplishment looks like. Our goal is for students to know the criteria for success and to believe that they can master the learning targets. We share criteria in different ways, but students need conversations about the criteria and models to follow. Quality work grows out of quality conversations! Below we show the links between the key questions on which teacher–student partnerships are built.

Teacher Perspective	Student Perspective
1. What are the lesson goals?	1. What am I trying to learn?
2. How can I determine what the students are learning?	2. What do I understand and what do I still need to learn?
3. Where do I go next with instruction?	3. What help do I need to learn this?

When students are partners in establishing criteria for success, the descriptions and examples have meaning for them. They take greater responsibility for their learning, and classrooms become places where everyone is working smarter. For example, by giving students the opportunity to compare two responses to the same problem and to suggest ways to improve the answers, we enable students to establish their own understandings about the criteria. Having a clear vision of what they need to learn and what mastery looks like eliminates the mystery surrounding success.

As we plan instruction, it is our responsibility to keep the teacher–student perspectives in mind. For each unit, lesson, and assessment, we need to be able to articulate what we would like the student outcomes to be; one strategy for making certain that our instruction is focused on a productive path is to create final assessments during initial lesson planning. This way, as instruction proceeds we have a reference for what we want our students to be able to do and ideas about how well they must perform to meet our expectations. The tasks and clear learning targets that we plan for instruction are paralleled in our final assessments.

Telling students in simple language what the day's lesson will encompass and alerting them to what you hope they will accomplish is one way to encourage students to take greater ownership of the learning targets. Consider the following scenarios, in which different teachers give their students a heads-up about the learning targets.

Three Scenarios That Support the Communication of Learning Targets to Students

Scenario 1

Today we're going to practice ordering fractions. The goal is for you to be able to put fractions in order between zero and one. We'll use pattern blocks, a human number line, and a fraction array to compare fractions. Think about how these models can help you see relationships among the numbers and then know how to order the fractions.

Scenario 2

Yesterday we used base ten blocks to model decimal numbers and you all were able to build models of decimal numbers and explain the models. Today our goal is for you to be able to add and subtract decimal numbers. Talk to your partner about what you know about adding and subtracting two numbers. Also talk about what you did yesterday modeling decimal numbers that might help you understand addition and subtraction of decimal numbers.

Scenario 3

We've been working on number relationships this week. I see from the work you handed in that there is still some confusion about how to determine which numbers are prime and which are composite. Today you and your partner will use color tiles to determine whether the numbers on this worksheet are prime or composite. Be prepared to talk about three things you know about prime and composite numbers. My goal is for you to be able to determine from a new list of numbers which are prime and which are composite and to tell why.

Developing partnerships with students has important implications for our teaching practices. It is likely to mean that we move away from what we experienced when we were the students. We may have to change the way we have always conducted our classes. We may need to rethink how we use class time, what kinds of questions we ask, and who does most of the talking.

Classroom Implications When Developing Partnerships with Students

- When students discuss solutions to open-ended problems or describe different ways to approach a task, assignments must have fewer problems.

- If students are to help establish criteria for success for different learning targets, they need opportunities to work with another student or with a group.

- When the emphasis is on scoring student work to identify what they have learned and what they still need to work on rather than scoring to assign a grade, it may mean redesigning the questions on the smaller quizzes we use throughout the unit and rethinking how we will provide feedback to students.

There is no question that evaluating student performance (grades) is appropriate at different points in time. But equally valid are tasks and assessments that are scored, but not graded, so that students have

Developing student–teacher partnerships has important implications for the classroom.

opportunities to find out what they know and what they still need to learn. They need feedback that helps them make adjustments in their thinking and relates their current performance to the criteria for success that the group has discussed. In later chapters we discuss environments and strategies for supporting student self-assessment (see Chapter 7) and for assessment methods to gather information about students' thinking and reasoning (see Chapters 4 and 5).

Step 3: Connecting Learning Targets to Mathematical Goals and Assessment

Connecting learning targets to mathematical goals and assessment illustrates how important it is to plan tasks carefully so that when students complete assignments, they have learned the mathematics. (See Figure 3–5.)

Notice that long-term learning goals are usually broad and complex; they are explored, taught, and revisited throughout the school year or even over multiple years. The objectives that support long-term goals involve factual, conceptual, and procedural knowledge. When students are asked to deal with mathematics in contexts, long-term goals and objectives also are apt to require metacognitive knowledge. On a day-to-day basis, teachers break down these objectives into learning targets for their lessons, such as *students will build place-value models to show equivalent representations of numbers*. Teachers may plan the same learning targets for multiple days as they teach an instructional unit. Take a moment to look back at Figure 3–3 (see page 63) and think about how other place-value goals and learning targets fit together.

"Reflection 3–3: Formalizing Preparation for Instruction and Assessment" (see page 77) is a chart that novice teachers can use to assist in lesson planning or that veteran teachers can use to reflect on the manner in which their daily lessons and learning targets relate back to broad standards and mathematical goals. While completing this chart for each unit of instruction is ideal, we recognize that it is not practical as a long-term strategy because of the number of activities most of us plan each day. However, using this chart or the questions in "Reflection 2–3: Making Decisions About What to Teach: Guiding Questions" (see page 47) several times throughout the semester will help to internalize the relationships exemplified in planning

Reflection 3–3

Formalizing Preparation for Instruction and Assessment

Page 77

Reflection 2–3

Making Decisions About What to Teach: Guiding Questions

Page 47

for instruction, teaching mathematics lessons, and assessing learning. The guiding questions and columns in the chart reflect that planning is a critical component of INFORMative assessment.

Goals	Objectives	Learning Targets
Mathematics Facts	• Learn basic number facts, conventions, definitions. • Learn vocabulary and correct terminology.	• Know addition facts. • Know the names of polygons. • Know that the name given to the point (0, 0) is origin. • Know that (3, 5) indicates the point on a graph located three units to the right of the y-axis and five units above the x-axis.
Mathematics Skills and Processes	• Develop strategies for computation. • Learn to carry out standard procedures.	• Complete multidigit addition or subtraction problems. • Apply a formula to find perimeter or to find area.
Mathematics Concepts	• Explore basic principles, relationships, and generalizations. • Make models and representations. • Develop and test theories.	• Understand that one unit of ten is equivalent to ten units of one. • Generalize or extend a pattern. • Prove what the equals sign represents. • Model that subtraction is both "take away" and comparison.
Mathematical Reasoning and Proof	• Use knowledge of concepts and procedures to solve problems and justify solutions.	• Give reasons to justify that a square is a type of rectangle. • Choose appropriate operations to solve a problem and justify why the answer is reasonable.
Mathematical Applications	• Use techniques and strategies to complete tasks and solve problems.	• Classify quadrilaterals by a rule. • Develop strategies for finding the values of a variable. • Apply knowledge of concepts and procedures to solve problems.
Personal Attitudes, Confidence, and Competence	• Develop a positive orientation toward the mathematics. • Become confident, creative, cooperative, committed, and able to work as a team.	• Work as a team to complete a difficult task. • Suggest a variety of strategies to solve problems. • Commit to finding a solution rather than giving up quickly or quitting. • Enjoy math challenges and see themselves as mathematicians.

FIGURE 3–5. Mathematics Content Organized as Goals, Objectives, and Learning Targets (Adapted from *Dynamic Classroom Assessment* [Bright and Joyner 2004])

Think About: Are Familiar Goals Easy Goals?

Sometimes the most familiar goals and learning targets are ones with which we struggle helping our students master. For example, suppose the goal is *students will be able to subtract with or without regrouping*. We know that completing many "naked number" computations may, for some students, lead to proficiency in applying a standard algorithm, while other students get correct answers sometimes and miss similar problems other times. Part of the difficulty may be that we fail to clearly articulate for ourselves that conceptual, factual, and procedural knowledge are involved and may be thought of as different learning targets leading to this goal.

Obviously, students need to know the subtraction facts (or understand subtraction as an inverse of addition facts). If they wish to apply a standard algorithm, they must know the appropriate steps. Defining subtraction narrowly as *take away* leaves out an important conceptual understanding of subtraction as a relationship of differences between the numbers. Without a clear understanding of all of the different kinds of knowledge embedded in the larger mathematical goal, students may never think beyond following steps rotely and ignore the need for modifying procedures because of the numbers or context involved. Rote applications of procedures may have students struggling to remember what to cross out and what to write down in the problem 4500 – 374. Knowing that taking the same amount from both the minuend and the subtrahend creates a new problem that maintains the same difference allows students to turn 80 – 37 into 79 – 36 or 500 – 374 into the easier problem of 499 – 373. The concept that the difference between two numbers remains the same when the same number is added to or subtracted from each is an understanding that we want students to develop. Conversations with individuals or class discussions often reveal this information if we are alert to noting it. Without discussions, however, we may never recognize students' misconceptions or incomplete understandings and unintentionally provide students with practice "doing things wrong."

INFORMing My Practice

Mathematics, like all disciplines, has a body of knowledge on which ideas build, grow, and extend. This foundational body includes learning targets that are concepts and generalizations, factual information, applications, procedures, and processes. The mathematics we are responsible for helping our students learn includes all of these processes and types of knowledge. With clear targets we are better able to plan, visualize, and describe for our students what they need to learn. With clear targets we can be better prepared for moment-to-moment decisions as instruction moves forward. With clear targets, both students and teacher know "where we are headed." Good instruction begins with clear learning targets.

> Good instruction begins with clear learning targets.

It is our responsibility always to keep the learning targets and their criteria for success in mind. For each unit, lesson, and assessment, we need to be able to articulate what we would like the student outcomes to be. By creating final assessments as we initially plan lessons, we are better able to be certain that our instruction is focused on a productive path. In planning a unit of instruction or creating daily lesson plans three questions should guide our decisions about what and how to teach impending mathematics:

- Am I clear about the learning targets for each day's lesson?

- Am I prepared to communicate what I want my students to understand and be able to do in terms that are meaningful and clear to them?

- Am I using ongoing assessment strategies to INFORM my daily planning?

Before leaving this chapter, turn to "Reflection 3–4: INFORMing My Practice: Looking Back to Plan Ahead" (see page 78) and record your thoughts about learning targets.

> **Learn More About Planning Mathematics Instruction**
>
> *About Teaching Mathematics: A K–8 Resource, Third Edition* (Burns 2007)
>
> *Teaching Student-Centered Mathematics: Grades 3–5* (Van de Walle and Lovin 2006a)

> **Reflection 3–4**
>
> INFORMing My Practice: Looking Back to Plan Ahead
>
> Page 78

Reflection 3–1: Learning Targets to Illustrate Types of Knowledge

Complete each section after reading the corresponding text on pages 58–62.

Types of Knowledge	Examples of Related Learning Targets
Factual	
Conceptual	
Procedural	
Metacognitive	

Why is it important for your mathematics program to include all of these types of knowledge?

Reflection 3-2: Classifying Problems: Intersection of Knowledge Types with Cognitive Processes

		Cognitive Processes					
		Remember List Memorize Name Describe Recall	**Understand** Classify Compare Interpret Explain Give Examples	**Apply** Carry Out Use Implement Calculate Illustrate Demonstrate	**Analyze** Organize Differentiate Construct/ Deconstruct Compare/ Contrast	**Evaluate** Judge Derive Hypothesize Validate Estimate	**Create** Generate Devise Design Invent Synthesize
Types of Knowledge	**Factual**						
	Conceptual						
	Procedural						
	Metacognitive						

(Adapted from Anderson and Krathwohl 2001, 28.)

Classification	Problem
_____	1. Eric has 18 stickers. He gave 2 stickers to his sister. How many stickers does Eric have now?
_____	2. Hallie is 1 year younger than her brother Joey. She thinks that someday she can catch up to his age. Will Hallie's age catch up to Joey's age? _____ Explain. How old will Hallie be when Joey is 8 years old? _____
_____	3. Kee and her brother are collecting cans. Kee has 4 cans and her brother has 6 cans. How many more cans does her brother have than Kee has?

(continued)

Classification	Problem
_____	4. The price of popsicles last summer was 60¢ each. Last summer Mrs. Wilson bought 1 popsicle for each of her 9 grandchildren. Now the same popsicles cost 75¢ each. How much more will popsicles cost this summer than last summer for all 9 grandchildren?
_____	5. Ray has a colored pencil that is 14 cm long. Every time he sharpens the pencil it gets 1 cm shorter. If he sharpens it 6 times, how long will the pencil be?
_____	6. Mr. Bright needs 5 new lightbulbs for his home. He can buy them separately for $1.25, or he can buy a package of 6 bulbs for $6.00. Which is the better buy? Why?
_____	7. Jane's dad wanted to know how far she had walked their dog Boots. Jane wasn't sure. "We walked about sixty steps every minute and we were gone for twelve minutes. I think my steps were about a yard long." About how far did Jane and Boots walk?
_____	8. If 3 lbs. of potatoes costs $2.10, how much should 5 lbs. of potatoes cost?
_____	9. Max surveyed his friends about the number of pets they have in their families. His survey results were 0, 3, 0, 4, 2, 38, 2, 0, 1. Explain why each measure of central tendency (mean, median, mode) may or may not be appropriate to describe the number of pets for these families?
_____	10. Classify the following numbers as prime or composite: 2, 9, 10, 11, 17, 18, 23, 36, 51. How do you know?

Reflection 3-3: Formalizing Preparation for Instruction and Assessment

State/District Goal (Standard): _____

Objectives: _____

Learning Targets	Background Needed	Instruction (Tasks)	Assessment (Tasks)	Evidence of Learning

Misconceptions to watch for:

Questions to pose during instruction:

Reflection 3-4: INFORMing My Practice: Looking Back to Plan Ahead

Think about the chapter you just read. Use this space to record your ideas.

Ideas about the importance of learning targets:

Changes in my thinking about INFORMative assessment:

Ideas I envision becoming a more important part of my practice:

Questions I have:

Frustrations/concerns I have:

Section III

How Do I Assess?

Strategies to Support Oral INFORMative Assessments

In this chapter, we begin by discussing the importance of using oral assessment methods that fit with our purposes for gathering information—that is, with the teaching decisions we need to make every day. Using INFORMative assessment, in particular, we can gather valuable information through conversations with individuals and small groups, interviews, class discussions, and observations of students at work. We end the chapter with strategies for documenting what we learn about our students' thinking from oral assessments.

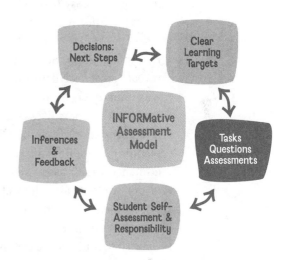

Overview

As we think about INFORMative assessment and move into assessment strategies, we need to keep in mind that there is no single "best" assessment method. Different assessment methods are likely to reveal different kinds of information. Some assessment methods are easy to administer and to score. Some give us more information than others. There are types of assessments that are easy to create but do not give us very rich information. Still others are difficult to design yet reveal a great deal of information. With some assessments we evaluate accomplishment of learning targets directly, while with others we sample performance and make inferences about learning. The purposes of diagnosing, planning, monitoring, and evaluating are likely to influence which assessment methods we use. The ages of our students and their abilities to express their ideas in written formats also influence our choices. By knowing the advantages and disadvantages of different assessment methods and being able to match the method with what we wish to find out, we can use a variety of strategies effectively and efficiently.

> "The point of classroom discourse is to develop students' understanding of key ideas. But it also provides opportunities to emphasize and model mathematical reasoning and problem solving to enhance students' disposition toward mathematics."
>
> —*Adding It Up* (National Research Council 2001, 345–346)

In this chapter we focus on strategies for informal oral formative assessments—class discussions, interviews with individuals, conversations with groups of students, and observations as students are at work. Anecdotal records (observation checklists, calendar grids, and so on) are ways in which we document these oral assessments and observations. Making use of these strategies allows us to quickly recognize students' misconceptions, become better INFORMed, and make adjustments in our lessons. Following are the three critical strategies that support oral INFORMative assessments:

Critical Strategies That Support Oral INFORMative Assessments

1. Initiating Class Discussions
2. Observing Students at Work
3. Creating and Maintaining Anecdotal Records

Strategy 1: Initiating Classroom Discussions

The best sources of information about our students come from our own classroom interactions. It is helpful to remember that as teachers we are always gathering information, informally and formally, about our students. Focusing on INFORMative assessment, however, allows us to more strategically use the information we gather.

Informal Conversations

When we engage students in informal conversations in our classrooms, we sometimes become aware of students' misunderstandings by accident, and many times are surprised at what we learn. Often what we expect that our students know and what they really think are different. At times students are like mirrors, reflecting back what we say and do but not really understanding why or how. If we focus on *understanding* student thinking, we become more certain about our inferences. Consider the following classroom scenarios; in each situation, notice the opportunities the teachers have to learn about and understand their students' thinking, even though they are not intentionally assessing students.

Three Scenarios Illustrating Informal Classroom Conversations

Scenario 1: Mr. Frierson's Third-Grade Class

Most students by third grade identify right angles in figures. In Mr. Frierson's third-grade classroom, however, one of his students kept referring to the "left angles" in a figure.

Mr. Frierson: *Leah, what is a "left angle"?*

Leah: *The lines from the corner go like this* (holds arms to show a right angle but turns herself so that one hand is pointing to the left).

Mr. Frierson: *I thought Will just used his arms the same way to model a right angle.*

Leah: *Left angles are the same as right angles. They just go the other way.*

(continued)

(continued from page 83)

Scenario 2: A Student Council Meeting

When the newly elected student council members assembled for their first meeting, the advisor asked the student secretary to get a list of students' names and homerooms. Mr. Murdoch added, "Please record the minutes for us, Kobe." After the meeting, the student brought the teacher a list of names. At the bottom of the page he had written, *Minutes 8:45–9:10.*

Scenario 3: Ms. Wade's Second-Grade Class

Early in the school year, Ms. Wade was reviewing harder addition facts with her second-grade students.

Ms Wade: *What is seven plus nine?*

Student: *Fifteen.*

Ms Wade: *No, think again.*

Student: *Seventeen?* (replying with a question in his voice)

Ms Wade: *No, seven plus nine is sixteen.*

Student: *That can't be right. Sixteen is already taken. You just said eight plus eight is sixteen.*

In Scenario 1, Mr. Frierson discovered Leah's misconception related to right angles and their orientation in space. In Scenario 2, the issue was not a mathematical misconception related to time, but a lack of understanding of what the teacher meant when he asked Kobe to "record the minutes" of the meeting. We assume that our instruction and our use of phrases or mathematical vocabulary have the same meanings for our students as for us. By verifying when these assumptions are correct and when our students' thinking diverges from what we anticipate, we become better prepared to help our students be successful. In Scenario 3, Ms. Wade's conversation with the student revealed a major misconception about addends that result in the same sums.

These scenarios are examples of situations in which unplanned, brief conversations with individual students within day-to-day routines can uncover misconceptions. We must be good listeners—paying attention to statements by our students that alert us to the need for further conversations with them.

Assessment Tip ✓

If assessing by listening for evidence of students' understanding during class discussions is not your current practice, begin by jotting down one mathematics idea you will listen for specifically in tomorrow's math class.

By listening carefully to our students, we may find they know more than they can record with traditional, symbolic notations; for example, they may write answers but find it difficult to spell out the steps they used or explain how they arrived at solutions.

Conversely, many young students know more mathematics for their age than we expect and accept challenges willingly. In one fourth-grade classroom, for example, the teacher brought in eight large chocolate bars. She explained to her eighteen students that each bar was divided into twelve sections and asked them to figure out how many squares each student would get if she shared the bars equally among the students. The students determined that there would be ninety-six small squares to share.

As it happened, a second-grade student was temporarily seated in the classroom (a time-out strategy used cooperatively by the teachers in the small school); he asked if he could be counted also, and the teacher said yes. While some of the fourth-graders set up a division problem and others tried other methods to decide how to divide each of the eight bars, the second-grader quickly drew nineteen circles and began putting tally marks in them. He counted as he made marks until he had ninety-five (five in each circle). He confidently declared that each student would get five squares with one left over for the teacher.

> **Learn More About Class Discussions**
>
> Classroom Discussions: Using Math to Help Students Learn, Grades K–6, Second Edition
> *(Chapin, O'Connor, and Anderson 2009)*
>
> Let's Talk Math: Encouraging Children to Explore Ideas
> *(Lilburn and Rawson 1994)*

Class Discussions

Discussions in the classroom not only give us a feel for how the majority of our students are thinking, but also are essential in assessing the depth of our students' conceptual and factual knowledge and their grasp of procedures. The key to judging how well a class understands the mathematics in a lesson is to listen for students' thinking beyond just the right answers.

What we learn during class discussions often guides our moment-to-moment decisions about what to do next. Suppose we are in the middle of a lesson; we might say, "Show me what you think. Have we identified all of the possible ways to combine these two shapes? If yes, put two thumbs up. If no, put thumbs down. If you are undecided, hide your thumbs behind your fingers." Using another strategy, one that requires students to have their own *yes* or *no* flash cards or *a, b, c, d* cards, we can get quick responses to simple questions by asking students to display the card that indicates their answer choice.

Increasingly, many schools have access to technologies that teachers can use to compile data—for example, students' responses to questions. Teachers

> The key to judging how well your class understands the mathematics in a lesson is to listen for students' thinking beyond just the right answers.

can also use technologies such as voting devices to see which students chose correct answers. Using technology in our classrooms and being able to respond right away based on the results means that we need to invest more time in planning questions we will ask our students. Our probing questions during class discussions can both prompt and reveal student thinking about answer choices; our questions help us move students' understanding in positive directions and at the same time give us information about their progress.

Becoming adept at informally assessing students' thinking through discussions has powerful benefits, such as the following.

Benefits of Informally Assessing Through Discussions

- We become encouraged to modify the number of questions we ask and to modify how to use the information we gather through our questioning.

- We become more diligent about listening carefully to students. Rather than focusing on what our next question will be, we pay attention to the student speaking and look for agreement or disagreement in the comments of other students.

- We see the importance of giving students time to think about their replies and are cautious not to draw conclusions too quickly from brief responses.

- We make sure we call on students randomly, not just those with their hands raised, which will likely help reveal students' understanding and misconceptions.

- We recognize that talking with a student in an individual three-minute conversation is a way to avoid misinterpreting the student's answers. We are less likely to make incorrect inferences about what students have mastered or take action because of an unintentional bias (for example, what we *expect* versus what the student really *understands*).

- And last but not least, our moment-to-moment decisions about what to do next become better INFORMed.

In-Class Interviews

Pulling up a chair beside a student, stopping by a student's desk, or calling a student to join a small group at a table while other students are engaged in productive work are opportunities to probe an individual student's misconceptions or incomplete understanding—or advanced ideas that need challenging. Such in-class conversations, which we refer to as interviews, give us a better feel for the class as a whole and alert us to students whose understandings we will want to probe more intensely.

An ideal time for in-class interviews is while students move through learning stations or centers or complete their morning work. We may remember a student's response during a class discussion or wonder about a student's lack of conversation about particular mathematics and write a couple of questions to ask the student while the class is working on an assignment. These questions are the basis of quick interviews.

One key to getting the most out of in-class interviews is knowing a continuum related to the concepts we are currently teaching and being aware of specific learning targets. Identifying what information we are looking for allows us to plan appropriate questions. In all of these discussions it is important to remember that our purpose in understanding what individual students know and what they still need to learn is *not* to create thirty different lesson plans; rather, we want to judge our students' levels of understanding about particular learning targets to make decisions about how we can shape our plans for the class in ways that better meet the needs of all students. Following are examples of situations in which brief interviews with individuals during regular mathematics lessons guide us in making adjustments in our planning.

> Brief interviews with individuals during mathematics lessons guide us in making adjustments in our planning.

Example 1: Interviews in K–1 Classrooms

If you are a kindergarten or first-grade teacher, put cubes in your pocket and move around the room, asking different children to count the collection. Noticing how they count—randomly, with purposeful one-to-one correspondence, or by twos—gives you information about the strategies they are using. If a student counts by ones, ask him if he would get the same results if he recounted by fives or snapped the cubes into tens and ones. Kindergartners and first-grade students learn to count by rote, "five, ten, fifteen, twenty. . . ." However, this does not necessarily mean that they understand groups of five, or the relationship of twenty to twenty-five, or that counting the same group of objects by fives results in the same total as counting the group by ones. Identifying what students know is the purpose of these brief interviews.

Often it is the simple follow-up question that gives us insight into what a child knows. Consider the following conversation between a kindergartener and her teacher:

Ms. Simmons asked Katie to count out eight cubes, then she covered part of the collection and asked her to count those that were visible and tell how many were hidden. Katie did the task successfully and said:

Katie: *Ask me a multiplication problem.*

Ms. Simmons: *Okay. What is three times two?*

Katie: (After a pause) *Six!*

Ms. Simmons: *How did you know the answer?*

Katie: *I just counted the ducks in my head.*

Ms. Simmons: *What do you mean you counted the ducks?*

Katie: *My sister taught me how to figure out multiplication. You just count all of the ducks in the groups.*

Ms. Simmons: *So how would you multiply two times four?*

Katie: (Looks away and silently "counts" one, two, three, four; hesitates, recounts, and then continues, five, six, seven) *Eight!*

At first, Ms. Simmons's plan simply was to check on Katie's knowledge of sums of eight, but Katie wanted to talk about multiplication—because her older sister was in third grade and that's what she had learned. By asking follow-up questions ("How did you know the answer?"; "What do you mean you counted the ducks?"), Ms. Simmons learned that Katie understood that multiplication involved adding equal groups.

Example 2: Interviews in Second- and Third-Grade Classrooms

Second- and third-grade students, when asked to solve a three-digit subtraction problem requiring regrouping, will say to cross out the number in the tens place and "make it one less," then "put a one" beside the number in the ones place. Sometimes they begin by crossing out the number in the hundreds place and making it one less, crossing out the number in the tens place and making it one less, and then adding one beside the number in the ones place. They explain these actions as making each place "one less," without relating their actions to renaming their original number with one less hundred or ten and more ones. If you are a second- or third-grade teacher, you have seen many variations of this scenario.

Obviously, when students' answers are incorrect, we talk with the students to try to uncover the misunderstanding or incomplete knowledge that causes their mistakes. However, even when students compute three-digit subtraction problems correctly, it is important to have short interviews to make certain they have a conceptual basis for the procedures they are doing. The planned interview might be two questions—a computation we ask the student to complete while thinking aloud, and a question about what each number represents as it is regrouped.

Example 3: Interviews in Fourth- and Fifth-Grade Classrooms

In Mr. Alvarez's fourth-grade class, Timothy consistently and correctly completed worksheets and weekly quizzes about creating equivalent fractions. During the following three-minute interview, however, Mr. Alvarez discovered that Timothy's successful application of a procedure was hiding a conceptual misunderstanding.

Mr. Alvarez: *Tell me what you know about finding equivalent fractions.*

Timothy: *You just multiply the top number and the bottom number by the same thing* (writes $\frac{2}{3} \times \frac{4}{4} = \frac{8}{12}$ and $\frac{1}{4} \times \frac{2}{2} = \frac{2}{8}$). *You can reduce fractions by dividing the top number and the bottom number of a fraction by the same number* (writes $\frac{6}{12} \div \frac{2}{2} = \frac{3}{6}$).

(continued)

(continued from page 89)

Mr. Alvarez: *Why do these strategies work?*

Timothy: *I don't know, but I can give you more examples (writes several more examples, including $\frac{3}{4} \times \frac{2}{2} = \frac{6}{8}$).*

Mr. Alvarez: *If I draw two circles that are the same size and shade three-fourths of one of them and six-eighths of the second circle, will the amount shaded be the same?*

Timothy: *No, the circle that has six-eighths shaded would be more.*

Mr. Alvarez discovered Timothy's lack of conceptual understanding of equivalent fractions because he regularly made it a practice to talk individually with his students about the content he was teaching. In the above example, Mr. Alvarez focused on Timothy's thinking, not just his ability to apply an algorithm. If he had looked only at Timothy's worksheets and quizzes, he might never have known about the gaps in Timothy's thinking about equivalent fractions.

> **When our students respond with wrong answers, we want to know the logic behind those mistakes.**

Stop and reflect on one of the interviews in the previous examples—either the kindergartner's ideas about multiplication (see page 88) or the fourth-grade student's understanding of equivalent fractions. What might you infer about each student's thinking? What questions would you like to ask the student? Complete these questions and more in "Reflection 4–1: Making the Most of Interviews: Inferences About a Student's Thinking" (see page 107).

The reasons why students make mistakes are likely to be varied, and our lessons, whether for differentiation or interventions, need to address the different misunderstandings. When our students respond with wrong answers, we want to know the logic behind those mistakes. When students respond to answers correctly, we want to know how confident they are in their answers. When we focus on the depth and breadth of students' understandings and specifically address gaps in their understanding, we position our students to achieve at higher levels.

Reflection 4–1

Making the Most of Interviews: Inferences About a Student's Thinking

Page 107

Individual Interviews

We have been talking about three- or four-minute planned interviews that take place during our regular mathematics lessons. Traditionally, elementary teachers schedule longer individual conferences around reading and writing; however, the same rationale for making time for conferencing with individuals in language arts applies just as much to mathematics. One-on-one conferences—extended interviews—may give us the most accurate information about our students' understandings. When we meet one-on-one with a student to discuss samples of their work and probe their thinking about specific mathematics, we use the conversation as a guide in modifying instruction to meet the student's needs. Individual conferences also are important opportunities for us to give feedback to students about the quality of their work and how they might improve. Individual conferences are times to set and review goals—those set by the student and by the teacher. Biweekly conferences are ideal, but planning a ten- to fifteen-minute interview outside of classtime with each student every grading period is a positive first step.

> One-on-one conferences— extended interviews— may give us the most accurate information about our students.

For these interviews it is important that we arrange a time and place where we are not likely to be interrupted. Both teacher and student need to feel comfortable and not worry about others overhearing the conversation. These interviews might be before or after school, during a portion of the lunch period, or at a time when another adult is working with the rest of the class. Having materials ready (pencil, paper, manipulatives, problems written out) means that no time is wasted getting organized.

There are basically three types of extended interviews. One type relates to content that we are planning to teach; we use these diagnostic interviews to help determine what the student knows before we begin instruction. A second type of interview arises from current instructional topics. We may base the interview around several samples of the student's work or plan new tasks related to content we are teaching. There are times when a student's thinking is not at all clear to us based on written work, and more than a quick conversation is necessary. The third type of interview focuses on a student's problem-solving strategies and is likely to include a variety of topics.

Beginning an interview with several easy questions, such as "What number comes after fifteen?" or "What is three times five?" or "What is half of sixty?" will help the student relax. While we want the student to be comfortable, we do not want to spend ten minutes on general chitchat; having printed questions ready so that the student can respond to them immediately in writing is helpful.

It is very difficult not to slip into a teaching mode when talking with an individual student—our impulse is to explain what the student seems not to understand; it is tempting to take the pencil from the student's hand to show how to get the answer. Keep in mind that the purpose of the interview is to identify what the student knows and what misconceptions he or she may have related to the content. Our job is to listen—not talk. If the interview relates to identifying specific needs and determining whether interventions—not just differentiation—are necessary, we need to use the interview to help us determine exactly what those interventions are. Recording the interview in audio or video and saving the student's work allows us to reflect back on what the student said and did. We can focus on watching and listening, rather than taking copious notes during the interview.

Suggestions for Getting Started with Student Conferences

- Choose the mathematics topic and write the questions.

- Identify a time and place to avoid interruptions.

- Listen carefully and use wait time.

- Converse but do not teach.

- Keep the interview positive for both you and the student.

- Record the conversation and keep the student's work.

For example, finding out if a student recognizes that letters can be used to represent numbers in different ways allows us to make assignments that expand the student's knowledge of variables. Does the student understand that a letter may name a specific unknown quantity ($3 + n = 7$)? Does the student realize that a letter used as a variable can represent many values ($n > 6$)? Does the student recognize that letters can name specific objects in formulas (area of a rectangle $= l \times w$)? Preparing for an interview related to this content would include creating problems using letters for numbers in each of these ways as well as one or more word problems that involve this content.

Strategy 2: Observing Students at Work

Observing students is what teachers do. We look for students' expressions that indicate they are excited, engaged, and eager to share. We notice when they look puzzled or when they are not tuned into the mathematics lesson. We listen in on conversations between partners and discussions of small groups. Using observation as an INFORMative assessment strategy means that we intentionally listen and look for evidence of what students know—we look for the logic behind their answers. One advantage of observations is that we may see more evidence of mathematics understanding for students who struggle with language and have difficulty explaining their thinking on written assessments.

Listening to students as they work and asking them to explain their thinking gives us more information than their written work alone reveals. We also use students' solution strategies—or misconceptions— as teachable moments for providing feedback to them. By observing students as they work, we may be able to redirect those who have started along an incorrect solution path.

In the following examples, students are working on classroom assignments while their teachers are carefully observing what individual students are doing.

> "Observing, questioning, and listening are the primary sources of evidence for assessment that is continual, recursive, and integrated with instruction."
>
> —*Assessment Standards for School Mathematics* (NCTM 1995, 46)

Example 1: First-Grade Classroom

In Mr. Cox's first-grade classroom, students used paper plate clocks to practice showing time to the hour. He had them set their clocks to 8:00, then 3:00, then 10:00. Moving around the room to see which students moved hands on the clock to the correct positions with confidence and which ones needed to watch their neighbors, Mr. Cox noticed that Erin seemed to be setting her clock at different times. The student looked confident as she worked. As Mr. Cox approached, Erin said, "Look. I set the hands on my clock to seven fifty-five. That is the time my bus comes each morning." This was the same student, Mr. Cox remembered, who had told him that she could not show her age using pennies and nickels because she did not have any "half-pennies" and she was six and a half. At this point Mr. Cox recognized that he needed to find a moment to talk further with Erin to determine what mathematics explorations would extend her learning.

Example 2: Fourth-Grade Classroom

By using INFORMative assessment strategies on a day-to-day basis, we are able to intervene as soon as we observe students making mistakes or misinterpreting a task so that their efforts in mathematics have positive results. In the example shown opposite, notice that the student misinterpreted question 1 and answered it incorrectly. (See Figure 4–1.) To solve questions 2 and 3, the student used the incorrect response from the first question. This caused him to use the wrong numbers for the computations even though he interpreted the tasks correctly and used an appropriate process for each question. If you were this student's teacher, how would you help him discover his misinterpretation of question 1? Since one purpose of formative assessment is to help students move along productive pathways and not to "catch them in their mistakes," talking with students as they are working allows us to help them avoid situations such as this. At this juncture our purpose is not to evaluate but to support learning. How we provide that support—that is, the questions we ask the student or the feedback we give—may vary.

Example 3: Fifth-Grade Classroom

As a review for ordering decimals, Mrs. Tucker gave her fifth-grade students large cards on which she had written different decimal numbers and then directed them to line themselves up from least to greatest without talking. Tory, who had the 0.1 card, positioned himself in the line to show that his number was less than 0.01. The other students kept motioning for him to move, but he was adamant that he was in the correct place. Finally,

The Centerville Pet Shop

The Centerville Pet Shop has 12 large parrots that belong to the owner. The parrots eat eight packages of a special fruit mixture each day. The shop owner buys the fruit mixture in boxes that have four packages of fruit mixture in each box.

1. How many boxes are needed each day for the parrots' lunch? How do you know?

$$
\begin{array}{llllllll}
4 & 8 & 12 & 16 & 20 & 24 & 28 \\
1 & 2 & 3 & 4 & 5 & 6 & 7 \\
42 & 46 & 50 & 54 & 58 & 62 & 66 \\
8 & 9 & 10 & 11 & 12 & 13 & 14 \\
70 & 74 & 78 & 82 & 86 & 90 & 94 \\
15 & 16 & 17 & 18 & 19 & 20 & 21
\end{array}
\qquad
\begin{array}{r}
12 \\
\times\ 8 \\
\hline
96
\end{array}
\quad \boxed{21}\ \text{boxes}
$$

Because $12 \times 8 = 96$. And $96 \div 4 = \boxed{21}$.

2. How many boxes are needed for one week? Explain your thinking.

If there are 21 boxes in one day, and there are 7 days in a week, then $21 \times 7 = \boxed{147}$.

$$
\begin{array}{r}
21 \\
\times\ 7 \\
\hline
147
\end{array}
$$

3. How many packages are used in one week? __588__ How did you use the information from question 2 to answer this question?

Well if there are 147 boxes in one week, and each box has 4 in it, than $147 \times 4 = \boxed{588}$

$$
\begin{array}{r}
147 \\
\times\ \ \ 4 \\
\hline
588
\end{array}
$$

FIGURE 4–1. The Centerville Pet Shop Problem

Mrs. Tucker asked everyone to take a seat except Tory, with his 0.1 card, and the student with the 0.01 card. "Why do you think that your card names the lower value?" Mrs. Tucker asked Tory. "Because," he replied, "her number is one-hundredth and my number is one-tenth, and ten is less than one hundred."

Before continuing, take a moment to think about Tory's misunderstanding. Answer the questions in "Reflection 4–2: Tory's Misunderstanding" (see page 108) before continuing.

Reflection 4-2

Tory's
Misunderstanding

Page 108

You can begin using observation as an INFORMative assessment strategy tomorrow—your lessons plans do not need to change. Observations can take place any time—during center time, directed math activities, class discussions, group work, or as students are working on projects. You will begin to discover more and more opportunities when you can gather information about several students at once.

By paying careful attention to how individual students respond, it is possible for us to gather information about a number of students simultaneously. For example, many of us routinely use hundred charts or ninety-nine charts in our classrooms. As we ask questions, students use counters on the charts to indicate their responses, and we carefully focus on the responses of several students at the same time. Even when there is no writing involved in the questions and answers, we can do checks of factual knowledge and simple procedures (mental math) very quickly:

- Cover these sums: 5 + 5, 7 + 9, 6 + 4.

- Cover 10 more than 25, 10 more than 16, 10 more than 81, 10 less than 44, 10 less than 39.

- Cover the number that tells how many pennies equal a dime, how many nickels equal a quarter, the value of one dime and two nickels.

- Cover the number that is 3 tens and 4 ones, 7 tens and 2 ones, 1 ten and 5 ones.

- Cover the number of inches in a yard, the number of ounces in a pound, the number of centimeters in a meter.

- Cover the number that is 3 more than 24, cover 2 more than 39, cover 4 less than 61.

During these times, notice who responds quickly and who glances around. We can see when students hesitate or cover an incorrect number. As with all assessments, we may decide to follow up with an individual conversation or a similar activity in a center. Also, simply "filing away" the information in your head for future planning is always an option.

Strategy 3: Creating and Maintaining Anecdotal Records

Observations, such as classroom discussions and interviews, are assessment strategies we use to gather information that usually do not include documentation. However, documentation is important; creating and maintaining anecdotal records mean that we have easy access to information that we can review as the school year progresses.

How any teacher creates anecdotal records is a matter of personal preference. We use anecdotal records to provide information for conferences with students and their parents, to share evidence when we work with assistance teams, and to organize flexible groups when interventions are required. We use charts that include information about all students in the class as efficient references for lesson planning. If we are technologically savvy, we use computer programs to record information in one format and print it out in multiple ways.

Because it is close to impossible to remember exactly what mathematics understanding each individual student in an entire class demonstrates during conversations, it is helpful to know a variety of ways to keep notes about our students. In the following sections we suggest multiple ways to create anecdotal records: observation checklists, calendar grids, mailing labels and sticky notes, index cards, photographs and videos, and journals and other narratives. Keep in mind that making notes should never be "busywork"; we need to use anecdotal records to help us meet the needs of individuals as we work with all students in our classes.

Six Ways to Create Anecdotal Records

1. Observation Checklists
2. Calendar Grids
3. Mailing Labels and Sticky Notes
4. Index Cards
5. Photographs and Videos
6. Journals and Other Narratives

Observation Checklists

Using observation checklists, or group charts, we can look for patterns in student performance as we make instructional decisions. At a glance, we can look for students who are excelling and for students who may need extra help. An easy way to create observation checklists is to make a chart with the names of all students in the rows and the content to be observed—for example, skill clusters or an instructional unit's learning targets—in column headings. If we use a class roster to make a master chart, we can duplicate the page multiple times and record different headings on different pages. The way in which we note the success or the needs of individual students on charts varies; deciding on one recording system (after experimenting with a few) and sticking with it on all observation checklists is helpful.

For example, one kindergarten teacher used minimal notation to record her information. Rather than mark every item for every student, she chose to mark students who were absent on the days she recorded information, students who exceeded her expectations (+), and students who needed extra help with the content (–). (See Figure 4–2.) No mark in the grid indicated that the student was working at the expected level. You can see at a glance that one student, Luz, was performing most content in a manner that exceeded the kindergarten-grade expectations and that Trina, another student, was struggling.

Some teachers prefer to make a notation for each child for each item. A teacher might use "+" when students exceed expectations, "✓" when students progress satisfactorily, and "–" when students have difficulty. If the teacher does not have a clear picture of what the student understood, she might use a "?" on the chart. A blank space may indicate that the student is absent. Notice that whatever way a teacher chooses to record information, it is possible to tell which students need additional assistance or experiences, though we may not know the exact nature of the problem. The more specific the lists of skills, facts, concepts, and processes in the labels across the top of the columns, the more specific the information is.

Calendar Grids

Another way to record information about the entire class on one sheet is to use a calendar grid. (See Figure 4–3, page 100.) These grids are different from observation checklists in that a calendar grid is focused on only one learning target. Calendar grids have the advantage of providing a small space for noting the nature of students' misunderstandings or providing space for notes about unusual or advanced student ideas. Using a calendar grid, we can write

Teacher: **Mrs. Robinson**   Grade: **K ?**   OBSERVATION CHECK LIST

Sample

Name	TOPIC 4	11-17 Describes Groups	11-18 Numbers 0-9	11-24 Numbers 0-9	11-26 Write 0-5	12-1 Match quantities to numerals	12-4 Ordinals 1st-6th	TOPIC 5	12-8 Sort by size	12-10 Long & Tall	12-11 Heavier/Lighter	12-12 Which holds more	12-15 Pan Balance Activities	12-17 Fire Station Fun	12-17 What's the order	12-18 Time
Abby									+		+					−
Beth																
Cullen											+					
David																
Franco											+					
Ivan											+					
Jill L.											−					
Jill R.																
Kenny																
Luz		+	+	+		+			+	+	+	+		+	+	
Maria																
Mark											+					
Pedro							−				+			−		
~~Roseanne~~						A	A	[withdrew from school								
Stefan							−				−			−		
Trina						−	−		−		−			−	−	−
Tyler				+		+										
Victor																
Laura	12/8	Entered school						[			−			−		+

FIGURE 4–2. A Kindergarten Teacher's Observation Record-Keeping Checklist

Simple patterns ↓ ↓↓
simple patterns + some harder 11-30 1,3,5,7,— / 76,70,65,—;—;—/ 4,9,14,19;—;—;—
Pattern Assessment Sheet (1 out of 20) 1-20
Round About – index cards w/ patterns (4 cards) 4-14

_____Date _____/_____Function

MATH ASSESSMENT

Michael	April	Tanner	Garrison	Sydney
✓✓ 21/20 all	wanted to repeat said inspected 5/20 simple only	✓ 19/20 all	no only 5's 12/20 simples only	wanted to repeat no +5 4÷3 14/20 all

Austin	Kelsea	Brandi	Joseph	Brooke
2,5%,10% only not +5 18/20 all	✓ 14/20 all except -1	✓ 19/20 all	no wanted to repeat -9×+5 11/20 simples only	wanted to repeat only 5's 16/20 much better — all except

Naomi	Jacob	Andrew	Lindsay	Brandon
✓✓ 20/20 all	2,5,10 only ✓ 16/20 all except -1	2,5,10 only 17/20 all	wanted to repeat not +5 ÷3 14/20 all	✓+ knew number ✓ wrote some of his own 20/20 all

Danyei	Cody	Savannah		
no no-tried to repeat 4/20 simple only	✓ not +5 ÷3 17/20 all except	wanted to repeat not +5 17/20 all		

FIGURE 4-3. A Kindergarten Teacher's Observation Record-Keeping Calendar Grid

something about every student or we can record only problems and simply put a check mark when no misconceptions or incomplete understandings are evident.

We can use observation checklists and calendar grids as the basis for grouping students, choosing tasks for the class, and identifying questions to ask individual students. Note that copies of these should *not* be included in any individual student's mathematics folder because they show information about all students, which is not appropriate for other students or their parents to see.

Mailing Labels and Sticky Notes

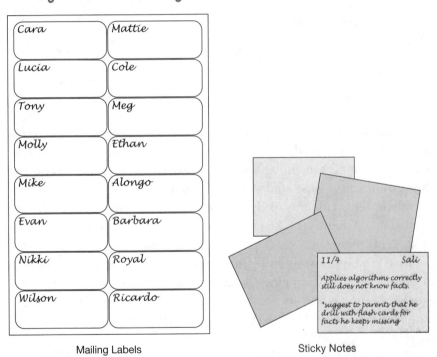

Cara   Mattie

Lucia   Cole

Tony   Meg

Molly   Ethan

Mike   Alongo

Evan   Barbara

Nikki   Royal

Wilson   Ricardo

Mailing Labels

11/4   Sali

Applies algorithms correctly
still does not know facts.

*suggest to parents that he
drill with flash cards for
facts he keeps missing

Sticky Notes

There are numerous strategies for taking notes about individual students. Some teachers write notes on blank mailing labels as they move around the classroom; later they attach the labels to file folders or charts for each student. Other teachers prefer to use sticky notes in the same manner. Both of these are quick and relatively inexpensive ways to record what we observe.

The primary disadvantages of these types of records are that we have to remember to file them before they get lost and, more importantly, we tend to make many notes about some students and few, if any, about others. One way to ensure that we observe all students is to preprint students' names on mailing labels.

Index Cards

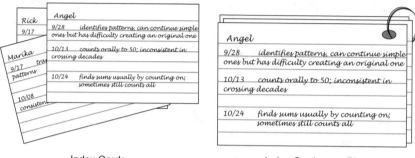

Index Cards   Index Cards on a Ring

Index cards can be used and easily stored in student folders or in a recipe file box. The most casual way we use cards is to write about a student only when we observe something special we want to remember. While any observation about what students understand is good, using index cards casually in this manner is likely to mean that we do not have records for all students. A more structured way for us to use index cards is to write all students' names on cards periodically so that we will be reminded to observe and talk with each student in our class. Punching a hole in an upper corner and slipping all cards on a large key ring to keep them together is an easy way to carry the cards around. When a student's card is full, we then either file it or keep it on the ring and add a new card for the student.

Another way to assemble class sets of index cards is to attach the cards to a clipboard. This record-keeping strategy is handy because the clipboard provides a sturdy writing surface as we move around the room. To make assembly easy, we write the students' names on the bottom of the cards and attach them to the clipboard from the bottom up, taping each card along its top edge. Once a student's card is filled, we replace it on the clipboard and file the card with observations with other student records.

Cara	Warren
Alonzo	Tony
Maya	Luc
Will	Aubry
Sonia	Kaneka
Joseph	Enrico
Evan	Meg
Mattie	Cole
Rusfika	Ben
Jose	Lucia
Marika	Tinamarie
Jimmy	Mike

Index Cards on Clipboard

Sometimes we create a class set of index cards, sorting the cards into eight to ten groups and focusing on one group of students per day. This method of anecdotal record keeping works especially well in self-contained classrooms where teachers can pay extra attention to two to four students each day, purposefully talking with them to probe their understanding related to the current learning targets and long-term goals. We take notes throughout the day and then summarize our observations at the end of the day. By the end of two weeks, we will have focused on the mathematical understandings of every child in the class.

Photographs and Videos

Many teachers use photos and short videos to record students at work, jotting notes on the backs of photos to explain the situation, the students' solutions, or the products they have created.

Using Photographs for Recording Students at Work

Digital cameras have made the costs of this method of documentation much more affordable. As an bonus, multiple copies of small digital photos allow students to attach photos of themselves to mathematics papers of which they are particularly proud.

Short videos have the advantage of documentation with sound as well as images. We use a small video camera to make multiple videos of short interviews or group work, load and save the videos onto our computers for later reflection and planning. The videos are evidence of learning that parents enjoy seeing, and we will be able to show rather than just describe for parents how their child completes tasks.

Another advantage of video is that when we capture students engaging in class discussions and explaining how they solve problems, we can use the video later to talk with individual students about their participation. Video is also an especially valuable tool for helping students take greater responsibility for improving their work habits. Videoing students as they are "doing good" is a powerful positive reinforcement.

Technology changes so rapidly that it is hard to predict what will become available to classrooms at reasonable costs in the near future. What we need to keep in mind is the potential for us to engage students in self-assessment, to have greater depth of understanding of students' thinking, and to take advantage of the ease of documenting evidence of learning.

Journals and Other Narratives

Some teachers keep personal journals, taking notes on a day-to-day basis and periodically reflecting on what they know about each student.

One way to organize a journal is to set aside one page for each student. This is helpful during parent and student conferences because it allows others to easily see student progress over time. As an alternative, we may write or tape daily problems at the top of the page and record observations about how students respond to the task. (See Figure 4–4.) The advantage in this type of journaling is in planning; knowing how groups of students respond to certain types of problems helps in decisions about "what's next."

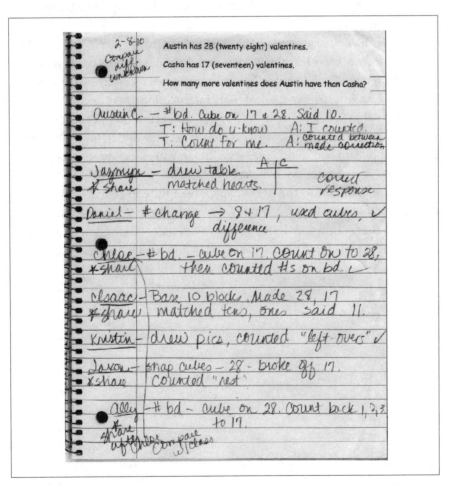

FIGURE 4–4. A Page from a Teacher's Observation Record-Keeping Journal

INFORMing My Practice

As we integrate oral assessment strategies into our instruction, we recognize that there are many ways we can gather information about our students' understandings and misunderstandings. Our goal is to merge ongoing assessment with instruction so that both are a natural part of what we do each day. When our students respond to questions incorrectly, we want to know the logic behind those mistakes. When they respond to questions correctly, we want to know how confident they are in their answers. In other words, we want to be able to make adjustments to our teaching while the learning is taking place.

> When our students respond to questions incorrectly, we want to know the logic behind those mistakes.

INFORMative assessment means that we work hard to make certain that we have clear learning targets and that our students understand our expectations. By becoming better listeners, we recognize what students need to do to improve and can design interventions that keep them from falling far behind. For example, one of our colleagues told her students that she asked questions to help her assess daily what they understood. One of her students spoke up and said, "No, Mrs. Gunter, you assess us *minute-ly*." That is perhaps the ultimate "assessment compliment."

Before going on to the next chapter, take time to reflect on your own thinking about discussions, interviews, and observations as assessment strategies. "Reflection 4–3: INFORMing My Practice: Gathering Information About Students' Thinking" (see page 109) is provided for you to record your ideas.

Reflection 4-3

INFORMing
My Practice:
Gathering
Information
About Students'
Thinking

Page 109

Reflection 4–1: Making the Most of Interviews: Inferences About a Student's Thinking

See pages 88–90. On which scenario are you reflecting, the kindergartner's ideas about multiplication or the fourth-grade student's understanding of equivalent fractions?

1. What might you infer about the student's thinking?

2. What questions would you like to ask the student?

3. What do you know about this student's confidence in himself or herself?

4. What opportunities for continued exploration of the mathematics might you provide?

Reflection 4-2: Tory's Misunderstanding

"Why do you think that your card names the lower value?" asked Mrs. Tucker. Tory replied, *"Her number is one-hundredth and my number is one-tenth, and ten is less than one hundred."*

1. Was this student's misunderstanding conceptual or procedural?

2. How might the teacher address this fifth-grade student's misconception? What experiences would you plan?

3. What questions would you like to ask the student?

Reflection 4-3: INFORMing My Practice: Gathering Information About Students' Thinking

Think about the chapter you just read. Use this space to record your ideas.

Ideas about discussions, interviews, and observations I envision becoming a more important part of my practice:

Anecdotal record strategies I am using or plan to use:

Changes in my thinking about INFORMative assessment:

Questions I have:

Strategies to Support Written INFORMative Assessments

Every assessment helps us make decisions about next steps in our teaching. In this chapter, we continue the discussion of assessment methods, focusing on two primary categories of written assessments: constructed response and selected response. In the final section of this chapter we address portfolios, sources of collected evidence from which we gather the big picture of a student's progress.

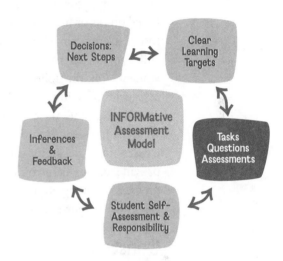

Overview

Traditionally we grade students' written work on small quizzes, tests, classwork, and homework and use these as the primary source of evidence about our students' progress and what we should plan next. Parents look at answers on students' papers that we have marked correct or incorrect and judge their child's progress based on his or her grades. While grades seem to satisfy most parents, for instructional planning a grade is not sufficient to tell the whole story about any particular student. On the following pages we discuss two key categories of written assessments: constructed-response assessments and selected-response assessments. These written assessments, along with oral assessments—classroom discussions, interviews, and observations—provide useful information for monitoring students' progress, planning our instructions, and, most importantly, INFORMing our next steps.

> "Making valid inferences about students' learning requires familiarity with every student's responses in a variety of modes, such as talking, writing, graphing, or illustrating, and in a variety of contexts."
>
> —*Assessment Standards for School Mathematics* (NCTM 1995, 52)

Constructed-Response Assessments

Constructed-response assessments are made up of tasks and problems that require student-generated answers, including responses to short-answer questions, single- and multistep problems, and open-ended tasks. Journal entries and learning logs, pictures with captions, exit cards, written reports, mathematics probes, and investigations are other examples that we can classify as constructed-response tasks or assessments. In most instances there is one correct answer to the assessment questions, but many of these tasks are designed for students to explain how they got their answers. Equally important to student-generated answers are explanations that provide insight into how well students are grasping the mathematics. In some open-ended tasks, there may be multiple correct responses depending on the justification that students give or the approach they take to answering a question.

Notice that in the following constructed-response task, students not only are allowed choices, but also must attend to parameters; they are prompted to make a specific list to identify their choices and to compute the results of their shopping.

Sojoan is shopping for school clothes. She has $110 to spend. A pair of jeans costs $32 and the T-shirts she likes cost $18 each. Long scarves are $15 each. She plans to buy at least 1 of each item. She wants to spend as much money as she can until she can't buy even 1 more item! Create a list of what she might purchase, identifying each item separately to show how many pairs of jeans, scarves, and T-shirts she can buy. According to your list, how much will Sojoan spend? How much money will she have left?

Let's now take a deeper look at three categories of constructed-response assessments: computations and short-answer questions, multistep and open-ended questions, and journals and learning logs.

Three Categories of Constructed-Response Assessments

1. Computations and Short-Answer Questions

2. Multistep and Open-Ended Questions

3. Journals, Learning Logs, and Exit Cards

Computations and Short-Answer Questions

We think of computation exercises and short-answer questions as those that reveal basic fact knowledge, assess recall, and reveal competence with applications of algorithms. They are typical of much of our students' work since they are the types of questions asked frequently on worksheets and textbook pages. Short-answer questions may ask for a single number or one-word answer: *Cora has 38 invitations to mail for the school picnic. Stamps cost $.47 each. How much will the stamps cost to mail the invitations?* Verbs like *name, list, tell, compute,* and *identify* are frequently used in short-answer questions. Being brief, however, does not mean that short-answer questions are trivial. Consider the following short-answer task: *Find the missing number:* $4 \times 3 = \square \times 6$. Think about the misconceptions that become evident when our students respond "seventy-two" or "twelve."

Having students solve so-called naked computations may not reveal a great deal of information about the thinking of those students who answer the problems correctly, but the computations do alert us to talk with students when their answers are not correct. What we want to avoid is having students practice applying incorrect strategies. Examine the following problems from a third-grade student's worksheet. What do you notice?

49	53	18	38
14	19	26	78
26	47	34	27
+32	+18	+55	+19
112	137	133	153

After scoring her paper, the teacher asked Sybil to work through the problems with him and to think aloud as she worked. She orally added correctly in every case. What the teacher discovered was that the Sybil's rule for carrying numbers was to always write down the larger number in the sum and carry the smaller one. This strategy meant that most of the time she solved addition problems correctly, but occasionally her answers were wrong and she did not understand why. By talking with Sybil rather than just assigning a grade, the teacher could help her understand why her rule was not appropriate.

In INFORMing ourselves of students' thinking through their written work, we need to remember that sometimes the problems we pose to our students have different meanings for them than they do for us. How we think about questions as we create worksheets or quizzes may not match the thinking of our students. For example, students in a second-grade class had been practicing adding ten and one hundred to two-digit numbers. When their teacher asked them to give examples of numbers that had two fours in them, she was disappointed in the results because she had anticipated that most students would write *44* and *144*. In "Reflection 5–1: Numbers with Two Fours" (see pages 128–29), look at the collection of student work. What questions would you have as the teacher? Answer the questions in Reflection 5–1; these questions prompt you to consider the possibilities of how to think about our students' work even on very simple tasks. Asking ourselves what we know from students' responses and deciding which of our questions are most important to have answered is the first step in examining students' written work through an INFORMative assessment lens.

Reflection 5–1

Numbers with
Two Fours

Pages 128–29

Multistep and Open-Ended Questions

Often our students respond to the tasks and problems we assign as if the questions required short answers. Helping students learn to put their ideas into words and to create representations that reveal thinking is challenging at every grade; however, it is one that is worth the effort. Being able to explain ideas and communicate reasoning is a workplace skill that everyone needs. When students solve complex or nonroutine problems, we have opportunities to uncover both common misconceptions and ideas that are unique to individual students. The problems might be multistep or ones in which students must explain how they got their answers. They might be unusual contexts or open-ended tasks. These questions usually take longer to score, but the payoff is great—we gain information to use in giving feedback to our students and to plan our future instruction.

Take a moment to solve the following *Rainbow Robots* task. What are the mathematics understandings students need in order to solve the problem?

> Rainbow Robots, Inc. was putting on a big demonstration. Everyone came to watch the colorful robots wash the windows at the Miller Building. First, the big Red Robot washed $\frac{1}{2}$ of all the windows. Then the smaller Green Robot washed $\frac{2}{3}$ of the windows that were left. Next the Blue Robot washed $\frac{1}{2}$ of the windows that were left. To the cheers of everyone watching, the tiny Yellow Robot washed the last 10 windows. In all, how many windows did Rainbow Robots, Inc. wash? Explain how you got your answer.

After you have solved the problem, turn to "Reflection 5–2: Rainbow Robots" (see pages 130–31). Look at the student responses. Do their representations reveal some of their thinking—and their lack of understanding? With a task such as this one, unpacking the problem in a class discussion can both reveal students' knowledge related to fraction concepts and help build fraction knowledge for many in the class. Answer the reflection questions before continuing to read further.

Even simple open-ended questions allow us to assess critical thinking and make judgments about the depth and clarity of students' understandings. For example, in one fifth-grade class, the teacher frequently asked students to create problems. One student, Chloe, appeared to have a procedural

Assessment Tip ✓

Look for the connections students are making on graphic organizers and charts that they create. Ask them to explain the placement of information.

Reflection 5–2

Rainbow Robots

Pages 130–31

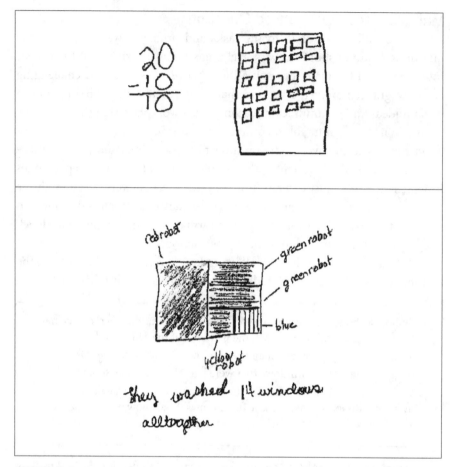

FIGURE 5–1. Jacob's and Madison's Responses to the "Rainbow Robots" Problem (See Page 130 for More Student Responses)

understanding of division but the problem she wrote indicated a lack of conceptual understanding. (See Figure 5–2.) Were we only to have Chloe compute long-division problems, we might not discover the gaps in her understanding of the meaning of division. One strategy for helping students connect concepts and related procedures is having them work with partners to complete tasks such as this.

Open-ended tasks that have multiple appropriate responses provide opportunities for diverse thinking. These tasks with more than one possible

Make up a problem that $7.20 ÷ 6 solves.
Write your problem and then solve it.

Rudi has $7.20. His friend
gave him 50¢ and his
mother gave him three
more dollars. How much
money does Rudi have
now?

$$\begin{array}{r} \$1.20 \\ 6\overline{\smash{)}7.20} \end{array}$$

FIGURE 5–2. Chloe's Response to a Division Prompt

response need to prompt students to justify their answers. Unless students explain their thinking, we might not recognize the logic behind their answers and mark them wrong. Notice how a fifth-grade teacher handled the following situation:

Mr. Lewis:	*Think of the pattern one, three, nine. . . . What comes next?*
Rusty:	*Eleven.*
Millen:	*Twenty-seven.*
Cary:	*Ten.*
Mr. Lewis:	(Oh my gosh, he thought. Have they missed the point of patterns or did I not give them enough numbers for them to see the pattern I had in mind?) *Tell us what the next three numbers in your pattern are.*

(continued)

(continued from page 117)

Rusty: *Eleven, seventeen, nineteen, twenty-five. My pattern is plus-two, plus-six.*

Millen: *Twenty-seven, eighty-one, two hundred forty-three, seven hundred twenty-nine. In my pattern you just multiply times three to get the next number.*

Cary: *Ten, thirteen, nineteen, twenty. This pattern is add ten, then add twenty, then add thirty.*

(Adapted from Reys et al. 2009, 313.)

Helping students know how to write a strong explanation or explain orally is often a challenge. Age, fluency with language, and experiences influence how successful students are likely to be. Students who are very articulate often give the impression that they know more than they do; the reverse is also true. As we study explanations of thinking, we need to be conscious of the differences between a student who knows the mathematics but is not able to explain it well and the student who writes lengthy explanations but does not exhibit depth of understanding of the mathematics. For very young students it may be recognizing when a child computes correctly, but writes answers as mirror images. We may need to talk with some students about properly organizing their work because there are numbers and pictures all over the page, making their response difficult to understand. Using open or extended-response tasks with several parts related to the same scenario can also be a strategy for working with students who are performing at different levels of expertise related to the same learning target.

When tasks are challenging, groups of students can have rich conversations as they work together to solve problems. These conversations do not happen without some guidance. Taking time to model and discuss how to unpack and solve multistep problems pays off when students become comfortable with working in groups.

A common language arts practice is to discuss, write, edit, revise, and rewrite. In a self-contained class, we can use a math task during a writing period. In this scenario, the students have an audience—the teacher and the classmates—and their task is to describe their thinking and their solution. One student might recap the discussion while another student records what

Learn More About Lessons That Reveal Students' Thinking

A Collection of Math Lessons from Grades 1–3

(Burns and Tank 1987)

A Collection of Math Lessons from Grades 3–6

(Burns 1987)

is being said. Once the group finalizes the notes about the process, they are ready to record their solution and edit or add any additional explanation before sharing with the rest of the class.

INFORMative assessment means that while we are teaching content we also are looking carefully at how our students' understanding is progressing along the path from not knowing to fully understanding. Taking the pulse of the group means we do not wait for a quiz at the end of the week to adjust instruction; rather, we use the information we collect from class work and homework problems to make ongoing adjustments.

Journals, Learning Logs, and Exit Cards

Many teachers use journals, learning logs, and exit cards (or minute-math cards) to invite students to reflect on their thinking and identify what they know and what they don't understand. Students' writing serves as an artifact for use in conferences or in portfolios. There are numerous resources with descriptions of writing for different purposes and guidelines for different types of journals and learning logs. We usually think of journal writing as *reflective* and learning logs as more *records* of activities and tasks. Our purpose here is not to specify a definition but to point out that student writing can be INFORMative assessments that reveal students' diverse thinking.

Some teachers have students include a problem of the day in their journals or logs, dating each entry. Usually the more explicit the prompt, the better information we are able to get from the students.

Examples of Math Journal Prompts

- Name two things that you learned in math today.

- Tell what you know about Venn diagrams and how they are used. Make up a Venn diagram with labels to illustrate your ideas.

- List everything you know about equilateral triangles and squares that might help you figure the measure of the interior angles of pattern blocks.

- Explain how counting by threes is different from getting into three groups.

While we collect exit cards at the end of the lesson, we less frequently review journals and learning logs formally—perhaps once a week or once every several weeks. Our feedback to students may be explicit to one journal entry or overall comments about their work. Since we continually look for evidence of student thinking to inform our planning, we can use journal writing more informally by moving around the classroom as students are writing. Statements that are unusual prompt us to stop and ask questions to clarify our understanding or help students clarify their own thinking. Journals and learning logs are valuable as a means of encouraging student metacognition. Since reflections are thinking about our own thinking, we encourage metacognition when we ask students to write how they know something ("How do you know a square is a special rectangle?") or why something is true ("Why did you say that the area of Figure B is larger than the area of Figure A?").

> **Assessment Tip** ✓
>
> Use exit cards to sort students into groups for follow-up instruction.

Selected-Response Assessments

Selected-response assessments are sometimes known as *forced-choice* assessments, and include multiple-choice, matching, and true-false assessments. They are designed to include items with less complex cognitive demands as well as items designed at more advanced process levels that require students to integrate knowledge and interpret information. Multiple-choice, matching, and true-false items also have the advantage of being easy to score by hand or machine and are widely available through textbooks, item banks, and computer management systems.

The distinguishing characteristic of selected-response questions is that students must select from among answer choices determined by others. Some short-answer questions that assess factual information—such as single-word, fill-in-the-blank questions or simple computation questions—are included in the selected-response category, and are usually scored right or wrong. However, we prefer to include these types of short-answer questions in the constructed-response category since the answers, though brief, are student-generated.

Perhaps the most appropriate use of selected-response items in the classroom is to measure factual knowledge. For example, multiple-choice tests, used as summative assessments for accountability purposes, can sample a broad range of student knowledge, give global information about individual student achievement—what has or has not been learned—and provide valuable program information when scores of all students are analyzed together.

For ongoing monitoring of student learning, however, overusing selected-response assessments is likely to give us an incomplete picture of what our students understand and what they can do independently. When students select from answers that are provided in forced-choice assessments, they are responding to someone else's thinking rather than providing their own ideas. For example, think about an iceberg: Sailors know it is there because they see what is above the surface of the ocean, and they know that beneath the surface is much more to the iceberg that is not visible. Selected-response assessments are like the tip of the iceberg: They provide information that is visible above the surface. Beneath that surface is hidden much more information about students' understandings that can best be uncovered by using multiple assessment strategies, especially those in which students are asked to explain or demonstrate their thinking. (See Figure 5–3.)

For ongoing monitoring of student learning, however, overusing selected–response assessments is likely to give us an incomplete picture of what our students understand and what they can do independently.

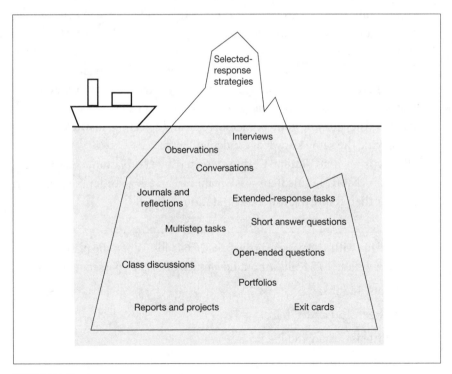

FIGURE 5–3. An Assessment Iceberg

Multiple-Choice Assessments

Multiple-choice items that are well constructed can provide information for instructional decisions, but quality multiple-choice questions are not easy to create. The question (prompt) must be clear to students and have the same meaning for them as it does for the teacher. The foils (answer choices) include distracters (wrong answers) that usually represent common student mistakes along with a correct answer. When the distracters are well chosen, we are likely to be comfortable with the inferences we make about students' wrong answers. For example, if the response chosen is the correct answer to the first part of a two-step problem, we infer that the student only recognized the need to do the first step.

When students respond by choosing the correct answer, we usually infer that they understand the mathematics. Because many students learn to identify correct answers by a process of eliminating some incorrect answers, however, we may not be able to rely on our inferences and may not recognize students' incomplete understandings. When we do not have an opportunity to see the steps or procedures that students use in determining answers or if students do not explain their thinking, the correct answers may be the results of informed guesses rather than solid understanding. The nature of the thinking required of a student to select an answer may be very different from the thinking required to construct a response. Students may guess and get scores that give the impression they know more than they do. They may be good at memorizing and selecting answers but weak at applying the same knowledge independently.

> When we do not have an opportunity to see the steps or procedures that students use in determining answers or if students do not explain their thinking, the correct answers may be the results of informed guesses rather than solid understanding.

Below is an item similar to those created by the National Assessment of Education (NAEP). This item was created to assess a student's estimation skills rather than requiring exact computation:

An airplane with 100 passengers weighs 26,643 lbs. When the plane is empty, it weighs 10,547 lbs. About how much does each passenger weigh?

A. About 145 lbs.

B. Between 150 and 170 lbs.

C. A little less than 180 lbs.

D. A little more than 180 lbs.

If a student misses the item, we cannot know the reason for the wrong answer. Is it the result of inappropriate reasoning or a lack of understanding of estimation? Think about how much more you might learn about your students' thinking if you followed the multiple-choice options with the direction to "Explain what you thought about or what you did to help you decide which answer to choose." For example, we may find out if the student rounded the numbers and then subtracted and divided, or we may discover that the student guessed because the explanation did not match the situation.

There are other disadvantages to multiple-choice assessments. If students are poor readers, they may know the content but have difficulty choosing the correct answer because of the wording. For creative students who think outside the box, none of the answer choices may allow them to demonstrate their knowledge. Likewise, young students tend to be very literal and may focus on aspects of the questions that lead them away from the correct answer choice. For students who do not see the answers they believe to be correct, random marking of answer choices may give the teacher misinformation about what the student does not understand. When an answer choice of "I don't know" is an option and students mark that choice, the answer is true for the student but will be counted as incorrect.

> Unless we take the time to analyze incorrect responses, we may have no clue as to why students miss questions.

In the classroom, a reliance on multiple-choice tests as the primary means of gathering information about what the students are learning is problematic. Unless we take the time to analyze incorrect responses, we may have no clue as to why students miss questions. What process or thinking was involved when students selected the incorrect responses? Were there misconceptions or merely misreading of the questions that led them to choose the wrong answers? Do the correct responses tell us that students have grasped that information or was it purely luck that caused them to select the correct response? Because multiple-choice items are so readily available, it is worthwhile considering how we might use them to give us, and our students, better information. We'll revisit multiple-choice in Chapter 9 when we discuss benchmark tests.

Other Selected-Response Assessments

We have not addressed true-false assessments because we believe they are no longer a major part of most classroom assessment routines. Unless we ask students to make the false statements true or we use some other strategy to determine why students chose their answers, our inferences about students' understanding may not be accurate. Since students have a fifty-fifty chance of answering a single true-false question correctly, there is no way to determine if the response reflects knowledge or a guess. However, using oral true-false or yes-no questions, with all students responding electronically or by hand signals, can give us a quick idea of the students' knowledge of facts. Asking a series of true-false or yes-no questions related to the same mathematics can help to provide clarity about students' thinking. For example, we might show students a right isosceles triangle and ask the following yes-no questions. Thumbs up if yes; thumbs down if no.

- Is angle A greater than 75 degrees?
- If angle B is 90 degrees, is it a right angle?
- If side AB is congruent to side BC, is this figure a scalene triangle?
- If side AB is congruent to side BC, is this figure an isosceles triangle?
- Could this figure be identified as a right triangle?
- If side AB is congruent to side BC, are angles A and C congruent?
- If angle B is 90 degrees, can angles A and C each be 60 degrees?
- Is the height of this triangle the length of side AC?

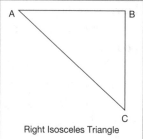

Right Isosceles Triangle

Matching assessments tend to be used by other disciplines more than in mathematics. One way to be more confident in these assessments is to have more possible answer choices than are needed and to alert students that not every answer choice will be used.

Portfolios as Collections of Students' Work

We think of portfolios—collections of students' written work—as more structured than just a folder containing all student work for a period of time. Portfolios may include artifacts such as pictures of projects in addition to work samples. Sometimes, if there is a special purpose for the portfolio, we give students specific guidelines for what to include in them:

- *Showcase portfolios* include selected examples of the student's best work, similar to an artist's portfolio that is designed to highlight the very best work of the student.

- *Progress portfolios* include samples of student work about similar learning targets that show growth over time. These portfolios are often compiled for student and parent conferences.

- *Pass-along portfolios* include selections from each grading period—some districts specify certain documents to include—and accompany a student to the next grade.

> "Effective assessment reveals the differences between what was taught and what was learned."
>
> —*Constructive Assessment in Mathematics: Practical Steps for Classroom Teachers* (Clarke 1997, 15)

In highlighting different assessment strategies, we mention portfolios and folders of student work not to have a lengthy discussion of guidelines for creating them but as a reminder that looking at multiple samples of work related to the same learning target often gives us a more complete picture than if we simply examine a single piece of student work. We'll revisit portfolios when we focus on student self-assessment in Chapter 7.

INFORMing My Practice

INFORMative assessment supports our efforts to meet the needs of each student within the context of the class as a whole. Whenever we teach a lesson, different students take away different understandings. It is helpful for us to try a variety of strategies for gathering information about what students are learning. There is no one right way to proceed—sometimes the way to begin using assessments more powerfully is to just jump in! Exploring assessment strategies that we have not traditionally used, one at a time, seems a reasonable approach to learning new techniques. Through experience, we determine what kind of information we can efficiently gather with a given strategy, how easy it is to use, and how valuable the information is in supporting our students. Just as mathematics must be sense making for our students, personal knowledge about the advantages and disadvantages of different assessment strategies grows out of our use of different methods.

In Chapter 4 and in this chapter, we have explored numerous oral and written assessment strategies. Now it's your turn to compare and contrast your assessment methods. Go to "Reflection 5–3: Comparison of Assessment Methods" (see pages 132–34). In this reflection we have provided a chart for you to make notes about common assessment methods. Look back at Chapter 4 to review oral assessments. Then, as you examine students' written work, ask yourself questions such as these:

Reflection 5–3

Comparison of Assessment Methods

Pages 132–34

> *Five Guiding Questions When Assessing Student Work*
>
> 1. Are there any questions that a number of students are missing? If yes, do I have any ideas about why that is?
>
> 2. Are there obvious misconceptions that students are exhibiting?
>
> 3. Am I learning anything about individual students from these papers?
>
> 4. What written feedback would benefit the students?
>
> 5. In multiple-choice problems, are there any wrong answer choices that most students are choosing?

It is not a dramatic leap into using assessment strategies that is likely to improve the quality of education in your classroom. Rather, it is the thoughtful shifts that you make in your thinking about *what, how,* and *why* you are using assessments. Start with strategies that are most comfortable for you and continue throughout the school year to tease out information to guide your planning. The "formativeness" of our profession means that we are continually learning. Keep a journal about what you try, or record your ideas in "Reflection 5–4: INFORMing My Practice: Using a Variety of Assessments" (see page 135). Your recorded successes— and those times when hindsight suggests there were other

Reflection 5–4

INFORMing My Practice: Using a Variety of Assessments

Page 135

It is not a dramatic leap into using assessment strategies that is likely to improve the quality of education in your classroom. Rather, it is the thoughtful shifts that you make in your thinking about *what, how,* and *why* you are using assessments.

questions that should have been asked—will provide a reference for future planning and allow you to evaluate the effectiveness of your new or modified activities. Remember, INFORMative assessment is not an add-on; it is most effective when it is indistinguishable from instruction and when instructional activities and assessments are planned at the same time.

Reflection 5–1: Numbers with Two Fours

Connor

Megan is thinking of a number. Her number has two 4's in it.

What number could it be? _____ 44

What else could Megan's number be? _____ 8

Sierra

Megan is thinking of a number. Her number has two 4's in it.

What number could it be? _____ 44

What else could Megan's number be? _____ 1044

Kit

Megan is thinking of a number. Her number has two 4's in it.

What number could it be? _____ 44

What else could Megan's number be? _____ 144

Aisha

Megan is thinking of a number. Her number has two 4's in it.

What number could it be? _____ 8

What else could Megan's number be? _____ th
thats the only one

Daniel

Megan is thinking of a number. Her number has two 4's in it.

What number could it be? _____ 44

What else could Megan's number be? _____ 454

Emily

Megan is thinking of a number. Her number has two 4's in it.

What number could it be? _____ 8

What else could Megan's number be? _____ I dont no!

Derrick

Megan is thinking of a number. Her number has two 4's in it.

What number could it be? _____ 44

What else could Megan's number be? _____ 044

Brittany

Megan is thinking of a number. Her number has two 4's in it.

What number could it be? _____ 8

What else could Megan's number be? _____ 4+4=8

Carlos

Megan is thinking of a number. Her number has two 4's in it.

What number could it be? _____ 8

What else could Megan's number be? _____ 9

Ava

Megan is thinking of a number. Her number has two 4's in it.

What number could it be? _____ 14

What else could Megan's number be? _____ 44

Students' Responses to the *Numbers with Two Fours* Problem

(continued)

Reflection 5–1: Numbers with Two Fours
continued

Look at the student work (see page 128). Answer the questions below.

1. What different interpretation did some students make about the questions?

2. How could the teacher have worded the question to help eliminate the interpretation?

3. What was positive about the students' responses when they replied "eight"?

4. What do you want to know about Sierra's answer of 1044?

5. Do you think that Derrick's second response of 044 is a legitimate answer? Explain.

6. What suggestions might you make to Aisha and Emily, or what questions would you ask?

7. If you were going to call on students to explain their answers, which students would you call on first? Why?

8. What experiences might help students develop a greater understanding of "one hundred more"?

Reflection 5-2: Rainbow Robots

Sofia

120 windows

Red Robot | Green Robot / Green Robot / Blue Robot | Yellow Robot

Jacob

$$\begin{array}{r} 20 \\ -10 \\ \hline 10 \end{array}$$

Madison

redrobot

green robot

green robot

blue

yellow robot

they washed 14 windows

alltogether.

Jayden

G   R

10   B

110 windows were washed

We drew a square that represents all the windows. Then we went through the passage and we divided the square into 10 parts, counted them and got our answer

Frosty

yellow = 10

Green = $\frac{2}{3}$

Blue = $\frac{1}{2}$

Red = $\frac{1}{2}$

Teagan

Red Robots $\frac{1}{2}$

$\frac{1}{3}$ Robots Green | $\frac{1}{3}$ green | Blue Robot $\frac{1}{2}$ | 10

10 windows + Blue Robots part = 20 - $\frac{1}{2}$ of $\frac{1}{2}$ of windows + the green's $\frac{2}{3}$ - 40 + 20 = 60 windows + Red Robots half - 60 + 60 = 120 windows

Students' Responses to the *Rainbow Robots* Problem

(continued)

Rainbow Robots, Inc. was putting on a big demonstration. Everyone came to watch the colorful robots wash the windows at the Miller Building. First, the big Red Robot washed $\frac{1}{2}$ of all the windows. Then the smaller Green Robot washed $\frac{2}{3}$ of the windows that were left. Next the Blue Robot washed $\frac{1}{2}$ of the windows that were left. To the cheers of everyone watching, the tiny Yellow Robot washed the last 10 windows. In all, how many windows did Rainbow Robots, Inc. wash? Explain how you got your answer.

Look through the student responses (see page 130), and think about what you might infer about each student's grasp of the task and the underlying mathematics.

1. Which students do you feel understood the situation described in the task?

2. For students who did not seem to grasp the situation, is there evidence of some understanding that you might build upon?

3. How might a class discussion help students clarify their own thinking so that they could identify incorrect portions of their responses and improve their explanations? What question(s) would you pose to begin the discussion?

4. If you were planning a class discussion about the Rainbow Robots task, in what order would you ask these students to share their solutions? Why?

Reflection 5-3: Comparison of Assessment Methods

Method	Advantages	Disadvantages	Documentation
Conversations and Interviews			Anecdotal records
Class Discussions			Anecdotal records
Observations			Anecdotal records

(continued)

Reflection 5-3: Comparison of Assessment Methods
continued

Method	Advantages	Disadvantages	Documentation
Open-Ended and Extended Problems			Student work
Journals and Learning Logs			Student work
Portfolios			Student artifacts

(continued)

Reflection 5-3: Comparison of Assessment Methods
continued

Method	Advantages	Disadvantages	Documentation
Short-Answer			Student work
Multiple-Choice			Answer sheet
True-False			Answer sheet
Matching			Answer sheet

Reflection 5-4: INFORMing My Practice: Using a Variety of Assessments

Think about the chapter you just read. Use this space to record your ideas.

INFORMative ways I am already using written assessments:

Ideas on ways to incorporate a greater variety of assessment strategies:

Ideas I envision becoming a more important part of my practice:

Questions I have:

Frustrations/concerns I have:

Strategies for Choosing Mathematically Rich Tasks for Instruction and Assessment

In this chapter, we talk about the decisions we as teachers make when choosing tasks for our lessons. Every task has potential to be used in a diagnostic manner, as an instructional task, or as an assessment. The difference is not how students respond to tasks, but how we use their work. If we use tasks to guide our instructional planning or to monitor students' progress, the task becomes part of our INFORMative assessment. Specific questions focus our decisions and sharpen our skills in identifying rich tasks for our students.

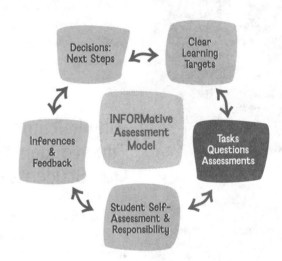

Overview

Why Is It Important to Take Time to Identify Rich Tasks for Our Students?

Where Can I Find Good Tasks?

How Am I Planning to Use This Task?

What Mathematics Knowledge Does the Task Require?

What Defines a Rich Mathematical Task?

Are There Different Ways That Students Could Engage with and Learn from the Task?

What Can I Learn About the Students' Thinking from a Variety of Tasks?

Does the Task Have Sufficient Complexity to Challenge a Range of Students' Thinking?

    Differentiated Instruction

    Interventions

    Parallel Tasks

INFORMing My Practice

> "Students gain insight into their thinking when they present their methods for solving problems, when they justify their reasoning to a classmate or teacher, or when they formulate a question about something that is puzzling them."
>
> —*Principles and Standards for School Mathematics* (NCTM 2000, 60–61)

Choosing the tasks we use in our classrooms is far from trivial. Through the tasks we select, we support students' learning and their engagement with mathematics. If our students' experiences are limited to applying memorized procedures, their opportunities for thinking are limited as well; they are not likely to develop the kind of thinking that encourages them to choose from a variety of strategies or possible solution paths, to make connections with other mathematical ideas, or even to make sense of the mathematics they are using. The same quality tasks we choose for instruction we can also use for assessment.

Why Is It Important to Take Time to Identify Rich Tasks for Our Students?

Because the tasks we assign our students directly affect their opportunities to learn, we must become more aggressive in choosing problems that challenge our students to unpack the tasks, reason about numbers and operations, make connections among different representations, and apply efficient strategies to solve the problems. A universal problem for classroom teachers is that we never have enough time for everything. However, we buy time by being selective in the tasks we assign our students, eliminating exercises that are redundant or problems that do not advance students' acquisition of important mathematics. There are no laws that we know of that say students have to do every problem in the textbook. Nor must we assign tasks that are boring, less intellectually complex, or lacking in value for the learning targets we have identified.

> "There are three features of tasks that are critical: First, the situation must be one that students can treat problematically. . . . Second, the tasks need to connect to something the students know and are able to do. . . . Third, what is problematic about the task should be the mathematics of the situation so that what gets left behind is something of mathematical value."
>
> —*Making Sense: Teaching and Learning Mathematics with Understanding* (Hiebert et al. 1997, 161)

Does this require more of our time in planning and preparing our lessons? Absolutely. Do we need to always choose new tasks? Of course not. Many times the best strategy is to analyze the problems in the textbook lessons we are using and to choose which of the problems are most likely to reveal students' thinking or which problems raise issues we want to discuss with our students as a group.

Remember, assigning problems and providing time for students to complete the work is only the first step. Examining students' work through the lens of understanding their thinking and debriefing tasks with students as a group are powerful strategies for supporting students' learning. Are there paybacks for investing our time and energies on choosing rich tasks? Certainly. When we choose wisely the tasks we assign our students, we are better able to do the following:

Taking a Thoughtful Approach Choosing Tasks Enables Teachers to . . .

- support students' conceptual understandings and factual knowledge;

- evaluate our students' procedural skills;

- identify and address individuals' misconceptions, errors, or overgeneralizations;

- evaluate the effectiveness of our instructional activities;

- determine the status of the class and decide whether to move on or revisit the mathematics;

- plan ways to differentiate instruction to more appropriately engage our students; and

- identify specific needs and develop effective plans for interventions.

Where Can I Find Good Tasks?

Because of the number of decisions we must make each day, many of us rely heavily on textbook materials to identify problems and tasks for our lessons. With dual goals of engaging our students with mathematics content and assessing their progress in developing strategies, we continually evaluate when to use textbook pages and when our students would be better served if we modify or create different tasks. Chances are, someone in the district already has done an alignment of the textbook with the district's learning goals for each grade level. In addition, there may also be a pacing guide all teachers are expected to follow and district-prepared benchmark tests to be administered at specified times. Because currently no set of textbook materials is written specifically for a single district, local pacing guides may have teachers skip some chapters, supplement some pages, or even develop missing content.

Resources for good problems abound. There are collections of tasks with suggestions for instruction and rubrics for scoring. Some of our favorite references can be found in the "Learn More" boxes throughout this book. However, we also need to remind ourselves that the same tasks we might choose for instruction we might also choose for assessments. The standards-based textbooks' tasks are carefully chosen to engage students' thinking, but there are times when we decide to use tasks from other sources or create our own tasks because they are a better fit with our students. We may need to supplement textbook activities; we might decide to tap into the special interests of our students; we might want to make stronger connections to literature or a unit of science or social studies.

Whatever the source of tasks we choose, we always want to think carefully about why and how we are using them. Five questions, which we encourage you to routinely revisit to ensure successful task selection focused on instruction and assessment, frame this discussion. These questions sharpen our skills in identifying mathematically rich tasks for INFORMative assessment.

Learn More About Tasks for Instruction and Assessment

50 Problem-Solving Lessons: The Best from 10 Years of Math Solutions Newsletters
(Burns 1996)

Mathematics Assessment Sampler: Items Aligned with NCTM's *Principles and Standards for School Mathematics*, Grades 3–5
(Gawronski et al. 2005)

Mathematics Assessment Sampler: Items Aligned with NCTM's *Principles and Standards for School Mathematics*, Pre-K–Grade 2
(Huinker et al. 2006)

Uncovering Student Thinking in Mathematics: 25 Formative Assessment Probes
(Rose, Minton, and Arline 2007)

Guiding Questions for Choosing Quality Tasks

1. How am I planning to use this task?
2. What mathematics knowledge does the task require?
3. Are there different ways that students could engage with and learn from the task?
4. What can I learn about the students' thinking from this task?
5. Does the task have sufficient complexity to challenge a range of students' thinking?

How Am I Planning to Use This Task?

Most likely, the majority of the tasks we choose are for our daily instruction. Becoming more intentional in examining each task we plan for our lessons naturally has the potential to improve our instructional program simply because a task's major criterion is that it must help reveal information about students' understanding.

When the purpose of an assessment is diagnostic, even a few questions will help us identify students who are likely to need more support and those who seem to be ready for more challenges. We can use diagnostic assessments to decide how much time to allocate for different activities. For example, if being able to use a number line is a learning target for our students, it is helpful for us to identify the range of numbers that will appropriately challenge students—we want to know if they are secure with numbers to ten or twenty or one hundred. Can our students identify missing numbers when only one or two numbers in a sequence are left out? Can they identify missing numbers when only a few points are labeled? It is important for us to know if our students are equally comfortable naming points on number lines showing only decades or hundreds or thousands. Can they move forward and backward on their number lines in a fluid manner so that the number line becomes a tool for computation? Are students ready to use a number line as a model for rounding numbers?

> **Assessment Tip** ✓
>
> We need to remind ourselves that the same tasks we choose for instruction we might also choose for assessments.

> **Think About the Teaching Principle:** "Effective mathematics teaching requires understanding what students know and need to learn and then challenging and supporting them to learn it well."
> —*Principles and Standards for School Mathematics* (NCTM 2000, 370)

What Mathematics Knowledge Does the Task Require?

Thinking about the types of thinking that students are required to use for a task, for example, recalling factual information, demonstrating conceptual understanding, detailing procedural skills, or combinations of these, can help us make modifications that will enrich the task. Basic recall questions such as "How many sides does a hexagon have?" or "What is eight times seven?" let us know if a student can retrieve information from memory, but

INFORMative assessment is not an add-on; it is most effective when it is indistinguishable from instruction and when instructional activities and assessments are planned at the same time.

they tell us little about the student's thought process. By thinking about the mathematics knowledge a task may require, and modifying it as necessary to make the mathematics richer, we help our students develop stronger problem-solving strategies and reasoning skills. We want our students to make decisions about what a problem is asking them to do as well as apply an appropriate procedure accurately, either their own strategy or a standard algorithm. We want our students to become good communicators of their ideas.

What Defines a Rich Mathematical Task?

What defines a rich mathematical task varies among authors. Different authors use different terms: Some talk about *high-cognitive demand*, *open-ended* versus *closed* tasks, *routine* versus *challenging* tasks, *simple* versus *complex* tasks. Without oversimplifying, we suggest that *rich tasks* are those that offer students opportunities to engage in meaningful mathematics and reason through their answers. In rich tasks, students must explain how they arrived at their solutions. From our experiences, we believe that how teachers present a task and how they structure the class can change a routine exercise to a very engaging and rich task, and vice versa—if we give our students too many clues or walk them through a problem step by step, we are in danger of replacing their thinking with our guidance.

"A child's logic is chiefly inductive, which simply means that children learn from experiences."
—*Number Sense and Number Nonsense: Understanding the Challenges of Learning Math* (Krasa and Shunkwiler 2009, 150)

Reflection 6-1

Evaluating Tasks

Pages 157–59

In "Reflection 6–1: Evaluating Tasks" (see pages 157–59), we present eight tasks. Some of the problems are very simple; others are more involved. The tasks span a variety of grade levels, and all expect responses beyond one-word or single-number answers. While responding correctly may appear easy for students, we can often learn a great deal about their thinking by how they explain or represent their responses. Turn to page 157 and identify a categorization of the type of mathematical knowledge and the process each task represents. (The taxonomy table relating cognitive processes and types of knowledge from Chapter 3, Figure 3–4, is included as a reference.) Finally, decide if the question is a rich task and explain why or why not.

Are There Different Ways That Students Could Engage with and Learn from the Task?

Sometimes we choose or create complex tasks because we want to address multiple learning targets over several days of instruction and we want to include all of our students, opening the door for those who struggle as well as challenging our more advanced students. Following is a task titled *Fiddles Fudge Factory*. Take a few minutes to solve the problem.

Fiddles Fudge Factory: Part 1, Volume

Thelonious Fiddles owns a candy company that specializes in making delicious fudge. For the upcoming season Thelonious wants his designers (you) to create new packaging for a Mother's Day box containing 60 one-inch cubes of fudge. His plan is to package the fudge in an open box that has no top but is covered in colorful plastic wrap. What are some possible ways the fudge can be packaged into rectangular boxes?

Reflect on what skills you needed to solve this problem. If you assigned the task to your students, what understandings would you be looking for? What misconceptions might you anticipate? How would you introduce the task? Would your expectations change for fourth-, fifth-, or sixth-grade students?

In one fourth-grade classroom, Ms. Stuart wanted her students to explore volume and decided to present the *Fiddles Fudge Factory* problem—a task in a context. She also planned for her students to explore the relationship of surface areas to the volumes of different-sized rectangular candy boxes. She assigned students to work in groups of four and provided cubes for each table. What happened in Ms. Stuart's classroom was not what she had hoped for: In most of the groups, one person often manipulated all of the cubes without giving other students a chance to participate. There was not much communication about the problem or the mathematics in the task. When a design did not work, the students made no adjustments—instead, they took all of the cubes apart and started randomly again. Only one group worked with more than one layer of fudge; they used words like *rows* and *columns* and *layers*, but they were not consistent. See the examples of student work; what do you infer about their understanding of volume? (See Figures 6–1 and 6–2.)

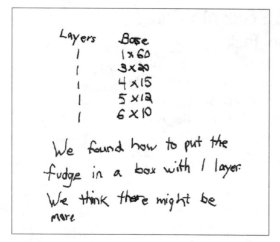

FIGURE 6-1. Makoto's Group's Solution to the *Fiddles Fudge Problem*

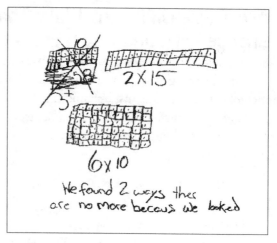

FIGURE 6-2. Rusty's Group's Solution to the *Fiddles Fudge Problem*

"When I brought the class back together to talk about the different sizes and shapes of the boxes," Ms. Stuart said, "the students had a hard time understanding each other. Their three-dimensional drawings were not clear and their lists were not organized. It was hard for me to follow some of their explanations and I suspected that many of my students didn't really understand the task. The students' work was not what I had anticipated, so I decided to work with the class as a whole before I let them go back to the *Fiddles Fudge Factory* problem.

"As a warm-up the next day," Ms. Stuart continued, "I gave each student six cubes and told the groups to make a rectangular prism that was two-by-three-by-four cubes. They could only touch their own cubes, so they had to communicate about where the cubes should go. I told the class that I noticed that they pulled their cubes apart and started over whenever they got stuck instead of making adjustments. I built a figure that didn't work and showed it to the whole class. The figure had multiple layers where the top layer wasn't completely filled in (to get that idea across as a possibility without saying 'do more than one layer'). I asked them to discuss with a partner for a minute how I might make a change. After a minute, I had them tell me how to adjust my figure so they could practice communicating. We worked on several examples until they seemed to get it.

"I told them that I thought we should have both pictures and numeric descriptions to record what we were doing, and I offered to help them begin a chart. We decided that since so many students had trouble drawing in three dimensions, we would draw a rectangular base and then write the height. I made a chart labeled *l, w,* and *h* and we recorded different shapes. We talked about the language they had used the day before (*rows, layers,* and *columns*) and connected the vocabulary to the labels for length, width, and height. All of this took up most of the math class period."

Ms. Stuart had the students continue to work on the original *Fiddles Fudge Factory* problem and record possible arrangements the next day. Later in the week, the students worked on the problem of what size and shape box they would recommend to Mr. Fiddles and why they thought it was the best one. They explored the amount of material it would take for each box (surface area). To introduce this part of the task, Ms. Stuart showed students several boxes without tops, and they all talked about the bottom and the sides. She also provided construction paper, scissors, and tape for students to make boxes if they wished.

Fiddles Fudge Factory: Part 2, Surface Area

Choose the box that you would like for Thelonious to use for the 60 pieces of fudge. What is the surface area of the box? Why would you recommend this box? Challenge: What are the dimensions of the box that uses the least amount of material?

Ms. Stuart decided not to present an extension of the problem—to create the most efficient net to cut a box from one rectangular piece of material—as she had originally planned, but rather to do another similar problem involving volume and surface area.

What happened in Ms. Stuart's classroom provides an example of how teachers can use INFORMative assessment to modify their instruction. The teacher identified the mathematics content that she wanted her students to learn, chose a task that provided several ways for students to engage in the mathematics, and observed her students at work. When the majority of the students did not seem to grasp the ideas firmly, she introduced the concept (in this

> What happened in Ms. Stuart's classroom provides an example of how teachers can use INFORMative assessment to modify their instruction.

case, volume) in a different way. Then she had students come back to the original task before going to a new one. In the end, she changed her plans for the next steps, omitting an extension and instead choosing to revisit the concept of volume with a similar task.

We are wise to capitalize on our students' interest and enthusiasm. Based on the *Fiddles Fudge Factory* scenario, Ms. Stuart presented another task that involved figuring sales tax (using a calculator) and comparing costs.

Extensions: *Fiddles Fudge Factory*

1. Thelonious Fiddles' company is going to sell special Mother's Day boxes of candy for $8.50 each. Sales tax is 6 percent and shipping is $2.00. What would be the cost of 1 box?

2. If Thelonious sells 10 boxes, including tax and shipping, for $125, would this be a bargain? Why or why not?

Also using the *Fiddles Fudge Factory* scenario as a model, Ms. Stuart presented a logic problem (see below) to her students. Interestingly, while she originally had planned the logic problem for the gifted students in the class, other students were successful when several of the gifted students wanted to give up—a reminder that thinking and reasoning is a goal for *all* students.

Logic Problem: *Fiddles Fudge Factory*

Thelonious Fiddles gave candy samples to different businesses. To the first business he gave $\frac{1}{2}$ of his samples plus 1 more sample. To the second, third, and fourth businesses he again gave $\frac{1}{2}$ of his samples plus 1 more sample. To the fifth and last business, he gave away $\frac{1}{2}$ of the remaining samples plus 1 more sample. Then he had no samples left. How many samples did he start with?

Ms. Stuart had students work in partners and directed each student to first explain the problem to his or her partner. She then said that if partners had questions, they should talk with another pair of students. Lastly, she directed partners to be prepared to convince the class that their answer is correct.

Focus on Teaching: Ways to Support Student Learning

Ms. Stuart supported her students' mathematics learning in very intentional ways, including

- having students work in groups or with a partner;

- providing manipulatives and models;

- giving additional directions without completing the students' task;

- specifically directing students to tell a partner what they thought;

- modeling a strategy for organizing data;

- providing an opportunity for students to revisit the original task; and

- building new learning on prior knowledge.

In what intentional ways, in addition to those that Ms. Stuart used, do you support your students' mathematical thinking?

What Can I Learn About the Students' Thinking from a Variety of Tasks?

When choosing tasks, it is crucial that we think about what we will learn from our students' thinking. Marking a student's answers wrong without delving into the thinking that led to the mistake allows students to continue along nonproductive paths. Rather than assume that a student's errors are careless—when he or she usually computes correctly—we need to talk with the student instead. We need to attend to an individual student's thinking and plan interventions appropriately.

For example, Marika was a fifth-grade student when her teacher asked her to talk about how she computed the following sums that were on a homework sheet. Look carefully at Marika's solutions. What do you notice about the correct and incorrect solutions?

98	177	854	1609	1378
+162	+ 53	+276	+ 1022	+2907
260	230	320	2100	3700

How did Marika arrive at her answers? Once you have looked at Marika's work, read the dialogue that ensued between the teacher, Miss Rucker, and Marika.

Conversation with a Fifth-Grade Student

Miss Rucker: *Tell me what* addition *means.*

Marika: *Putting numbers together.*

Miss Rucker: *What do you mean "putting numbers together"?*

Marika: *Like this. Nine* (points to the first problem) *plus eight is seventeen. One and six is seven and two more makes nine. Seventeen plus nine is twenty-six.*

Miss Rucker: *I see how you added, but where did the zero come from?*

Marika: *Well, there are three numbers there* (points to 162), *so you have to put a zero to have three numbers in your answer.*

Miss Rucker: *Show me how you did this problem* (points to the fifth one).

Marika: *One plus three plus seven is eleven. Plus eight is nineteen. Ugh . . . nineteen plus two is twenty-one plus nine is thirty plus seven is thirty-seven. Then you add two zeros so the answer has four numbers.*

Marika's method of solving addition problems was to add all of the digits in the problem as if each were a single-digit addend. In first and second grades, when the addends were single digits, she got correct answers. As she moved up in the grades, occasionally her solutions were correct (problems such as 105 + 25 or 76 + 154), sometimes they were close to the correct answer (problems such as 1279 + 1001), but most often they were wrong. She did not understand why she got the answers right sometimes and other times missed the problems.

We ask ourselves, how could Marika's misinformed strategy have been missed? A guess might be that over the years Marika's teachers scored her assignments, identifying correct responses and marking wrong answers. She got just enough answers correct and demonstrated a sufficiently acceptable knowledge of number facts that her teachers may not have talked with her about her strategy for addition.

Rather than focus on what should have happened whenever we make discoveries such as this, we are better served to use the example to remind ourselves that there is logic behind students' answers. When a student's responses to computations are consistently wrong, we always look for the reasons. However, when a student's answers to computations are inconsistently wrong, we need to dig deeper and identify the misconception. This is how INFORMative assessment supports student learning. If you were Marika's teacher and had made this discovery, what interventions would you plan? Turn to "Reflection 6–2: Plan for Addressing Marika's Misconceptions" (see page 160). We've provided questions to help you think about how this might apply to your own classroom.

Though we do not have detailed information about what Marika's teacher did, as we thought about the situation we realized that telling Marika that her strategy was incorrect and showing her how to add with regrouping was not a very good option. It is likely that Marika's teachers in her second-, third-, and fourth-grade classes had worked with traditional algorithms. If we could plan the intervention, we believe that Marika's number sense should be the starting point. We would ask questions that help to identify Marika's development of quantity and her sense of using numbers in real-world applications, such as "If you have a quarter and three dimes, how much money do you have?" or "If you have fifty pencils and I give you eight more, how many pencils would you have?" or "There are two thousand students and three hundred parents at the ball game. How many people are at the ball game?"

> When a student's responses to computations are consistently wrong, we always look for the reasons. However, when a student's answers to computations are inconsistently wrong, we need to dig deeper and identify the misconception. This is how INFORMative assessment supports student learning.

Reflection 6–2

Plan for Addressing Marika's Misconceptions

Page 160

If Marika responds appropriately to the questions, the next step could be writing down the same problems and asking her about the difference in the answers she gave to the oral problems and those that she would get with her method of addition. At this point we think she would need to be told explicitly that her strategy is not correct. This would be the time to provide her with opportunities to develop an understanding of how multidigit whole numbers combine.

> ### Addressing Marika's Computational Misunderstandings and Supporting Her Thinking
>
> - Review place value, breaking apart numbers (decomposing) and combining numbers (composing) in different ways.
>
> - Encourage Marika to first estimate answers to computations and then give a rationale for the estimate.
>
> - Engage Marika in conversations about traditional algorithms and why they work.
>
> - Discuss computations and story problems as Marika is solving them to be certain she is clear about the questions to be answered.

No student who needs serious intervention is likely to be well served by one preplanned program. Students' needs—from misconceptions and incomplete understandings—vary greatly. Interventions must provide opportunities for students to make sense of mathematics in order to connect new learning with what they already know. When students are far behind, it is imperative that we first identify the nature of their incomplete knowledge and their misconceptions and then plan an intervention. We all recognize that saying the same things again, slower and louder, is not an appropriate strategy. Telling students the same thing one more time, even in a one-on-one tutorial, is not likely to support the conceptual development that is needed. Often we must go back in the curriculum several years to prepare suitable early foundational experiences for the students.

Interventions must provide opportunities for students to make sense of mathematics in order to connect new learning with what they already know.

Every assignment a student completes has potential to inform both the teacher and the student about what he or she understands. Any task can serve more than one purpose; the same task that is used diagnostically by one teacher might be used as an instructional task by another. A task becomes an assessment depending on how the teacher responds. When we score students' work and assign grades, the assessment value is not very great if the end result is merely a score in a grade book. If we make notes of questions to ask particular students or divide the students into different groups for follow-up on identified problems, the assessment value of the task rises. These actions—examining students' responses and deciding what to do next—are at the heart of INFORMative assessment. If we do not explore with students what they know, we may miss a student's strategy that leads to a correct solution for one problem and a wrong answer for what we think is a similar problem. Without feedback from the teacher on their mathematical thinking regarding a task, students may never know why their strategies work sometimes and not other times.

> A task becomes an assessment depending on how the teacher responds to the student's work.

Does the Task Have Sufficient Complexity to Challenge a Range of Students' Thinking?

The need for identifying and addressing individual students' strengths and misconceptions is not a new idea. Many years ago, individualized instruction and Learning Activity Packets (LAPs) were educational trends. Teachers spent hours preparing packets of materials for individuals or small groups of students who then worked on their own to complete the different worksheets and various tasks. Pretests usually determined the groups and posttests ended the units. There were several shortcomings with this trend. Multiple-choice questions were usually the basis of what went into the packets. Students had few opportunities to share their thinking and hear others' ideas. Class conversations to debrief rich or complex tasks were rare. Teachers spent their time managing multiple groups and duplicating pages, and students often had many opportunities to "practice wrong." The intentions of these initiatives were good, but teachers often failed to focus on what students were thinking and why they answered as they did. Teachers rarely had time to focus on the logic behind students' answers or to expect students to elaborate on how they solved problems.

Assessment Tip ✓

Addressing misconceptions or incomplete learning usually involves identifying a different instructional pathway.

Differentiated Instruction

Today differentiation is likely to look different in each of our classrooms. While we all might want to be proactive in identifying and meeting the mathematical needs of our students, how we gather information and use that knowledge may be different. Some of us are comfortable having two or three mathematics groups that we configure and then reconfigure according to units of instruction or student needs. Others of us prefer to differentiate within whole-class lessons. There are numerous resources specifically about the philosophy behind differentiation and guidelines for implementation of differentiated instruction.

When differentiating instruction in our mathematics lessons, we need to remember that the mathematical learning targets should almost always be the same for all students. We want the same high expectations of accomplishment for all of the class, but we choose activities that provide alternative ways of developing the essential understandings, concepts, and key skills that students need to acquire. We use different tasks to provide for different learning styles and for the ways we provide access to the content students need to learn. One goal for varying the complexity of tasks is to build on what students already know, so that those who need additional attention or assistance have more structure and experiences that will allow them to learn the mathematics in meaningful ways. Likewise, those whose understandings are more advanced can work on tasks that challenge them intellectually, while still other students are developing mastery through the tasks chosen for them.

Interventions

Specific interventions are necessary when students are significantly behind or ahead of other students in the class and need mathematics instruction separate from the class. This does not mean excluding students from the class; it does mean that there need to be opportunities to learn in addition to those provided by the classroom teacher. The learning targets could be different from the class's current instruction because of the incomplete understandings or advanced knowledge of the students. The tasks would be specifically chosen to address the individual student's learning needs.

If we think carefully about what interventions need to accomplish, we realize the importance of having more specific information than "the student cannot multiply large numbers" or "the student missed sixteen items out of a twenty-item assessment." More extensive diagnosis and one-on-one conversations become critical for planning, monitoring, and evaluating the effectiveness of interventions.

Parallel Tasks

Within the regular classroom we frequently need to provide for two or three clusters of students who are at different places related to learning particular mathematics. Almost always we can informally place our students into three broad categories:

- not there yet;
- on target but need practice; or
- need challenges.

Varying the numbers within tasks is one way to provide both access and challenge to problems. For example, we might put groups of three numbers in appropriate places within problems. Students may choose to solve the problems using the first numbers in the set, the second numbers, or the third numbers. If a student chooses the second number in one group, he must use the second number in all other groups. Thinking carefully about the numbers we use allows us to provide computational practice with an appropriate range of numbers and problem-solving practice as students decide how to solve the same problems.

Same Task—Different Numbers

Yesterday there were (55, 73, 166) ants running around in the ant colony. (14, 48, 159) left to find food. How many were still in the ant colony?

My mom has a lot of seashells on the shelves. On the first shelf she has (16, 28, 105) seashells. On the second shelf she has (30, 57, 298) small seashells, and on the third shelf she has (13, 24, 127) seashells. How many seashells does she have?

Raul and Peter kept a list of books they read throughout the year. Raul read (38, 70, 106) books. Peter read (26, 45, 87) books. How many more books did Raul read than Peter?

A similar approach is to leave blank the spaces where numbers go in problems and then write in or tell individuals or groups of students what numbers to use as they solve the problems. Both of these strategies keep the processes the same but provide access and appropriate practice to students who have varying computational strengths and needs.

It is important to remember that challenging our advanced students does not always mean taking on content from the next grade level. There are many ways to delve deeper into the current content by increasing the complexity of the task or connecting it to other knowledge. For example, as students are learning multiplication concepts and facts, the typical practice problem might be $3 \times 4 = \square$. Think about the following problems. We challenge our students who memorized the previous fact quickly when we ask them to explain these new problems:

$3 \times \square = 12$

$\square \times 4 = 12$

How many pairs of two numbers can you find whose product is 12?

Parallel tasks, sometimes referred to as tiered tasks, address the same learning target at varied levels of difficulty. (See Figure 6–3.) Take a moment to think about and solve the tasks in Figure 6–3; continue reading once you've completed all three worksheets (Fractions of Areas I, II, and III).

If you were the teacher, what learning targets might you be addressing with the tasks in Figure 6–3? If you were a student in each group, what would you need to understand about area models for fractions to successfully complete the worksheet? Notice that unless the fraction models are large enough for students to fold or cut out or dimensions are given, the students must make some assumptions about lines that divide the figures. For example, each figure has a line dividing it into half.

Now turn to "Reflection 6–3: Fractions of Regions: Task in Three Levels of Difficulty" (see pages 161–62). In this reflection we have posed additional questions for you to consider as you think about reaching students at different levels who are studying similar learning targets. In Chapter 4 we suggested a number of ways to collect anecdotal records from classroom conversations

Reflection 6–3

Fractions of Regions: Task in Three Levels of Difficulty

Pages 161–62

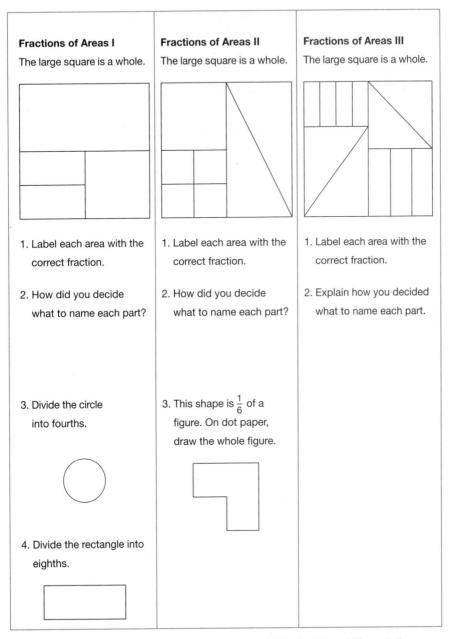

Fractions of Areas I

The large square is a whole.

1. Label each area with the correct fraction.

2. How did you decide what to name each part?

3. Divide the circle into fourths.

4. Divide the rectangle into eighths.

Fractions of Areas II

The large square is a whole.

1. Label each area with the correct fraction.

2. How did you decide what to name each part?

3. This shape is $\frac{1}{6}$ of a figure. On dot paper, draw the whole figure.

Fractions of Areas III

The large square is a whole.

1. Label each area with the correct fraction.

2. Explain how you decided what to name each part.

FIGURE 6–3. Tiered Tasks with Different Levels of Difficulty Allow Differentiation Within a Class

and observations. We use these records, along with samples of students' work, as a guide to group students according to their specific strengths and needs for tiered tasks such as those in Figure 6–3.

Reflection 6-4

INFORMing
My Practice: An
Action Plan for
Tasks

Page 163

INFORMing My Practice

As you think about the ideas in this chapter, refer to "Reflection 6–4: INFORMing My Practice: An Action Plan for Tasks" (see page 163). One action we encourage you to consider is to begin your own collection of good tasks and samples of student work that will become models for your classes in future years.

Reflection 6-1: Evaluating Tasks

		Cognitive Processes					
		Remember List Memorize Name Describe Recall	**Understand** Classify Compare Interpret Explain Give Examples	**Apply** Carry Out Use Implement Calculate Illustrate Demonstrate	**Analyze** Organize Differentiate Construct/ Deconstruct Compare/ Contrast	**Evaluate** Judge Derive Hypothesize Validate Estimate	**Create** Generate Devise Design Invent Synthesize
Types of Knowledge	**Factual**						
	Conceptual						
	Procedural						
	Metacognitive						

(Adapted from Anderson and Krathwohl 2001, 28.)

Read each task. Identify the classification for each one and decide if it is a rich task or not. Explain why or why not. Use the taxonomy table above (introduced in Chapter 3) to help you.

#	Task	Classification	Is this a rich task? Why or why not?
1	Draw 4 cats. Use your drawings to decide how many ears._____ How many paws. _____	*Procedural – Apply*	*For kindergarten students this is a rich task, but for third-grade students it becomes routine.*
2	Write a story problem that could be solved by the number sentence 4 × 8 = ___ .		

(continued)

#	Task	Classification	Is this a rich task? Why or why not?
3	Show or describe at least three different ways to find the product of 5 × 18 = ___ .		
4	Explain how 2 × 3 = ☐ is equivalent to ☐ = 3 × 2.		
5	Erica noticed that she has 3 different T-shirts, 3 different pairs of pants, and 2 different pairs of boots. How many different ways can she put the T-shirts, pants, and boots together before she has to wear the same exact outfit? Show or explain how you arrived at your answer.		
6	Mr. Kosloski did the grocery shopping this week. He bought vegetables for $17.49, meat for $22.81, dairy products for $13.54, and desserts for $9.98. When he got to the check-out register he realized he had only four $20 dollar bills in his wallet.		

(continued)

#	Task	Classification	Is this a rich task? Why or why not?
6 cont.	*He quickly estimated his total cost. Did Mr. Kosloski have enough money to pay for his groceries? Show or describe how you arrived at your estimate.*		
7	*Clarence and his partner had to complete a table to show information about the following growing pattern:* *Determine how the pattern is growing. Make a table to show what you found out.*		
8	*Draw a two-intersecting-circle Venn diagram. Decide how to classify the shapes and label the diagram. Place the letter for each shape into the sections and explain how you decided where to place them.* 		

How do you define rich mathematical tasks?

Reflection 6-2: Plan for Addressing Marika's Misconceptions

Study Marika's computation and the dialogue with Miss Rucker (see page 148). Reflect on Marika's understanding and answer the following questions.

1. Why is it critical that a specific intervention be planned for Marika?

2. If you were Marika's teacher, what interventions would you plan?

3. If you teach at another grade level, what inconsistencies similar to Marika's do your students have that you need to investigate?

4. In what ways does implementing INFORMative assessment strategies help us prevent our students from practicing misconceptions?

Reflection 6-3: Fractions of Regions: Task in Three Levels of Difficulty

If you were the teacher, what learning targets would you address with these tasks? What would students need to understand about area models for fractions to successfully complete each worksheet? Refer back to the three fraction worksheets (see page 155) as you respond to these questions.

1. What do you know about students who can successfully complete the Fraction of Areas I worksheet?

2. What do you infer about a student who labeled the fractions like the following?

3. Why are questions 2 through 4 on page 155 important for the inferences you might make about this student's understanding of fractions of a region?

4. What questions do you want to ask this student?

(continued)

5. What might you infer about a student using Fraction of Areas II worksheet who labeled the areas like the following and said that the small squares are each one-eighth pieces?

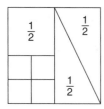

6. What error do you think the student made?

7. What feedback could you give this student so that he or she might identify his or her mistake?

8. How might question 3 on page 155 help you feel more certain about this student's understanding of areas of fractions?

9. How did you begin to think about the task on the Fraction of Areas III worksheet?*

10. What did you notice right away?

---

* The idea for this third square came from Dr. Catherine Swartz, who created a similar figure for her preservice teachers.

Reflection 6-4: INFORMing My Practice: An Action Plan for Tasks

1. What ideas from this chapter are most important to you?

2. Identify three actions you plan to take related to choosing tasks for your students.

3. What questions do you still have?

Section IV

How Can I Support My Students in Assessing Themselves?

Supporting Student Self-Assessment and Responsibility

In this chapter, we address ways that we can help students become significant partners in their own learning. We have organized our thinking around creating an environment that supports learning in order to respond to the question, "How do we encourage, facilitate, and support students in taking greater responsibility for their learning through INFORMative assessment?"

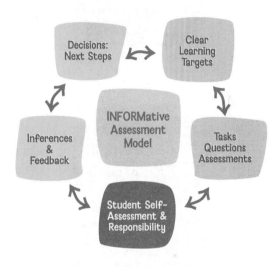

Overview

> "Students learn best when they monitor and take responsibility for their own learning."
> —"The Quest for Quality" (Chappuis, Chappuis, and Stiggins 2009)

> "Teaching is a cultural activity. We learn how to teach indirectly, through years of participation in classroom life, and we are largely unaware of some of the most widespread attributes of teaching in our own culture."
> —*The Teaching Gap: Best Ideas from the World's Teachers for Improving Education in the Classroom* (Stigler and Hiebert 1999, 11)

One major shift in our practice comes when we realize that formative assessment includes an emphasis on student self-assessment and responsibility. Teachers alone are not responsible for students' learning. The emphasis on students taking increased responsibility and becoming more engaged in assessing their own work is not an abdication of our responsibilities as teachers. Rather, we are expanding our goals for teaching and learning mathematics to include more emphasis on student metacognition and the development of work habits that will become lifelong skills for our students.

These shifts in practice are not easy nor are they usually very comfortable in the beginning. For most of us, the primary models we have for teaching are our own experiences when we were students. As students, many of us mimicked the examples that our teachers gave us, memorized what we were told we needed to learn, and moved forward at a steady pace. While we may have recognized that some of our friends did not do as well in school as we did, we probably did not spend much time thinking about why this was true.

Modeling Self-Assessment

Both research and experience suggest that helping students become significant partners in their learning strengthens what they learn (Black and Wiliam 1998). The dilemma is how to do this. How can we encourage, facilitate, and support students in taking greater responsibility for their learning? How can we guide them to learn and use strategies for self-assessment? To respond to these questions, we have organized our thinking into four broad categories that emphasize what both teachers and students can do:

Categories of Strategies to Support Student Self-Assessment and Responsibility

- Create Positive Learning Environments

- Motivate Students

- Encourage Quality Student Work

- Create Structures to Promote Student Responsibility

All of the categories overlap and provide opportunities for reflection about our own practices. Before you begin reading the next section about supporting student learning, turn to "Reflection 7–1: Evaluating My Current Practice" (see page 194) and take a moment to assess your current practices related to INFORMative assessment. This is a quick survey to encourage you to think about how your beliefs influence your teaching.

Reflection 7–1

Evaluating My Current Practice

Page 194

Creating Positive Learning Environments

Everyone agrees that classrooms should be positive environments for all students. We work hard to make our classrooms comfortable, inviting places. Yet there are times when a number of our students do not agree that school is a good place to be. Whether their perceptions are based on lack of academic success, their own personalities, or circumstances outside of school beyond our control, for these students their learning environment does not seem supportive. We pose four ways—establishing mutual respect, setting clear expectations, encouraging partnerships, and supporting group work—to develop a positive learning environment that in turn promotes student self-assessment and responsibility.

Establishing Mutual Respect

One fundamental component of a positive environment is an atmosphere of mutual respect. Respect means that everyone's opinion is valued, even when statements are clearly wrong. Establish from the beginning that mistakes are opportunities to learn—and students must know that it is OK to change their minds! For example, if Sam has a different idea from her first response, she needs to be comfortable saying, "I was wrong because . . ." or "At first I thought . . . , but now I think. . . ." Learning is all about incorporating new ideas and skills into what we already know.

> "Mistakes simply are outcomes of methods that need to be improved." —*Making Sense: Teaching and Learning Mathematics with Understanding* (Hiebert et al. 1997, 48)

Respect also means that when we ask questions, we provide time for students to think about their answers.

Thinking takes time, and thinking is what is important in our mathematics lessons.

Good questions almost always require more than one-number or one-word answers. Thinking takes time, and thinking is what is important in our mathematics lessons. Respect demands that we practice patience and listen carefully as a student is answering. Modeling attentive listening sends a message to the class that we believe what each student has to say is important.

Students need to learn to listen to others and agree or disagree with dignity. Encourage students to say "I have a different idea" or "My answer is different" or "I think the answer is (a different number or word)" rather than "No way" or "You're wrong." Differences of opinion are good—they indicate that students are thinking. When everyone's opinions are valued, there are opportunities for class discussions about strategies, number relationships, procedures, and interpretations of problems. If students are able to join into conversations without being laughed at or feeling foolish, they are more likely to become risk takers who attempt more challenging mathematics.

This type of positive environment does not happen overnight. One second-grade teacher shared with us that she usually works on building mutual respect with each new class for six to eight weeks. "By the end of October my students are usually good at saying positive things to each other and adding to other students' ideas," she reports. "But it is not easy. We have many discussions about the importance of listening carefully to each other and disagreeing politely."

Related to respecting different ideas is the notion of what it means to respect personal space and personal property; for example, while it is evident to us that reaching over to take another's pencil is not respecting personal property, students may need specific examples.

Setting Clear Expectations

Knowing what is expected is important for students both in terms of behavior and in terms of quality of work. As teachers, we need to be very explicit about what we want students to be doing—regardless of whether they are working independently, with a partner, or in a group. For example, we can:

If one of the goals of schooling is to create lifelong learners, from the earliest grades we need to encourage and assist students in being confident and responsible as learners.

- Post class rules—few, but well-chosen ones—as a reminder for appropriate behaviors.

- Help students know what it means to work thoughtfully and productively on mathematics tasks.

- Model different scenarios, especially situations that illustrate our expectations for how students should work with a partner or in a group to solve a problem.

Consider the following dialogue between a teacher and his third-grade students. What does he do to ensure his expectations are explicit?

A Third-Grade Teacher Models Expectations in a Class Conversation

Mr. Kratzer: *What are we trying to figure out in this problem?*

Laura: *The question is, "How many more ball games did the Bulls play than the Cardinals?"*

Mr. Kratzer: *There are a lot of numbers in this story. Which ones do you think we need to use?*

Trae: *It says the Bulls played thirty-seven games and the Cardinals played forty-six games.*

Laura: *And it says that teams usually play thirty-eight games each season.*

(continued)

> **Mr. Kratzer:** *Which numbers will help us answer the question?*
>
> **Laura:** *Bulls played thirty-seven and Cardinals played forty-six games.*
>
> **Mr. Kratzer:** *OK. Let's all work the problem. We can compare our answers and see if we did the problem the same way.*

Being explicit helps students know that all students are expected to complete assignments, that they will have opportunities to revise work that is incomplete or incorrect, and that assistance is available when they need help. However, we also need to be explicit that *assistance* means helping each other get started with tasks and having conversations to clarify ideas—not expecting someone else to do the thinking or work for them!

Encouraging Collaboration: Partner Work

More and more of our classrooms are populated with diverse learners. Differences in habits, interests, language, abilities, and experiences make it difficult to meet the needs of all students if the teacher is the sole source of information and assistance. Encouraging students to collaborate with each other helps them become more confident in their work as well as becoming more self-sufficient. As partners, students become informal mentors for each other. If a task is not clear, they help each other. Think about how much easier it would be for students to go to the front of the room to share their work if a partner could come along.

An important guideline for most partner work is to have students talk about the task and then solve the problem independently. Once students have a solution, they can compare answers with their partner and work to resolve any differences. The message in this guideline is that though every person is expected to learn to use the mathematics, collaboration will help all students be more successful. Talking about their ideas with a partner encourages students to become secure about their own thinking and gives them practice communicating with others. With multiple partner groups in a classroom, students have many more opportunities to share than in

> Though students are expected to solve each problem, collaboration can help all students be more successful.

whole-class discussions alone. There is also the advantage that students are not as likely to tune out when working with a partner, as happens more frequently during whole-class discussions.

Encouraging Collaboration: Group Work

Having students work in groups of three or four to solve complex tasks allows us to bring more challenging mathematics into our lessons while providing support for learners. Group work does require guidelines for how students interact; for example, it is not the physical arrangement of desks in a cluster but the participation of each member that makes successful groups. Equally critical is that groups not be static, because students thrive through opportunities to work with different classmates.

We need to be clear on our own guidelines for assigning groups. If students remain in groups of red birds (the more advanced students), blue birds (the average students), and parrots (the less advanced students), they quickly identify those in the "smart" group and those who are "buzzards"— exactly the opposite of a supportive, positive environment for all students.

How Does Creating a Positive Learning Environment Benefit Teachers?

For all that students gain in a positive learning environment, there are many benefits for us as well. One of the most important is that students are more likely to be engaged with their learning. Classrooms where students are involved in their work give us opportunities to:

- move around the room and observe students close at hand;
- engage in short but needed conversations with individual students;
- converse with students to better understand their thinking about the mathematics in their assignments;
- steer students to more productive paths if they are misinterpreting tasks; and
- discuss issues that relate to individual students rather than the class as a whole, such as improving a specific response, giving feedback when an answer is wrong, or nudging a student to attempt more complex problems.

Very often the information we gather from several students provides a general view of where the class is in relation to the topic and helps us make decisions about our next instructional plans. (See Chapter 9 for more on individual conversations.) Note that sometimes the conversations relate to management issues, such as staying on task, doing one's share of the work, and so on, which helps enforce the positive learning environment.

As already noted, spending time up front to establish clear class guidelines for working together ensures more successful collaboration. While a "no-talking" classroom does not facilitate intellectual growth, neither does a chaotic classroom. Our goal is to create a supportive environment in which students think about their own ideas and those of others. In every classroom, students sometimes work alone and many times with other students. Students may not recognize that this environment facilitates their learning, but we will. Our opportunities *and* our students' opportunities to monitor understanding and identify misunderstandings set the stage for everyone to believe success is within their reach.

Motivating Students

Motivation is extremely important in encouraging student responsibility and self-assessment. Following is an email from a sixth-grade student to her grandmother, in which the student describes a task recently done in her math class. As you read the email think about the task's motivational qualities. What tasks do you consider as highly motivating for your students?

Gmom,

Last Friday my math class went to the mall and then we were divided into groups of four. Each group had a chaperone. We "had" $75 and a calculator. Each group was given the name of a boy or girl and a list of [their] interests. We then went out and "shopped" for them. We wrote down the items we found, the store and the tax (the lesson was all about % so finding tax using a calculator was that practice). We then calculated the total. The group who got the closest to $75 dollars without going over got to go back and purchase the items for the child. At lunch we again calculated our tax and total for our meals. We had to do lots of math to get our purchases to come close to $75. My group had $74.68 and we thought we would win but another team had $74.89. It was a really COOL field trip! XXOO, Meg

It is clear from her email that in Meg's class students had opportunities to make decisions, evaluate their answers, and make changes in the final product. Obviously, not all of our mathematics lessons can be field trips. However, if we read between the lines of the email, we observe thoughtful planning on the teacher's part. The students knew that they were to practice finding percents. Though they had a specific monetary target, there was flexibility in the task, which motivated students to make decisions about what to buy. Competition was present but was designed for teamwork. Students were able to evaluate their efforts and make adjustments in their choices of purchases before they had to turn in their shopping list.

Over time, responsibility and self-assessment can become habits of mind.

Strategies for Motivating Students

- Establish mistakes as opportunities to learn.
- Encourage partner and group work.
- Create an open, positive environment.
- Help students know their ideas are valued.
- Provide many opportunities for success.
- Set high but realistic expectations.
- Relate applications and tasks to students' interests.
- Be enthusiastic about mathematics.
- Emphasize learning, not grades.
- Give students choices.
- Use real-world contexts.
- Provide feedback frequently.
- Involve students in decisions.
- Help students set goals.
- Avoid intense competition.
- Treat students with respect.

Learn More About Ongoing Assessment

Assessment for Learning: Putting It into Practice
(Black et al. 2003)

So You Have to Teach Math? Sound Advice for K–6 Teachers
(Burns and Silbey 2000)

In classrooms where students are motivated, students prove that they can take greater ownership for their learning. We all work hard to help students identify where they are in relation to where they need to be. We help students have clear understandings of what they are to learn, encourage them to ask questions, and give them opportunities to seek additional learning opportunities if needed. Students need motivation to begin thinking about their own thinking and learning.

Encouraging Quality Student Work

In this section we focus briefly on the students' perspective of what constitutes quality work. In order for students to improve their work, they have to know not only *what* they are trying to accomplish but also *how* they are to demonstrate their learning. All of us have had students respond to our questions about how they got their answers with comments like "I just know it." Even when we include directions on worksheets or assessments such as *show your work* or *explain how you got your answer*, students often do not include much information. What it means to *explain* takes time and class discussions to develop. What we feel is that a strong explanation and what the students perceive as quality work are often very different. For example, one fourth-grade student felt his explanation was adequate when he wrote *I used my caculator* [sic] to explain how he figured out his answer.

Interestingly, the opposite is sometimes true for young children. Some youngsters tend to turn a response to a math question into an elaborate art project, taking so long to complete it that they only finish part of the assignment. Sometimes we need to show young students that they can, for example, count the ears on three rabbits to solve a math problem without making detailed drawings of the rabbits—complete with eyelashes, whiskers, paws, and cotton tails.

More often we see a student's bare-bones response that leaves us wondering how the student arrived at the answer. (See Figure 7–1.) Did the student compute mentally, use logical reasoning, or copy the answer from a neighbor's paper? Sometimes we have situations in which we believe that an individual student has a strong understanding of the mathematics in a particular task, and we do not want to discourage him or her from using mental math. The student reaches an answer through mental computations

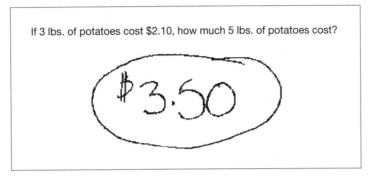

If 3 lbs. of potatoes cost $2.10, how much 5 lbs. of potatoes cost?

$3.50

FIGURE 7–1. Student's Bare-Bones Response to the *Cost of Potatoes Problem*

and reasoning and sees no need to explain in writing what is obvious to him or her. In these situations, class discussions illustrate the need for explanations about how answers are obtained.

Rubrics and Quality Student Work

When we use rubrics with our students—especially when we assign complex problems that include multiple steps and require written explanations, such as the *Fiddles Fudge Factory* problems (see Chapter 6, pages 143, 145, and 146)—they are better equipped to judge the quality of their own work. We then can gather a range of responses from weak to outstanding, which in turn support discussions about characteristics of the work and ways to improve different responses. There are many resource books about using rubrics to help students evaluate their work. See Chapter 9 for a more in-depth exploration of rubrics.

Establishing Characteristics of Quality Student Work

General descriptions that we use to guide our students in understanding the characteristics of quality responses, such as those listed on the following page, can be elaborate or very simple. How detailed the criteria we use in our classrooms will likely depend on the age of the students and the nature of the tasks.

Characteristics of High-Quality Student Work

- All parts of the problem are solved and answers are correct.

- Appropriate processes and/or tools are used.

- Computations and/or diagrams, graphs, charts, and representations are clearly labeled.

- Solution methods are clearly explained in words, pictures, and/or numbers using appropriate mathematical vocabulary.

Descriptions of criteria are best brought to life for students by anchor papers and/or models of quality work. Class discussions about what makes quality work—comparing two quality responses or one strong sample and one that needs improvement—encourage students to compare their own work to see what they can improve. (Since students are quick to recognize each other's work, trading student samples with a colleague or using samples from previous classes may be more appropriate than using work from students in the current class.) By looking at samples of good responses and then discussing and agreeing on a class criteria, students develop the skills needed for self-assessment, discussing work with partners, and revising work.

Class conversations and discussions with individuals and small groups are great opportunities for us to help students become better at articulating their ideas and critiquing their own and others' work.

Class conversations and discussions with individuals and small groups are great opportunities for us to help students become better at articulating their ideas and critiquing their own and others' work. Asking a more specific question related to the task and what the student has just said may prompt a richer response than a general question. For example, "What did you first notice in this problem?" or "What did this problem ask you to figure out?" are alternatives to opening a conversation with "How did you solve this problem?" As students suggest ways to improve sample responses, they get ideas for making changes or adding to their own work, thus gaining the motivation to take more ownership of their learning.

Encouraging students to work with a partner to critique each other's work, as they often do in a writing class before they turn in their papers, gives students additional opportunities to talk about mathematics. In one feedback strategy we use, called *Two Stars and a Wish*, students make two positive statements about their partners' work and then a suggestion (wish) for a way to improve the response. Through all discussions regarding student responses, it is important for us to remember that students need our guidance in learning to talk about the work, not about the student.

Through the self-assessment process, and in establishing characteristics of quality student work, we want our students to recognize that mathematics learning involves more than just getting a correct number. We want students to routinely ask themselves if they have answered questions as completely and clearly as they can, and to challenge themselves to give details in their work. (See Figure 7–2.) We support students in becoming strong users of

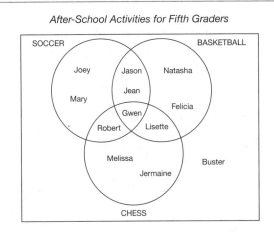

After-School Activities for Fifth Graders

What can you tell from the Venn diagram about these fifth graders' after-school activities? Give as complete an answer as you can.

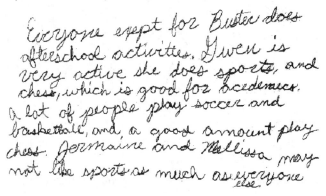

Everyone exept for Buster does afterschool activities. Gwen is very active she does sports, and chess, which is good for acedemics. A lot of people play soccer and basketball, and a good amount play chess. Jermaine and Mellissa may not like sports as much as everyone else.

FIGURE 7–2. We Encourage Students to Use a Venn Diagram to Give More Detailed Responses to Their Work

mathematics (mathematicians) by recognizing and acknowledging good work and offering praise when their work goes beyond expectations, for example, when their work elaborates on or makes unsolicited connections.

The following student responses illustrate additional types of tasks and samples that we can use to initiate discussions on what makes a quality response. Before examining each student sample, think about how you would solve the problems and what you would consider to be quality responses. It is important also to consider how you would begin discussions with your students about the samples and what mathematics you would highlight.

Second-Grade Example: Tuyen's Response to the *Popsicle* Problem

Popsicles cost 5¢ each. How much will it cost for Mrs. Martin to buy 9 popsicles for her grandchildren?

One way to begin is by asking students what they notice about Tuyen's answer. Other questions you might ask include:

- "What mathematics does this student show you that she knows?"

- "How did this student solve the problem?"

- "Can you think of another way to solve this problem?"

We can help students focus on the importance of answering the question posed in the problem by saying, "What sentence could you write to answer the question in the problem?"

Fifth-Grade Example: A Student's Response to the *Tangram* Problem

This teacher chose a money context and a value that would have "friendly numbers" as the answers:

If the whole square costs $4.00, how much would each piece of the puzzle cost? Explain how you know.

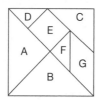

Now look at the student work below. The student's answers are correct and the explanation fits the answers. It is clear that the student solved the problem using proportional reasoning and his understanding of fractional relationships. What question could begin a discussion of this work sample? What features of the student's response should be highlighted?

A = $1¼

B = $1¼

C = 50¢

D = 25¢

E = 50¢

F = 25¢

G = 50¢

Explain your strategy and your thinking. I figured out my answer by fractions. I knew that 1 of the big triangles was 1/4 of the tile so 1/4 of $4 is $1, so A and B are $1. I knew 2 f's or d's equals 1 g or 1 e or 1 c. Next I knew that 4 f's or 4 d's equals 1 A or B. So 2 e's or g's equal 1 A or B. So g, e and c are 50¢ each. If 2 D's or 2 F's equal 1 g, e or c, and g, e and c are 50¢ they're 25¢.

Models of quality student responses are always linked to specific tasks. For conversations about samples to be helpful, students usually need to solve the problems and write their own answers first. Discussions should focus on the mathematics in the tasks, appropriate answers, and how the students conveyed their solutions. For example, compare how two second-grade students explained their thinking in the following *Jelly Bean Problem* samples from the end of the school year. (See Figure 7–3.) Note that this would be a good problem-solving task for third graders also.

Having two responses to the same problem reinforces the idea that there are multiple ways to solve most problems and to explain thinking. Each sample reveals a different approach to the task. Study Roshanda's response in Figure 7–3 especially carefully; her response is a good one to illustrate to students the importance of using an appropriate process to solve a problem, giving a clear explanation of how the problem was solved, *and* getting a correct answer. *Almost right* is not our goal—imagine if, in the working world, builders calculating where to bury a pipe so that it would connect to a main drain just got it *almost right*, or a driver passing another car on the freeway *almost passed*.

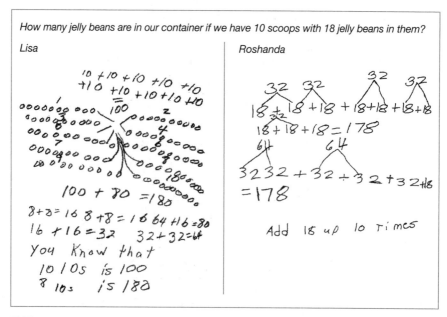

FIGURE 7–3. Lisa's and Roshanda's Responses to the *Jelly Bean Problem*

Now turn to "Reflection 7–2: Establishing Characteristics of Quality Work with Students" (see page 195). Choose a sample of student work that is close to the grade that you teach and respond to the questions in the reflection.

Reflection 7–2

Establishing Characteristics of Quality Work with Students

Page 195

Improving Responses in Daily Student Work

When we establish characteristics of quality work for our students, daily practice problems give us information that is helpful in knowing what our students understand and where we need to give more instruction or practice time. Take, for example, the *Potato Problem*, a routine item we might see in a textbook or we might put on a worksheet:

> If 3 lbs. of potatoes costs $2.10, how much should 5 lbs. of potatoes cost?

This is not an item that requires an elaborate explanation; however, we still want our students to be clear in their responses. Fifth-grade students Dakota and Wendy, for example, did not write an explanation, but their numbers clearly show how they arrived at their answers. Greg and Serena, on the other hand, had incorrect responses. (See Figure 7–4.)

As teachers, we have many examples of student work that are similar to the responses in the *Potato Problem*. The challenge we face is how to use sample student work wisely and efficiently to promote our students' understanding and daily practice of self-assessment. What level of detail do we want for a quality answer? Pause and think about this question and others; turn to "Reflection 7–3: Improving Responses in Daily Student Work: The *Potato Problem*" (see pages 196–97), and answer the questions before continuing to read.

Reflection 7–3

Improving Responses in Daily Student Work: The *Potato Problem*

Pages 196–97

The value students place on their work determines the ultimate quality of their responses, the effort they invest, and the commitment they make. For students to become good self-assessors, they need to have a clear understanding of the learning targets and the criteria that will be used to judge their work. They will be able to improve as they recognize the differences in their work and models that are considered quality performance. Students will also learn to evaluate their growth in mathematics knowledge over time. Since early experiences in which students have success set the stage for lifelong learning,

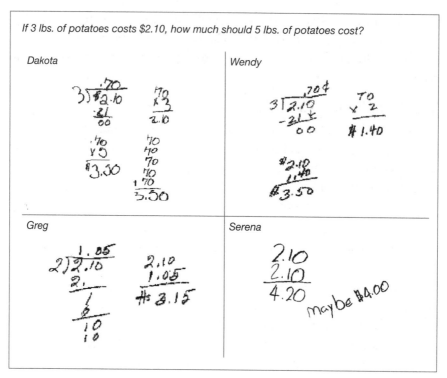

FIGURE 7–4. Four Responses to the *Potato Problem*

time we devote to helping students learn to assess their own work and create quality responses is time well spent.

Creating Structures to Promote Student Responsibility

The word *structure* brings to mind many different aspects of teaching and learning. In the classroom there are physical structures such as the arrangement of desks and the availability of manipulatives; there are operational structures such as students working with mentors or other students; and there are instructional structures such as graphic organizers and scaffolded questions. Since INFORMative assessment takes place during instruction as well as through specific assessment tasks, all of these structures are part of creating classrooms where students become more active partners in monitoring and evaluating their learning. Students need encouragement to begin thinking about their own thinking and to develop skills and strategies for being responsible. Although we have chosen seven examples as illustrations of structures to promote student responsibility, we are sure you will think of many more.

Seven Structures to Promote Student Responsibility

1. Classroom Routines

2. Checklists

3. Portfolios

4. Analysis and Revision of Work

5. Yellow Pages

6. Menus

7. Student-Led Conferences

Classroom Routines

If we want our students to be responsible learners, we must take time to teach them what responsible behavior looks like. Simple classroom routines such as teaching students to date their work, giving students folders to store their work, helping students learn to file their materials, and providing students with a table of contents for their notebooks become the starting points for becoming more responsible learners. Create daily routines—habits of mind—in which students are responsible for checking in, indicating lunch choices, and putting papers in certain places. And always provide clear directions so that students never have to ask, "What am I supposed to be doing?"

> If we want our students to be responsible learners, we must take time to teach them what responsible behavior looks like.

Efficient classroom routines are clearly a component of positive environments that help students understand what is expected of them. These routines, along with clear guidelines for quality work, support students' positive feelings about themselves as learners of mathematics.

> ### Students' Perceptions Make a Difference
>
> Students must believe that . . .
>
> - Success in math is within their reach.
>
> - They know what success looks like.
>
> - Assessment supports their learning.
>
> - Feedback can be helpful.
>
> - They will have chances for improving. (Bright and Joyner 2004)

Reflection 7–4

Student
Self-Assessment
of Everyday
Work Habits:
Templates

Pages 198–99

REPRODUCIBLE

Reflection 7–5

Student Self-
Assessment of
Test-Taking:
Template

Pages 200–201

REPRODUCIBLE

Checklists

To encourage students to be more responsible, we need to help them see benefits for their efforts. Sometimes the place to begin is with general habits. We have provided templates for two reproducible work habits checklists and one testing checklist at the end of this chapter; take a moment to look at them and think about how they are appropriate for your students: "Reflection 7–4: Student Self-Assessment of Everyday Work Habits: Templates" (two checklists; see pages 198–99) and "Reflection 7–5: Student Self-Assessment of Test-Taking: Template" (see pages 200–201). We include opportunities in the work-habits checklists for students to set goals for themselves and advice for students in the test-taking checklist. Use these checklists to generate ideas for ones that fit your classroom. The age of your students and the goals you want to accomplish will guide your planning. While checklists will not guarantee changes in students' behavior, they are discussion starters for the conversations that help students understand what behaviors are productive.

Portfolios

In Chapter 5, we briefly discussed portfolios (see page 154), purposeful collections of evidence that we and our students judge to be important. Portfolios differ from students' work folders in that they contain carefully chosen samples rather than housing all of a student's work. They are also different in their design according to their purpose and audience:

- *Showcase portfolios* are celebrative; like an artist's portfolio, they house collections of a student's favorite or best work.

- *Progress portfolios,* sometimes called *chronological* or *growth portfolios,* contain samples of student work about similar tasks, highlighting a student's progress over time from novice to more accomplished user of particular mathematics. The samples of work are usually a combination of those chosen by the teacher, such as for specific tasks or assessments, and by the students.

- *Anthologies* or *pass-along portfolios* contain a combination of on-demand tasks, best works, and samples that illustrate growth over time. Certain documents may accompany students through elementary grades—some districts may specify specific documents to include—with teachers supplementing the portfolios each year.

Key Questions for Making Decisions About Portfolios

- What is the purpose?

- Who is the audience?

- How will it be used?

- Who decides the contents?

- What will be included?

- When will it be created?

- How will it be evaluated?

There is no one right way to design portfolios, but there are ways to make them meaningful to the audience and useful to the students as a learning experience. Compiling portfolios should be primarily the student's responsibility. With our guidance and a list of requirements, even young students are able to assemble their portfolios. We designate certain assignments or tests to be included, and students choose papers of which they are proud. Students put dates on all of their papers, organize their work, and create a table of contents.

Portfolios provide opportunities for students to learn responsibility and to take greater ownership for their learning. Students customarily write a reflection about each entry; these reflections are not necessarily long, but they provide a context for the work and an opportunity for students to explain why they chose to include a particular piece in their portfolios.

> Portfolios provide opportunities for students to learn responsibility and to take greater ownership for their learning.

Technology opens new avenues for both assessing our students and sharing their accomplishments. We can use electronic portfolios, for example, to solve the issue of storage space, replacing the need for a file drawer devoted just to portfolios or, in the case of some teachers, a cabinet storing the unused pizza boxes that house each student's portfolio. In addition, with electronic portfolios, students have the option to include digital photographs, short videos, and electronic slideshow presentations to supplement their projects. Students can also type their reflections on the computer to accompany scans of their work.

Analysis and Revision of Work

One way we support self-assessment and student responsibility is by providing opportunities for students to redo assignments and assessments. Rather than assigning a grade, we can score papers and indicate answers that are wrong or incomplete; students then review their work to determine why they missed questions and make corrections or identify what they do not understand. We have provided "Reflection 7–6: Student Error Analysis of Tests: Template" (see page 202) for you to use with your students and to gain ideas for creating your own.

Reflection 7–6

Student Error Analysis of Tests: Template

Page 202

REPRODUCIBLE

As with other strategies for student self-assessment, we must invest time modeling how to look at wrong answers and determine why they were missed. Early in this process, students may not be able to identify the reasons for their errors and need encouragement to identify exactly what they do and do not understand. For some students, it may take a two- or three-minute conversation about their papers to get them started. For example, Mrs. Peterson, a third-grade teacher, said of modeling analysis and revision: "I had to spend a lot of time talking about why it is important to think about what you know and what you do not understand. The students' papers from earlier in the year were not as revealing. Many times I modeled explanations and corrections. The investment of time was worth it. My students make far fewer careless mistakes now and are able to ask me more specific questions when they do not understand."

During this process, Mrs. Peterson taught her students to make a simple three-column chart listing the problem number, their mistake, and the corrected solution. (See Figure 7–5.) Notice that the students' error analysis made evident that there might be a problem with item 9. Most of the students in the class missed that question, which indicated to Mrs. Peterson that a close look at the question was in order. Was the question ambiguous? Did the context confuse the students? Was the mathematics required to answer the question something that had not been addressed? Do students need more instruction and discussion about the mathematics?

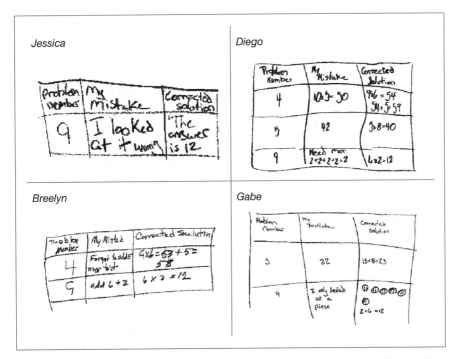

FIGURE 7–5. Examples of Third-Grade Students' Error Analysis from the End of the School Year

Student-Developed Yellow Pages

We use mathematics yellow pages to both assist students in learning and encourage them to take more responsibility for their work. Similar to phone book yellow pages, these booklets are personal resources that students develop for themselves. Using yellow paper, students define vocabulary terms to make a personal glossary, explain procedures, illustrate formulas with examples, and make other notes that they can use as a resource to help solve mathematics problems. These yellow pages become a structural support, a study guide, and a resource, especially for students who struggle with mathematics or for whom English is not their first language.

To help students get started creating their own yellow pages resource, give specific examples, such as asking students to draw a pentagon, an irregular polygon, and a rectangle with dimensions given and arrows going around the figures, and then asking them to write a definition for the perimeter of polygons as the distance around the figures and to include a formula for the perimeter of the rectangle: $p = 2l + 2w$.

Menus

Menus are another support strategy that provide differentiated tasks and include student choice. An advantage of menus is that a project, a range of tasks, or a collection of problems usually appears on one assignment sheet. Students are responsible for completing and organizing their work.

For example, one type of menu for primary students might include nine word problems based on *Cognitively Guided Instruction* problem types (Carpenter, Fennema, Franke, Levi, and Empson 1999). Three problems are assigned to each student based on the student's current performance. When finished, the student can choose two more problems to complete. When the students reconvene, they discuss an example of each problem type so that all students hear strategies for different kinds of tasks.

With other types of menus, we can list a variety of tasks, some of which may be worksheets, center activities, or small-group discussions. We can include a combination of assigned tasks—varying according to student strengths or needs—and student choices. We can use menus in centers or as regular class assignments.

Learn More About Ideas for Menu Activities

Facilitator's Guide to Groupwork in Diverse Classrooms: A Casebook for Educators
(Shulman, Lotan, and Whitcomb 1998)

It All Adds Up! Engaging 8-to-12-Year-Olds in Math Investigations
(Skinner 1999)

Student-Led Conferences

One of the most powerful strategies for developing student self-assessment and responsibility is the student-led parent conference. When well planned, these conferences build ownership and confidence. Students' achievement is validated as they present work samples to their parents, talk about their struggles and successes, explain criteria for good work, and set new personal learning goals. There is pride and an increased enthusiasm for learning that comes from describing well-done work.

Student-led conferences are never designed to be a substitute for teacher–parent conferences, nor should they occur without careful planning and coaching. We have many up-front responsibilities to ensure our students' success, beginning with obtaining the support of the principal, informing students and parents at the first of the year that student-led conferences are coming, and arranging for substitute parents if parents or caregivers cannot participate. Our responsibilities also include defining clear goals for the conferences, informing students about what work they need to include, sending invitations for the conferences, helping students be well prepared, and role-playing a sample conference with students.

Knowing the kinds of things that they will be sharing during the conferences, students have a reason to keep their work folders and portfolios—often a feature of student-led conferences—up to date and to pay special attention to the quality of their work. With opportunities to practice in modeling and role-playing sessions, students can focus on organizing their presentations and communicating mathematical ideas.

There is no one model for student-led parent conferences that fits every classroom. Our purpose is not to provide a template for planning these conferences; rather, we want to emphasize that student-led parent conferences are another way to develop and support student responsibility.

Scaffolding

We want the same expectations for accomplishment of mathematics learning targets for all of our students, but how students demonstrate their knowledge and skills may be slightly different. The student who races up the steps two at a time to reach the front door of the school, the one who moves deliberately one step at a time, and the student who rolls in a wheelchair up the ramp all

> ### Learn More About Student-Led Conferences
>
> Changing the View: Student-Led Parent Conferences
> *(Austin 1994)*
>
> How to Assess While You Teach Math: Formative Assessment Practices and Lessons, Grades K–2: A Multimedia Professional Learning Resource
> *(Islas 2011)*

reach the front door and enter the school. Whether we name the strategies as scaffolding or differentiating or individualizing, our jobs as teachers are to set high goals for learning mathematics content and then provide as many supports as we can to help students reach the goals. The same scaffolding and support structures we have always used to assist students in learning mathematics are ones that we need to continue to use in our assessments. It is always important to keep in mind that the small changes we make in the ways that we interact with our students and the opportunities we provide for them to learn mathematics can result in big gains for their mathematics learning.

> *Scaffolding as a Way to Support Student Responsibility*
>
> - Write each sentence in a problem on a separate line.
>
> - Provide highlighters for students to mark needed information.
>
> - Break multistep problems apart with an answer line for each part.
>
> - Use smaller numbers in the same problems as other students are solving.
>
> - Scribe for young students or those students who have identified difficulty with motor skills.
>
> - Encourage students to use graphic organizers and thinking maps.

Assessment Tip

If the purpose is to determine what students know and can do, provide the same support structures for formative assessments as for instruction.

Our intent here is not to model each of these structures, but to remind ourselves that we are probably already using most of these ideas at different times. We want to raise our awareness of their value in assessments as well as instruction. If the purpose of an assessment is to determine if our students are learning the content we are teaching, we need to include structures that help students reveal their understanding of that mathematics.

INFORMing My Practice

Throughout this book we hope that one message is clear: INFORMative assessment and the decisions that we make on a day-to-day basis are integrally linked. Our decisions have a profound influence on students and their success in learning mathematics. By creating positive learning environments, encouraging quality student work, and creating structures that support student responsibility, we are helping our students develop positive habits of mind and develop self-assessment strategies and that are likely to result in greater achievement and self-satisfaction.

Turn to "Reflection 7–7: INFORMing My Practice: Supporting Student Self-Assessment and Responsibility" (see page 203). As you answer the questions, make sure you list three things you are interested in trying in your classroom to encourage students to take greater ownership of their learning.

Reflection 7–7
INFORMing My Practice: Supporting Student Self-Assessment and Responsibility

Page 203

The Research: An Environment to Support Learning

Classrooms that function as communities of learners demonstrate four features identified in the research on teaching and learning mathematics with understanding.

- Students' ideas and methods are respected and valued because they have the potential to contribute to everyone's learning.

- Students choose and share with the class their methods of solving problems while recognizing that many strategies are likely to exist for solving problems.

- Students appreciate the value of mistakes as opportunities for learning by examining reasoning, thus deepening everyone's analysis of the mistakes.

- Students learn that decisions about whether something is correct and sensible lie in the logic and structure of mathematics rather than in the status of the teacher or the popularity of the student making the argument.

"Hence, in addition to selecting tasks with goals in mind and sharing essential information, the teacher's primary role is to establish a classroom culture that supports learning with understanding, thereby serving to motivate students to learn." (National Research Council 2001a, 344–345)

Reflection 7-1: Evaluating My Current Practice

• In planning, are you clear on the learning targets for your lessons?	Yes No Sometimes
• Do you establish criteria for what achievement of the learning targets will be?	Yes No Sometimes
• Do you have diagnostic information about what your students already know as you begin a new unit of instruction?	Yes No Sometimes
• Are you using INFORMative assessment strategies that are most effective in gathering information about your students' understandings?	Yes No Sometimes
• Have you increased the amount of time you spend listening to your students' explanations of their thinking?	Yes No Sometimes
• Are you looking for evidence of learning, growth in problem solving, thinking, and reasoning in a variety of situations?	Yes No Sometimes
• Are you incorporating a variety of assessment methods in your classroom?	Yes No Sometimes
• Are you more frequently looking at your students' work through the lens of understanding their thinking in order to plan rather than just to assign a grade?	Yes No Sometimes
• When you choose tasks, are you thinking about the mathematics students need to know or can learn?	Yes No Sometimes
• If observers came into your classroom, would they see INFORMative assessment in action?	Yes No Sometimes

Reflection 7-2: Establishing Characteristics of Quality Work with Students

Look back at the samples of student work on pages 177–84. Which student sample would be most appropriate for you to use in a discussion with your class about quality responses?

1. What features of the student work would you want to highlight with your students?

2. What mathematics understanding would you discuss with your students?

3. What questions might you pose to help students brainstorm ways to improve the sample or to generalize quality features?

If 3 lbs. of potatoes costs $2.10, how much should 5 lbs. of potatoes cost?

Dakota

$$3\overline{)\$2.10} = .70$$
$$-21$$
$$00$$

$$\begin{array}{r} 70 \\ \times 3 \\ \hline 2.10 \end{array}$$

$$\begin{array}{r} .70 \\ \times 5 \\ \hline \$3.50 \end{array}$$

$$\begin{array}{r} 70 \\ 70 \\ 70 \\ 70 \\ 1\ 70 \\ \hline 3.50 \end{array}$$

Wendy

$$3\overline{)2.10} = .70¢$$
$$-21¢$$
$$00$$

$$\begin{array}{r} 70 \\ \times 2 \\ \hline \$1.40 \end{array}$$

$$\begin{array}{r} \$2.10 \\ 1.40 \\ \hline \$3.50 \end{array}$$

Greg

$$2\overline{)2.10} = 1.05$$
$$2.$$
$$1$$
$$6$$
$$10$$
$$10$$

$$\begin{array}{r} 2.10 \\ 1.05 \\ \hline \$3.15 \end{array}$$

Serena

$$\begin{array}{r} 2.10 \\ 2.10 \\ \hline 4.20 \end{array}$$

maybe $4.00

(continued)

Reflection 7–3: Improving Responses in Daily Student Work: The *Potato Problem*
continued

Review student responses to the Potato Problem *(see page 196), then answer the questions below.*

1. What would you say to Dakota and Wendy, whose computations were correct, to encourage them to clarify what the numbers represent? Would labels be sufficient or do you want your students to write a sentence to answer the question in the problem?

2. What do you know about the misunderstandings (or incomplete understandings) of Greg and Serena? What discussion might you have with each student and with the class to address these mistakes?

Reflection 7-4: Student Self-Assessment of Everyday Work Habits: Template 1

Name_____   Date_____

	Never	Sometimes	Usually	Always
Are you in your seat and ready to learn when the mathematics lesson begins?				
Do you have your math materials ready for each lesson?				
Do you pay careful attention in class? Are you a good listener?				
Do you work cooperatively with other students?				
Do you ask your partner or the teacher for help if you do not understand?				
Do you complete and turn in your mathematics class work and homework?				
Do you keep your mathematics papers and worksheets neat and organized?				
Do you use your time in mathematics class wisely?				

1. School is your job. What habits do you need to improve?

2. Good students make learning their work each day. What actions are you going to take to improve your everyday work habits?

Reflection 7–4: Student Self-Assessment of Everyday Work Habits: Template 2

Name_____   Date_____

I am ready to begin when the math lesson starts.	☺	😐	☹
I listen carefully when the teacher or my friends are talking.	☺	😐	☹
I raise my hand when I have ideas to share.	☺	😐	☹
I work quietly with my partner.	☺	😐	☹
I write my answers neatly and show my thinking.	☺	😐	☹
I check my answers.	☺	😐	☹
I finish all of my math work.	☺	😐	☹

What is one thing you want to improve to be a better math student?

Reflection 7-5: Student Self-Assessment of Test-Taking: Template

Name_____ Date_____

	Never	Sometimes	Usually	Always
When you prepare, can you explain in your own words what you will need to know and be able to do on the test?				
Do you study for tests by reviewing your homework and class work papers?				
Do you get plenty of rest the night before the test?				
Do you read the directions on the test paper carefully?				
Do you think about what each question is asking you to do or what you are trying to find out?				
Do you answer each question completely and show all of your work?				
Do you give details to show your thinking if the question says to "explain"?				

(continued)

From INFORMative Assessment: Formative Assessment to Improve Math Achievement, Grades K–6 by Jeane M. Joyner and Mari Muri. © 2011 Scholastic Inc. Permission granted to photocopy for nonprofit use in a classroom or similar place dedicated to face-to-face educational instruction.

	Never	Sometimes	Usually	Always
Do you check your work carefully to be sure you completed every question?				
Do you try to do your best even if the mathematics is hard?				

A good test taker is a good student every day. Here are some ideas for being a better test taker. Check the ideas you think will help you the most.

☐ If you do not understand the directions, ask.

☐ If you do not know how to solve a problem, tell yourself what you do know about the problem.

☐ Say in your own words the question you are trying to answer.

☐ If there is a vocabulary word that you do not know, try to figure it out by reading the rest of the question.

☐ Use your time wisely. Don't daydream or spend too long being stuck on one question.

☐ Believe in yourself. You are the key to your own success!

Reflection 7-6: Student Error Analysis of Tests: Template

Use your test paper to answer the questions below and identify what you still need to learn.

1. Describe the mathematics you need to know for this test.

2. For each question that you missed, explain why and tell how you are going to fix the mistake.

Question I missed	Why I missed it	How I corrected it

3. Write one goal for yourself related to this mathematics test.

From *INFORMative Assessment: Formative Assessment to Improve Math Achievement, Grades K–6* by Jeane M. Joyner and Mari Muri. © 2011 Scholastic Inc. Permission granted to photocopy for nonprofit use in a classroom or similar place dedicated to face-to-face educational instruction.

Reflection 7-7: INFORMing My Practice: Supporting Student Self-Assessment and Responsibility

On a scale of 1 (very low) to 10 (very high), how would you rate your classroom as an environment to support student learning? _____

Is there anything you are considering changing?

What are three things are you interested in trying in your classroom to encourage students to take greater ownership of their learning?

1.

2.

3.

How is your thinking about INFORMative assessment changing?

Questions I still have:

Section V

How Do Good Questions Lead to
Quality Inferences and Feedback?

Good Questions Lead to Important Assessment Information

Questioning is at the heart of teaching and learning. Both teachers and students use questions to explore new topics, understand thinking, and determine competence. In this chapter, we organize our ideas about questioning into five broad, overlapping categories that describe ways we can use questions to support student learning. Since our questions often serve more than one purpose at a time, the five categories are not discrete. Throughout the chapter, we focus on how students' responses to our questions support the inferences we make about their learning.

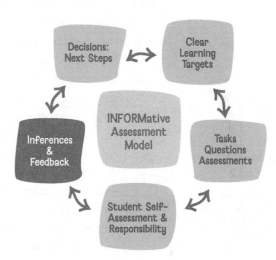

Overview

Students' responses to our oral questions are invaluable; when we strive to become better at carefully listening to what our students have to say, we can learn about their understandings and misconceptions. In this chapter, we focus on the importance of questioning as an INFORMative assessment strategy. How does posing good questions help us learn more about our students' understanding? How does our use of good questions help us decide *what's next* as we teach? As we plan tomorrow's lesson? As we give feedback to individual students and the class?

There are a variety of resources that we can use to frame better questions and create stronger assessments: some designed to promote thought-provoking, more advanced questions and discussions as opposed to less advanced, one-word response questions; others we use to create series of questions related to specific content, ask more questions during class discussions, and scaffold questions to help students develop mathematical understandings.

When we plan questions around the thinking that students might employ in their answers, use wait time, and have students respond to each others' statements, we usually ask fewer questions (Sullivan and Lilburn 2002). Ultimately, we become better prepared to ask questions and support student learning.

In this chapter we organize our ideas about questioning into five broad, overlapping categories that describe ways we can use questions to support student learning—inviting participation, guiding thinking toward essential elements of tasks, helping students unpack problems and rethink their responses, probing students' responses, and challenging students to extend their ideas, make connections, and apply their knowledge in new situations. As we plan questions, we need to first identify the mathematical concepts and procedures that underlie the tasks.

Learn More About the Importance of Questions in Mathematics Classrooms

Good Questions for Math Teaching: Why Ask Them and What to Ask, Grades K–6

(Sullivan and Lilburn 2002)

Categories of Questions for Formative Assessment

1. Questions That Invite Student Participation in Discussions

2. Questions That Guide Students' Thinking

3. Questions That Help Students Rethink Their Responses

4. Questions That Probe Students' Thinking

5. Questions That Encourage Students to Extend Ideas

Questions That Invite Student Participation in Discussions

Beginning a discussion with a question that all students can answer is a way to invite students—even those who may not be very successful in mathematics or are sometimes tuned out—into a class conversation. These questions are likely to be open-ended and may be either generic or specific to the task. Rather than asking, "What is the answer?," we can pose a question that has multiple possible responses, such as one from the list below, as a way to encourage all our students to contribute to the conversation. As you read the list, think of other questions you might ask.

Questions for Inviting Student Participation in Discussions

- "What do you notice in this problem?"

- "Who are the people in the problem?"

- "What is happening in this problem?"

- "What question are we trying to answer in this problem?"

- "How is this problem like the ones we talked about yesterday?"

- "What are some observations you can make about the data we collected?"

These introductory questions are not tough ones; they are open-ended and generic in nature. As we ask them, we have several purposes in mind: to provide an opportunity for all students to engage in the lesson, to increase student participation, and to send the message that we expect everyone in the class to be part of the discussion. We do this by our words and our actions; for example, when we momentarily ignore the hands that immediately go up, our nonverbal communication says that we are prepared to wait until more students are ready to respond.

It is important that we not allow students to opt out of discussions, especially those based on open-ended questions. Sometimes, for example, we may ask a specific question and call on a student who responds, "I don't know." This is a time for us to say something such as, "OK, tell me something

Learn More About Questions for Inviting Student Participation in Discussions

Classroom Discussions: Using Math Talk to Help Students Learn, Grades K–6, Second Edition

(Chapin, O'Connor, and Anderson 2009)

Classroom Discussions: Seeing Math Discourse in Action, Grades K–6: A Multimedia Professional Learning Resource

(Chapin, O'Connor, and Anderson 2011)

Our purpose in asking questions is never to catch students who might not be paying attention or who may not know an answer. We undermine the goal of greater student participation in discussions if we use questioning as a behavior management tool.

about this problem that you do know," or we can call on another student for a response, then come back to the first student and ask him or her to restate the same information. Our purpose in asking questions should never be to catch students who might not be paying attention or who may truly not know an answer. We undermine the goal of greater student participation in discussions if we use questioning as a behavior management tool. If we want to develop a classroom culture in which all students actively participate and in which not knowing is a chance to learn, our questions should be engaging and our conversations should be respectful of students' developing ideas.

Questions That Guide Students' Thinking

Skillfully using questions guides our students' to more advanced thinking and shapes classroom interactions. Helping our students make connections and recognize how to use knowledge that they already have is as important in kindergarten as it is in middle school.

In one first-grade classroom, a teacher prepared a lesson on exploring halves by first telling students about two children sharing a sandwich. In the following dialogue, consider how Mrs. Griffith gathered information about her students' various means of thinking before she asked them to fold and cut shapes for the exploring halves task:

Mrs. Griffith's Questions About Halves

Mrs. Griffith: *Caitlin cut her sandwich in half to share with her little brother who said, "I want the bigger half." What could we say to Caitlin's brother about sharing halves?*

Jason: *He should be polite and ask for the smaller half.*

Margie: *Whoever cuts, the other person gets to choose first.*

Mrs. Griffith: *Let's think about what we know about halves. Talk to your partner about halves and what we should tell Caitlin's brother* (gives students several minutes to talk and then calls the class back together).

> **Reggie:** *Can I come draw a picture?* (Goes to the board, draws a square, and then bisects it diagonally.) *I can take one part and lay it on the other part to show they are the same* (demonstrates with his hands).
>
> **Mrs. Griffith:** (Addressing the class.) *What do you think about the picture Reggie has drawn?*
>
> **Ethan:** *So halves have to match each other?*
>
> **Maya:** *Halves are only the same for the same thing.*
>
> **Mrs. Griffith:** *Tell us some more about what you just said, Maya.*
>
> **Maya:** *Well, when we have pizza, my mom and dad have a big one and they get a small one for my brother and me. We eat half of our pizza but it is not as big as half of Mom's pizza.*
>
> **Mrs. Griffith:** *So what does Maya's example tell us?*
>
> **Jenny:** *We have to know how big the pizza is to talk about half.*
>
> **Mrs. Griffith:** *Hmmm. Let's look at the shapes I've put on your tables and see what we can discover about halves. Then tomorrow, I want us to come back to the question of what to tell Caitlin's little brother.*

Our goal is to encourage our students to activate their own knowledge and to learn to look for patterns. Sometimes we pose questions to the class to help students who have trouble getting started or who are stuck. For example, early in the year in Mr. Zacchio's second-grade classroom, students worked on a farm animal problem:

> The farmer looked into the barn and saw some animals. He counted 12 legs. Use words, pictures, or numbers to tell what animals he might have seen.

Mr. Zacchio noticed that most students got right to work, but a few seemed to have difficulty getting started. Rather than telling students what to do, he used guiding questions, such as the following, to involve students in providing assistance to their classmates and focus attention in helpful directions:

"What are some animals that live on a farm? How does this information help you?"

"What do you know about the number of legs different animals have?"

When Mr. Zacchio sensed that some students needed even more ideas, he asked several students to show the class how they answered the question. (See Figure 8–1.) Mattie counted the legs of two ducks, one horse, and one cow, carefully placing the fence so that only the animals' legs were visible. Linda had a different idea; she said the farmer saw two cows and two chickens. With the students displaying their work, we might ask, "How are these answers alike? How are they different?"

There are times when we call for volunteers to share their ideas: "Who would like to show the class what the farmer might have seen?" Other times we want to be selective because of specific features of a student's response.

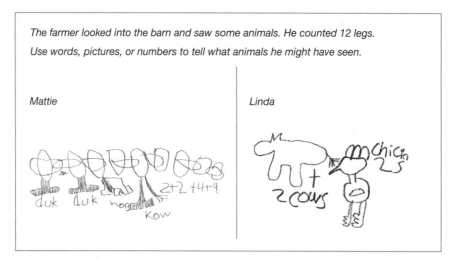

The farmer looked into the barn and saw some animals. He counted 12 legs.
Use words, pictures, or numbers to tell what animals he might have seen.

Mattie   Linda

FIGURE 8–1. Mattie's and Linda's Responses to the *Farm Animal Problem*

> The farmer looked into the barn and saw some animals. He counted 12 legs.
>
> Use words, pictures, or numbers to tell what animals he might have seen.

FIGURE 8-2. Joseph's Response to the *Farm Animal Problem*

For example, having Joseph share his answer might not be a wise choice for initial examples, though we definitely want to talk with him about his work. (See Figure 8–2.) His pictures show an owl plus an owl equals twelve (illustrated by another owl). The labels for the figures read *3 owls, 3 owls,* and *owls' legs.* As teachers, we recognize the thinking of this beginning second grader and are pleased that he recognizes that three owls times two legs, plus three owls times two legs, equals twelve legs. His example may be a good one to share after a number of other students have displayed their solutions.

If the class conversation is about computations such as 28 + 34 or 509 − 385 or 36 × 7, there are a number of possible questions that can direct students toward productive paths. Our questions should focus attention on number relationships and appropriate procedures, such as "Why do you think the answer might be more (or less) than a hundred?" or "Is there more than one way to solve these computations?" Somewhat less open but still important is a question such as "When you subtract three hundred eighty-five from five hundred nine, what might be a reasonable estimate?

How did you make that estimate?" On the other hand, asking, "What is the answer to number one?" or "Who can tell us the answer to the third problem?" is likely to lead students to focus on the answers only and not think about the process for getting the answers or consider whether there are alternative solution strategies. And do not forget that an engaging question, such as "Can you suggest a story problem that could go with these numbers?" or "What situation might this problem represent?" might start a discussion of computations.

Questions That Help Students Rethink Their Responses

As we encourage students to check their own responses, we often find out more about our students' thinking than just how many problems they got correct or how many they missed. We refer to these examples as *questions that help students unpack their thinking and rethink their responses.*

For example, we often quickly check over the answers to homework and worksheet pages—typical classroom activities designed to provide students opportunities to practice the mathematics they have learned—because we do not want our students practicing computations incorrectly. Sometimes the nature of students' errors are obvious, such as making a number fact error or not labeling the answer with the appropriate units. (Students will have difficulty recognizing a number fact error if they apply the same facts in an inverse operation. Thus, if they multiplied $6 \times 7 = 49$, they may check their work and write $49 \div 7 = 6$.)

Other times, we do not understand why students made mistakes and cannot identify the logic for their answers. We wonder if their mistakes were careless errors or if they represent a lack of conceptual knowledge or a misunderstood procedure. We need to identify and help our students identify where the errors lie so they can address the errors in a timely manner. We also want to help our students expand their understandings and hear how others solve the same problem. The questions and strategies in this category allow students to focus on their responses and identify different, appropriate ways to unpack problems.

Assessment Tip ✓

Often we ask questions that could be answered with "yes" or "no" even though we expect more information. Our task is to follow up with reminders such as "Explain . . ." or "Tell me more about . . ." to prompt students to give additional information.

Questions to Help Students Rethink Their Responses

Look through your work . . .

- Were there some questions that seemed easier than others? If so, why?

- If there is a problem you are not sure about, have you discussed it with your partner?

- What mathematics thinking did you use to complete the assignment?

- If any of your answers are different, can you and your partner explain why?

- Can you think of another way to solve this problem? Explain.

- Is there a hidden question in the problem that means the solution needs more than one step?

Many students have difficulty with two-step problems. For example, in the problem *Lucas buys gum for 89¢, an apple for $1.10, and carton of chocolate milk for $1.29. How much change does he get from a five dollar bill?*, the hidden question is "How much did he spend?" Students tend to complete the first step—often the hidden question—and stop with the results of this computation as their answer to the problem. Even if the second computation is one that is easy for them, they do not complete the task. Therefore, asking a question that focuses attention on the possibility of two computations causes students to rethink their work: "Did you notice that it took more than one computation to solve some of these problems? That is, were there hidden questions so that you needed to do two steps? Before we discuss the problems, look through your work with your partner to see if you have completely answered each problem." In situations such as this, we are giving students specific directions, but our ultimate goal is for students to take responsibility for checking themselves.

Even in these so-called unpacking conversations, we often find evidence of different depths of understandings among our students. For example, if a problem involves elapsed time, we might begin a discussion by

Information about students' understanding of mathematics is available in almost every conversation we have with our students.

asking, "What do you know about the different times in this story problem?" The student who suggests that you could write *4:45 – 4:29* to subtract and find out how long it would take Tanisha to get to the store is likely to have a different sense of number than the one who says, "I know it will take sixteen minutes for Tanisha to get to the store because you just add one more minute to fifteen minutes."

In other words, information about students' understanding of mathematics is available in almost every conversation we have with our class. Our task is to become better, INFORMative assessment listeners.

Questions That Probe Students' Thinking

Probing questions help us to clarify the strength of students' understandings and the nature of students' misconceptions. When a student correctly identifies a right angle as one with an opening of 90 degrees and then names the same angle when rotated counterclockwise as a "left angle," we need to find out more information. Is the confusion only in naming the figure because of the direction of the rays? How does the student define an angle? A right angle? Does the student focus more on the figure's orientation in space or the degree of turning of one ray from the other?

If a question requires deep thinking, we must give students time to think.

Wait time is critical for probing questions to be effective. When we pose a question for the group or an individual, then we need to pause. If the question requires deep thinking, we must give students time to think. There are times when we believe that the students understand but are having difficulty expressing themselves. Asking for a further explanation is an opportunity for students to clarify their own thinking. "What do you mean?" or "Tell me a little more about your idea" are generic probing questions. We might ask for students to express their answers in complete sentences to help them solidify their understandings. Keeping the emphasis on the students' ideas is not necessarily easy; students sometimes spend their energies trying to figure out what we want them to say rather than thinking about what they know and what they need to learn.

Keeping the emphasis on the students' ideas is not easy; students sometimes spend their energies trying to figure out what we want them to say rather than thinking about what they know and what they need to learn.

While probing questions help us understand an individual student's grasp of the content, they also give us information to guide us as we are working with our class as a whole. Using questions to take the pulse of the class does not require us to change the way we conduct our lessons as much as it requires us to find ways to absorb and use the information available through the students' responses. If we probe the thinking of five or six students whose work represents a range of performance, we are likely to be able to identify the group's understanding. Asking similar questions of two students who usually struggle, two who are in the middle, and one or two who are more advanced in their learning can help us INFORMally assess how well students as a whole are mastering the content.

For most of us, learning to ask questions that *probe* rather than *direct* students' thinking is a new skill. Following are three tasks, related to rational numbers in kindergarten, grade 4, and grade 6, that provide contexts for us to practice designing probing questions.

The Kindergarten Fraction Pretest

Knowing what and how students think about fractions is important in planning lessons. Fraction concepts develop over time through numerous, varied experiences; however, there is an assumption that if students understand whole-number relationships and operations, they will easily grasp rational number concepts and procedures. Textbooks and pacing guides move students quickly through hands-on activities designed to build fraction concepts into applications and procedural tasks.

In one kindergarten class, Julia Ellen's teacher gave her directions orally as she completed each part of her fraction "pretest." As she began coloring the rectangle, she said, "Tell me when to stop." Her teacher told her to go as far as she wanted to go to show one-half. (See Figure 8–3 on the following page.) If you were planning lessons involving fractions for kindergarten or first-grade classrooms, what concepts do you think are important for students to develop? What questions would you like to ask this student? What might you infer about her understanding and experiences with fraction ideas in preschool?

"Questions should support and encourage student thinking. If students are not thinking, they are not learning." —*Dynamic Classroom Assessment: Linking Assessment with Instruction in Elementary School Mathematics (Participant's Guide)* (Bright and Joyner 2005, 95)

"Questions can keep students focused on important mathematical ideas and can move discussions beyond short, discrete, unrelated responses to in-depth dialog that helps students make sense of mathematics." —*Dynamic Classroom Assessment: Linking Assessment with Instruction in Elementary School Mathematics (Participant's Guide)* (Bright and Joyner 2005, 95)

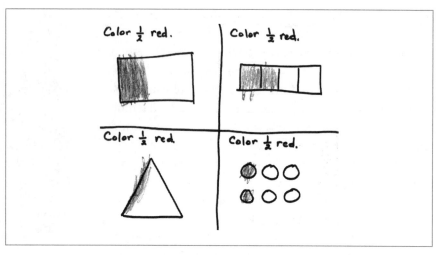

FIGURE 8–3. Julia Ellen's Responses to the Kindergarten Fraction Pretest

The Fourth-Grade *Kings' Melons Problem*

As you solve the following problem posed to a class of fourth graders, decide what you would expect as a good response before you look at the student work.

The Kings' Melons Problem

Some kings found 9 melons. They shared them equally. Then they found 6 more melons and shared them equally. How many kings were there and how many melons did each king get? Show your work and explain your thinking. (Brockhoff et al. 1992)

What can you infer from each student's response to the *Kings' Melons Problem*? What probing questions might you ask each student? (See Figure 8–4.)

The Sixth-Grade *Soccer League Problem*

It is easy to recognize the misunderstandings of some students and more difficult to know the thinking of other students. As you solve this problem (page 220), think about what probing questions you would ask each student.

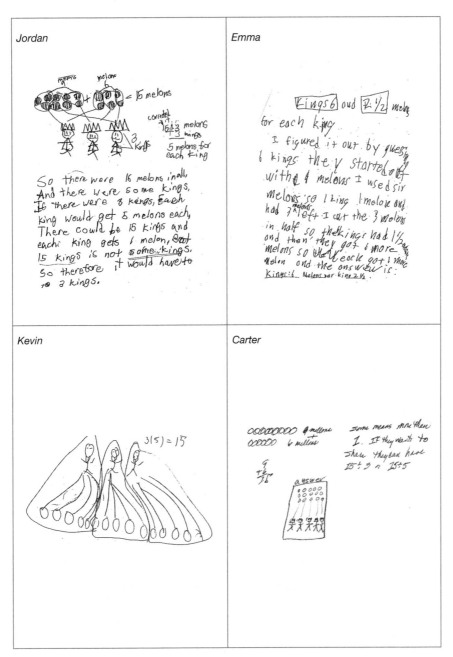

FIGURE 8–4. Four Students' Responses to the *Kings' Melons Problem*

> **The Soccer League Problem**
>
> Each team in the Appleton soccer league has $\frac{1}{4}$ of the members in the league. The Rockets are the only team with sixth-grade students. Two-thirds of the Rockets are sixth-grade girls. What fraction of all of the students in the league are sixth-grade girls?

What features of the problem do you think each student focused on in his or her response? What can you infer about what each student knows? What the student may not know? What might your next lesson be? (See Figure 8–5.)

Writing Probing Questions

Think about the fractions pretest, the *Kings' Melons Problem*, and the *Soccer League Problem*, and then revisit each student's work (revisit Figures 8–2 through 8–5). Refer to "Reflection 8–1: Writing Probing Questions for a

Reflection 8–1

Writing Probing Questions for a Kindergarten Student

Page 234

Michaela	Tracy
Only 1 team has sixth graders so 1/4 of the students are sixth grade girls.	$2/3 \text{ of } 1/4 = 1/6\text{th}$
Emanuel	Suzi
$\frac{1}{4} + \frac{2}{3} = \frac{3}{12} + \frac{8}{12} = \frac{11}{12}$ $\frac{11}{12}$ are sixth grade girls	This problem cannot be solved because the number in the leagues is not told

FIGURE 8–5. Four Students' Responses to the *Soccer League Problem*

Kindergarten Student" (see page 234), "Reflection 8–2: Writing Probing Questions for Fourth-Grade Students" (see pages 235–37), or "Reflection 8–3: Writing Probing Questions for Sixth-Grade Students" (see pages 238–39). Using the reflection closest to the grade level you teach, write questions you might ask to probe the understanding—or misunderstanding—of the students. Complete the reflection before continuing to read.

If you completed Reflection 8–2, did you think of some of the following probing questions for the *Kings' Melons Problem* (see Figure 8–4)? Do these questions help you think of others?

Reflection 8–2

Writing Probing Questions for Fourth-Grade Students

Pages 235–37

Reflection 8–3

Writing Probing Questions for Sixth-Grade Students

Pages 238–39

The Kings' Melons Problem: Probing Questions for Jordan

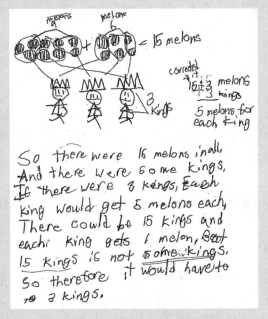

1. I see how you decided the number of melons for each king. How did you know how many kings to draw as you started dividing the melons?

2. You mentioned that there were fifteen melons in all, but you drew nine melons first and divided them and then six melons that you also divided. Why didn't you say fifteen melons divided by five kings?

The Kings' Melons Problem: Probing Questions for Emma

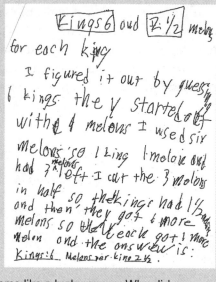

1. Six kings seems like a lucky guess. Why did you guess six?

2. The problem did not say that the melons had to stay whole. How would you solve the problem if you were not allowed to cut the melons?

The Kings' Melons Problem: Probing Questions for Kevin

1. When you read this problem, what do you know? What are you trying to find out?

2. Tell me about your picture and the numbers you used.

The Kings' Melons Problem: Probing Questions for Carter

1. You said there could be fifteen divided by five or fifteen divided by three. How did you decide on those numbers?

2. Read the problem to me. What might make me think there are two steps to this problem?

By combining strategies of probing the mathematics in students' answers and inviting students into discussions, we help all students become better problem solvers and communicators of ideas:

"Does anyone have the same answer but solved the problem in a different way?"

"How many of us think this will always work? What makes you say that?"

"What would happen to the area and the perimeter if we doubled the length of one side?"

"What would be another example when this process would work?"

We need to continually challenge the completeness and accuracy of our students' thinking in ways that help them expand their knowledge and self-confidence.

Probing Questions in Interviews

In Chapter 4 we talked about interviews that are short (three- to four-minute conversations) and extended (ten- to fifteen-minute conversations). On page 92 we included suggestions for getting started with interviews; in this section, we briefly revisit interviews through the lens of probing questions. The types of questions we ask are significant to an interview's success.

In one first-grade classroom, Mrs. Sears was interested in her students' developing sense of number relationships, their counting strategies, and patterning concepts, so she interviewed all of her students. While interviewing Matlynn, Mrs. Sears noted that she was organized as she counted cubes, moving them aside as she counted all thirty-six cubes on the table. Matlynn counted on confidently from single-digit numbers and hesitated only slightly when asked to count on from teen numbers. She understood one more and one less. The conversation continued and Mrs. Sears asked Matlynn about patterns:

Probing Questions in an Interview with a First Grader

Mrs. Sears: *Make a pattern for me using the cubes.*

Matlynn: (Assembles red and green cubes.) *This is an ABAB pattern.*

Mrs. Sears: *What do you mean, ABAB pattern?*

Matlynn: *It is red, green, red, green, red, green, so it is ABABAB* (points to cubes). *I can make a different one* (assembles a pattern with red, yellow, and blue cubes). *See—red, yellow, blue, red, yellow, blue. That's an ABC pattern.*

Mrs. Sears: *If I want to continue your pattern* (adds a red and yellow cube), *what would I put next?*

Matlynn: Blue.

Mrs. Sears: *OK, let's do a pattern with numbers.* (Thinking that Matlynn has a strong grasp of patterns, writes *2, 5, 8, 11, 14, ____.*) *Tell me about this pattern.*

Matlynn: *Well* (very hesitantly), *fifteen because it comes after fourteen.*

> **Mrs. Sears:** *Let's try this pattern* (writes 2, 4, 6, 8, _____). *Do you know what number would go in the blank?*
>
> **Matlynn:** *Ten.*
>
> **Mrs. Sears:** *How do you know?*
>
> **Matlynn:** *You just count by twos.*
>
> **Mrs. Sears:** *OK. What would come next in this pattern* (writes 3, 5, 7, 9, _____)?
>
> **Matlynn:** (Hesitating slightly) *Ten.*
>
> **Mrs. Sears:** *How do you know?*
>
> **Matlynn:** *Ten is the next number after nine.*

Mrs. Sears' interview revealed that Matlynn's concept of patterns was still developing. She could create simple concrete patterns and translate them into letters and actions; however, she needed more opportunities to talk about pattern units and how they are predictable. The conversation with Matlynn reminds us not to make generalizations and assumptions about what students know and to check for solid understanding of important concepts.

Questions That Encourage Students to Extend Ideas

Even when students respond to our questions with correct answers, we want them to continue to think about the mathematics. Whether our question is a relatively straightforward one that we pose to include a struggling student in the conversation or one that requires more complex application of mathematics, we have opportunities to extend our students' thinking by asking follow-up questions. This is a way to differentiate within lessons as well as probe to make certain that students have mastered what we think they understand. For example, if a student says that the least

> Whether our question was a relatively straightforward one that we posed to include a struggling student in the conversation or one that required more complex application of mathematics, we have opportunities to extend our students' thinking by asking them follow-up questions.

common multiple of three and four is twelve, we might respond by saying, "That's right. So what is the least common multiple of ten and eight?" Suppose the student replies, "Ten times eight is the same as two times eight, which is sixteen plus five times eight, which is forty. Then sixteen plus forty is fifty-six." We might say, "What you have said is correct, but you have not answered the question of what is the least common multiple of ten and eight."

There are times when we simply say "correct" or "yes" or "no" in response to students' answers to our questions. However, skillful use of questions allows us to support students at different levels of competence—points along a trajectory of incremental learning targets—related to the same mathematics content goal. Asking for students to justify an answer, use the procedure in a different setting, or simply asking "How do you know?" are ways that we help students extend their ideas.

Planning Our Questions

While our questions create opportunities for all students to engage in discussions, we need to plan what we will ask in order to keep those conversations focused on the mathematics in our lessons and tasks. This planning ties directly to learning targets (see Chapter 3), reflecting what we want our students to learn from the lesson. When we carefully plan and sequence our questions, we can:

- avoid situations in which we substitute our own thinking for our students' thinking;

- highlight and identify the mathematics important in the tasks;

- think through what aspects of students' performance indicate mastery of concepts and procedures;

- move discussions from simple step-by-step procedures to opportunities for students to demonstrate their understandings;

- encourage students to think about what appropriate answers would be (for example, making good estimates—being able to identify what answers will be in the ballpark or what range of numbers are likely to be reasonable responses—takes practice);

- encourage students to think about the mathematics they already know, and how that knowledge may be applicable to current tasks;

- become more observant of and analytical about our students' work; and

- more easily recognize when the majority of students are ready to move on and which students need more assistance.

Even if our lesson plan involves students completing certain pages in their textbooks, we still need to be reflective and think about the questions we will use to make the lesson more meaningful to students and to give us information about what they know. The quality and value of students' responses relate directly to the quality of our questions.

In "Reflection 8–4: Planning Questions for a Variety of Mathematical Purposes" (see pages 239–41), we offer prompts for planning questions for different purposes. Choose one of the following problems, depending upon the grade that you teach, and use Reflection 8–2 to help you write questions you would ask your students.

Reflection 8-4

Planning Questions for a Variety of Mathematical Purposes

Pages 240–41

Reflection 8-2

Writing Probing Questions for Fourth-Grade Students

Pages 235–37

Problem 1

Jose found 3 pennies in his pocket, 8 pennies in his desk, and 5 pennies in his coat pocket. He said that he has 15 pennies. Explain how you know if Jose is correct or not.

Problem 2

A stock clerk must display 140 cans of tomatoes. The clerk decides to make the display in the form of a square pyramid that will use all the cans. How many cans will make up 1 edge of the bottom layer? How many cans will be in each layer? (Yagi and Olson 2007, 377)

Planning questions that allow us to check for understanding throughout a lesson means that we can respond to incomplete understandings right away. Interventions do not need to wait until after a unit test—we can immediately identify students who need assistance and challenge those who appear ready to expand their ideas. We can tailor our next lessons to clarify vocabulary terms, reteach steps in a process, plan similar tasks, or reteach a concept in a different way. For example, we might offer an extension to the grocery store task such as the following:

> Suppose the stock clerk decides to make the display in the shape of a cylinder. How many layers will the cylinder have? How many cans will be in each layer? Is there more than one possible answer?

Asking more advanced questions during a class discussion is not easy; as we become more comfortable formulating probing questions as we plan, we will also become better at asking them on the fly.

During class discussions we are busy monitoring the class's interactions, listening for information that reveals students' understandings and misunderstandings, and thinking about "what's next." Thus, planning ahead will help us develop our own habits of mind and skills in asking good questions, especially if this planning involves conversations with colleagues about the mathematics in tasks. Collaboration, whether with a single teacher or a grade-level group, helps us set appropriate expectations and identify places where students often misstep.

Examples of Good Questions for Different Mathematical Purposes

Throughout this chapter we have talked about the importance of using questions for different purposes. Developing a personal collection of questions to use in a variety of situations helps us expand our expertise in using INFORMative assessment in a routine manner. Following is a collection of questions that we have gathered and always find to be particularly helpful in very specific situations (Stenmark 1994). Notice that these questions can be used for teaching or for assessing. As you read through these examples, highlight questions that you wish to begin using right away. You might use these questions as a starter list to build your own collection of good questions.

Questions for Many Mathematical Purposes

Problem Comprehension	Questions to Ask the Student
Can students understand, define, formulate, or explain the problem or task?	• What is this problem about? What can you tell me about it? • How would you interpret that? • Would you please explain that in your own words?
Can they cope with poorly defined problems?	• What do you know about this part? • Do you need to define or set limits for the problem? • Is there something that can be eliminated or that is missing? • What assumptions do you have to make?
Approaches and Strategies	**Questions to Ask the Student**
Do students have an organized approach to the problem or task?	• Where could you find the needed information? • What have you tried? What steps did you take? • What did not work?
How do they record?	• How did you organize the information? Do you have a record?
Do they use tools (manipulatives, diagrams, graphs, calculators, computers, and so on) appropriately?	• Did you have a system? A strategy? A design? • Have you tried [tables, trees, lists, diagrams . . .]? • Would it help to draw a diagram or make a sketch? • How would it look if you used these materials? • How would you research that?

(continued)

Relationships	Questions to Ask the Student
Do students see relationships and recognize the central idea? *Do they relate the problem to similar problems previously done?*	• What is the relationship of this to that? • What is the same? What is different? • Is there a pattern? • Let's see if we can break it down. What would the parts be? • What if you moved this part? • Can you write another problem related to this one?
Flexibility	**Questions to Ask the Student**
Can students vary the approach if one is not working? *Do they persist?* *Do they try something else?*	• Have you tried making a guess? • Would another recording method work as well or better? • What else have you tried? • Give me another related problem. Is there an easier problem? • Is there another way to [draw, explain, say . . .] that?
Communication	**Questions to Ask the Student**
Can students describe or depict the strategies they are using? *Do they articulate their thought processes?* *Can they display or demonstrate the problem situation?*	• Would you please reword that in simpler terms? • Could you explain what you think you know right now? • How would you explain this process to a younger child? • Could you write an explanation for next year's students (or some other audience) of how to do this? • Which words were most important? Why?

Curiosity and Hypotheses	Questions to Ask the Student
Is there evidence of conjecturing, thinking ahead, checking back?	• Can you predict what will happen? • What was your estimate or prediction? • How do you feel about your answer? • What do you think comes next? • What else would you like to know?
Equality and Equity	**Questions to Ask the Student**
Do all students participate to the same degree? *Is the quality of participation opportunities the same?*	• Did you work together? In what way? • Have you discussed this with your group? with others? • Where would you go for help? • How could you help another student without telling the answer? • Did everybody get a fair chance to talk?
Solutions	**Questions to Ask the Student**
Do students reach a result? *Do they consider other possibilities?*	• Is that the only possible answer? • How would you check the steps you have taken, or your answer? • Other than retracing your steps, how can you determine if your answers are appropriate? • Is there anything you have overlooked? • Is the solution reasonable, considering the context? • How did you know you were done?
Examining Results	**Questions to Ask the Student**
Can students generalize, prove their results?	• What makes you think that was what you should do? • Is there a real-life situation where this could be used? • Where else would this strategy be useful?

(continued)

Examining Results	Questions to Ask the Student
Do students connect ideas to other similar problems or to the real world?	• What other problem does this seem to lead to? • Is there a general rule? • How were you sure your answer was right? • How would your method work with other problems? • What questions does this raise for you?
Mathematical Learning	**Questions to Ask the Student**
Did students use or learn some mathematics from the activity? *Are there indications of a comprehensive curriculum?*	• What were the mathematical ideas in this problem? • What was one thing you learned (or two or more)? • What are the variables in this problem? What stays constant? • How many kinds of mathematics were used in this investigation? • What is different about the mathematics in these two situations? • Where would this problem fit on our mathematics chart?
Self-Assessment	**Questions to Ask the Student**
Do students evaluate their own processing, actions, and progress?	• What do you need to do next? • What are your strengths and weaknesses? • What have you accomplished? • Was your own group participation appropriate and helpful? • What kind of problems are still difficult for you?

(Adapted from Stenmark 1994.)

INFORMing My Practice

Before continuing to the next chapter, turn to "Reflection 8–5: INFORMing My Practice: Self-Evaluation of Questioning Techniques" (see pages 242–43). Complete the evaluation. Are you where you would like to be?

Reflection 8–5

INFORMing
My Practice:
Self-Evaluation
of Questioning
Techniques

Pages 242–43

Reflection 8-1: Writing Probing Questions for a Kindergarten Student

The teacher told Julia Ellen to color one-half of the figure in each part of the fraction pretest. As she began coloring the rectangle, the student said, "Tell me when to stop." Her teacher told her to go as far as she wanted to go to show one-half.

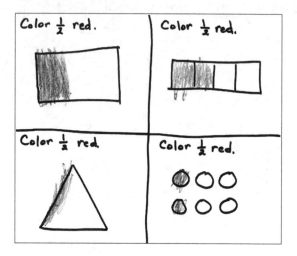

Before writing questions to probe Julia Ellen's understanding, think about:

1. What do you know about Julia Ellen's understanding of halves?

2. What do you want to know about her understanding of other unit fractions?

3. How would your questions be different for a student in first grade rather than one in kindergarten?

Probing questions to ask Julia Ellen:

Reflection 8-2: Writing Probing Questions for Fourth-Grade Students

> **The Kings' Melons Problem**
>
> Some kings found 9 melons. They shared them equally. Then they found 6 more melons and shared them equally. How many kings were there and how many melons did each king get? Show your work and explain your thinking. (Brockhoff et al. 1992)

Below are questions to prompt your thinking before you write probing questions to ask these fourth-grade students about their work on the Kings' Melons Problem. *(See Chapter 8, pages 218–19, for further insights.)*

- What do you know about each student's thinking based on the samples?

- What can you infer about what each student knows or may not know?

- What are strengths of each student's response?

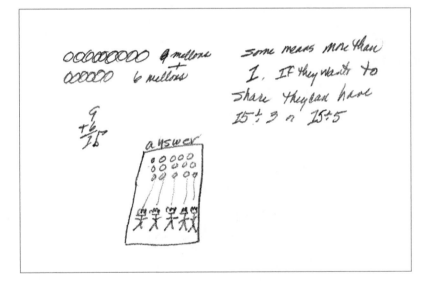

Questions for Carter:

(continued)

Kings 6 and 2 1/2 melons
for each king

I figured it out by guessing
6 kings. they started off
with 4 melons I used six
melons. so 1 king 1 melon and
had 3 melons left. I cut the 3 melons
in half so the kings had 1 1/2
and then they got 1 more
melons so they each got 1 more
melon and the answer is:
Kings: 6 Melons per king 2 1/2.

Questions for Emma:

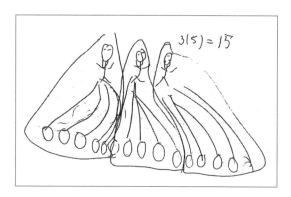

$3(5) = 15$

Questions for Kevin:

(continued)

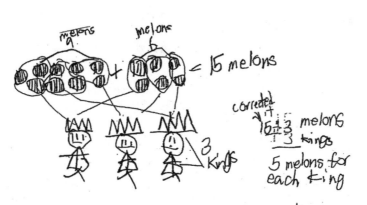

So there were 15 melons in all,
And there were some kings,
If there were 3 kings, Each
king would get 5 melons each,
There could be 15 kings and
each king gets 1 melon, But
15 kings is not some kings,
So therefore it would have to
be 3 kings.

Questions for Jordan:

Reflection 8-3: Writing Probing Questions for Sixth-Grade Students

---

The Soccer League Problem

Each team in the Appleton soccer league has $\frac{1}{4}$ of the members in the league. The Rockets are the only team with sixth-grade students. Two-thirds of the Rockets are sixth-grade girls. What fraction of all of the students in the league are sixth-grade girls?

Below are questions to prompt your thinking before you write probing questions to ask these sixth-grade students about their work on the Soccer League Problem.

- What do you know about each student's thinking based on the samples?
- What can you infer about what each student knows or may not know?
- What features of the problem do you think each student focused on?

> Only 1 team has sixth graders so 1/4 of the students are sixth grade girls.

Questions for Michaela:

(continued)

$$2/3 \, of \, 1/4 = 1/6th$$

Questions for Tracy:

$$\frac{1}{4} + \frac{2}{3} = \frac{3}{12} + \frac{8}{12} = \frac{11}{12}$$

$\frac{11}{12}$ are sixth grade girls

Questions for Emanuel:

This problem canot be
solved becase the number
in the leagues is not told

Questions for Suzi:

Reflection 8-4: Planning Questions for a Variety of Mathematical Purposes

---

Problem 1

Jose found 3 pennies in his pocket, 8 pennies in his desk, and 5 pennies in his coat pocket. He said that he has 15 pennies. Explain how you know if Jose is correct or not.

Problem 2

A stock clerk must display 140 cans of tomatoes. The clerk decides to make the display in the form of a square pyramid that will use all the cans. How many cans will make up 1 edge of the bottom layer? How many cans will be in each layer? (Yagi and Olson 2007, 377)

Which problem (problem 1 or 2 above) have you chosen? _____

1. What questions might you use to invite students into a conversation about this task?

2. What questions will help students unpack the task? Which questions would you ask before students work on the problem?

(continued)

240

Reflection 8-4: Planning Questions for a Variety of Mathematical Purposes
continued

3. What questions would you use in debriefing the task? What mathematical understandings do you want your students to exhibit?

4. What questions will you ask to uncover misconceptions when debriefing the task?

Reflection 8-5: INFORMing My Practice: Self-Evaluation of Questioning Techniques

When you have finished reading Chapter 8, evaluate yourself on your questioning techniques for all three categories. Use the scale that follows for the appropriate columns.

Self-Evaluation of Questioning Techniques

	Questioning Techniques	A. Helpful for Informing Instruction	B. Current Level of Use	C. Commitment to Improve/ Increase
1.	I provide time for students to consider answers to questions before calling on another student.			
2.	I invite students to answer each other's questions and comments.			
3.	I ask students to justify their answers.			
4.	I ask students to add to or enhance their answers when they are not complete.			
5.	I avoid asking "yes" or "no" questions.			
6.	I avoid asking "true" or "false" questions.			
7.	I avoid using questions as a disciplinary tool.			
8.	I use hand signals or other nonverbal ways for students to respond as a group.			
9.	I provide students think time before asking them to respond orally.			
10.	I rephrase questions to encourage students to reveal their thinking.			
11.	My questions help me learn the sources of misunderstanding or misconceptions.			
12.	My questions help me to determine "who knows" and "who still needs help."			

(continued)

Reflection 8–5: INFORMing My Practice: Self-Evaluation of Questioning Techniques
continued

A. Helpful for Informing Instruction	
How helpful are your questions for *informing instruction*?	1 = not helpful
	2 = somewhat helpful
	3 = helpful
	4 = very helpful
B. Current Level of Use	
What is your *current use* of your questioning techniques?	1 = never tried it
	2 = use occasionally
	3 = use often
	4 = use consistently, all the time
C. Commitment to Improve/Increase	
What is your *level of commitment* to using questions as better thinking probes?	1 = will not try
	2 = undecided
	3 = will try occasionally
	4 = definitely

Assessment to INFORM Inferences and Actionable Feedback

We continually make inferences about what our students know and are able to do. These inferences arise from conversations and class discussions, from homework and class work, from quizzes and tests. They are the basis for lessons we plan, feedback we give to students, and grades we put on report cards. Effective INFORMative assessment supports the inferences we make about our students' learning of mathematical concepts, skills, and applications. In this chapter, we revisit the inferences we make based on benchmark tests. We describe actionable feedback—a key INFORMative assessment strategy—and suggest rubrics as tools for guiding and supporting student learning.

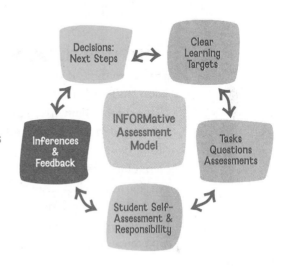

Overview

Inferences, as defined in the dictionary, are conclusions drawn from evidence or reasoning. They are deductions and assumptions made from available information. We make inferences by putting together knowledge of how students learn, what the learning targets are, and specific information about our students that we gather through our interactions with them.

Inferences are deductions and assumptions made from available information.

Inferring What Students Know

Effective INFORMative assessment supports the inferences we make about our students' learning of mathematical concepts, skills, and applications. Through the daily assessment of our students' work we continually evaluate their understanding and infer what they have learned. By listening carefully to students' responses to questions and examining written work through the lens of understanding their thinking, not just correct or incorrect answers, we decide how well students have mastered the learning targets. We decide where they fit along trajectories of content knowledge. In the following pages we focus on two types of inferences we make in understanding our students' learning: inferences from benchmark tests and inferences related to interventions.

Inferences from Benchmark Tests

Across the country, benchmark tests—either commercial products or those developed by school districts—are touted as a formative assessment strategy. Benchmark tests often are:

- designed to be administered at the end of grading periods;

- used as a tool to evaluate whether students have accomplished the content goals for that grading period (in hopes of immediately addressing any misconceptions and incomplete understandings);

- scored in-house with scanning programs so that teachers get the results in a timely manner; and

- summarized with a detailed item analysis providing details about how students responded to specific items.

The idea of using benchmark tests in a formative manner is a good one: the earlier that students' mistakes can be corrected, the better; if students get assistance as they need it, they are less likely to fall far behind; if there is a topic that almost all students miss, teachers are able to rethink their instruction and reteach the content.

The type of information that teachers get from benchmark test results, however, determines whether the tests are likely to be more summative than formative. In Chapter 2, we discussed the need for more specific data than just benchmark test scores (see page 37). In this chapter, we use a specific example of a benchmark test's results to help us think about inferring what students know in order to plan instruction. (See Figure 9–1.) What kind of information can we infer from this type of report?

The report shows the correct answer and each student's response to twenty multiple-choice questions. The questions are tied to specific objectives so that mastery of related objectives can be examined. From these data we know that the percentage of mastery of questions ranged from a low of 40 percent to a high of 95 percent. Six students mastered 80 to 95 percent of the content; twelve scored 55 percent to 75 percent; and four students were able to answer only 40 to 50 percent of the items correctly. All students answered question 5 correctly, but no students answered question 7 correctly. We notice that students did fairly well on the first five objectives and that there appear to be some weaknesses in the next set of five objectives. We also notice that, as a whole, the class did not do well on the five questions related to objectives 3.1 and 3.2. We may infer that we need to revisit this content with the entire class.

Some reporting systems generate charts and graphs with the same data as in Figure 9–1, just represented differently, such as the percentage of items that each student mastered or the percentage of students who got each item correct. (See Figures 9–2 and 9–3.) For those of us who are very visual, these graphs help us focus on an overall picture of our instruction and nudge us toward examining our instructional programs carefully. In addition, data graphs, such as those that follow, help us raise questions about how well our students are learning the content.

Items	1	2	3	4	5	6	7	8	9	10	11	12	13	14	15	16	17	18	19	20	
Objective	1.8	1.8	1.9	1.9	1.9	2.1	2.1	2.1	2.2	2.2	1.1	1.1	1.1	1.11	1.11	3.1	3.1	3.2	3.2	3.2	
Response	a	d	b	c	a	a	c	b	d	d	a	c	b	a	d	c	c	b	a	d	
Name																					% Mastery
Alvarez, M.	a	d	b	c	a	a	d	b	d	d	a	c	a	a	b	d	a	b	a	d	75%
Bright, G.	a	d	b	c	a	a	b	b	d	d	a	c	b	a	d	c	c	b	a	d	95%
Byrn, S.	a	d	b	c	a	a	d	b	d	d	a	c	b	a	c	c	c	b	a	d	95%
Clima, R.	a	d	b	a	a	b	b	b	d	d	a	b	c	a	b	c	c	a	a	b	55%
Diaz, C.	a	d	b	c	a	a	b	b	d	d	a	b	b	a	d	c	c	b	b	d	90%
Dolan, Z.	a	d	b	b	a	a	d	c	d	a	a	c	b	a	d	d	a	b	b	d	65%
Gaerner, K.	c	d	a	a	a	a	d	b	d	a	a	c	b	a	c	c	c	b	b	a	55%
Giani, J.	a	a	b	c	a	c	d	b	d	d	b	c	b	a	b	a	a	b	a	a	65%
Gutirrez, J.	a	d	a	c	a	a	b	b	a	a	b	b	b	d	b	c	c	a	b	a	45%
Hendricks, L.	c	a	b	d	a	a	b	b	c	d	b	c	b	a	d	c	c	b	c	b	50%
Kelsey, C.	a	d	b	c	a	a	d	b	d	d	a	c	c	a	d	c	c	b	a	d	90%
Kosloski, S.	a	b	b	c	a	b	b	b	d	d	b	b	b	b	d	c	a	c	c	d	55%
Laesser, G.	a	d	c	c	a	c	b	b	a	d	a	c	d	d	d	c	c	b	c	d	70%
Langdon, O.	a	d	c	c	a	a	b	b	c	d	b	d	b	a	b	d	a	c	b	d	50%
Murdock, J.	a	d	b	c	a	c	d	d	a	d	b	d	b	b	d	d	c	a	a	b	60%
Quacchia, R.	b	c	b	c	a	c	b	b	a	a	a	c	c	a	b	a	a	b	c	b	40%
Sears, D.	a	d	c	c	a	c	d	b	a	d	a	c	d	d	d	c	c	b	a	d	70%
Torres, B.	a	b	b	c	a	b	d	b	d	d	a	d	b	a	d	c	a	b	a	a	70%
Warren, J.	a	d	b	c	a	b	d	c	d	a	c	d	b	a	d	d	c	b	c	a	60%
Waters, A.	a	d	b	c	a	a	d	b	d	d	c	d	c	a	b	c	c	b	a	d	80%
Weaver, B.	a	d	b	a	a	b	b	b	a	d	a	b	c	a	d	c	c	a	a	b	55%
Williams, G.	a	d	b	c	a	a	d	b	d	d	a	c	b	a	d	c	c	b	a	d	95%
% Mastery	86%	77%	73%	73%	100%	55%	0%	86%	64%	77%	73%	59%	64%	73%	68%	68%	69%	73%	64%	50%	

FIGURE 9–1. Benchmark Test Results

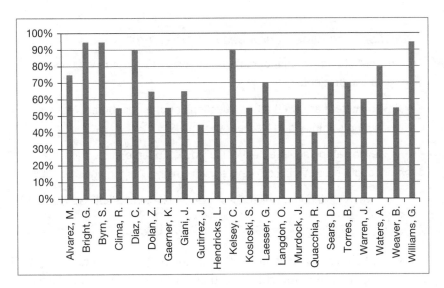

FIGURE 9-2. Benchmark Test Results: Percentage of Mastery of Individual Students

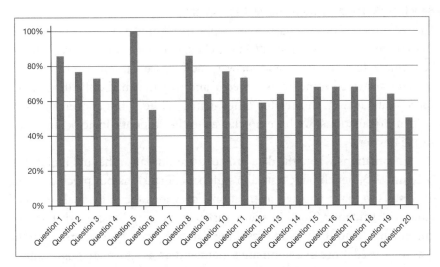

FIGURE 9-3. Benchmark Test Results: Percentage of Students Answering Each Item Correctly

Questions to Guide Inferences from Benchmark Tests

- How certain are we that our instruction was meaningful and engaging for our students?

- How confident are we that the questions on the benchmark test are measuring our intended learner outcomes?

- As we look at the achievement of individual students, did we feel that more of our students should have shown a higher percentage of mastery?

- Have we made incorrect inferences about what our students are learning?

We all believe that it is not sufficient for us to say "I taught it" or "I provided opportunities for students; they just didn't learn it." However, program evaluation and individual assessment of what each student knows and what he or she still needs to learn often require complementary but different sources of data.

Benchmark Tests as Summative Assessments

The data in each of the charts and graphs in Figures 9–1, 9–2, and 9–3 tell us something about the students in the class. However, without access to the benchmark test questions and answer choices, we cannot determine why students answered some items correctly and why they had difficulty making appropriate answer choices for other items. Without the conversations or written explanations, we have no clue as to the students' logic behind their wrong answers.

In situations where the data provided are similar to that in Figures 9–1, 9–2, and 9–3, benchmark tests allow global conclusions but preclude using the results to make targeted instructional decisions for individuals or small groups of students. Thus, in many districts the way benchmark tests are implemented and the way the resulting data are given to teachers cause the tests to be used more in a summative manner than as a formative assessment. And since most benchmark tests are multiple-choice and designed for easy machine scoring, they lack the richness of information that is available in constructed-response and open-ended questions.

Inferences are conclusions about students' understandings. High inference procedures such as multiple-choice tests measure the understandings that the student may or may not have less directly than classroom conversations and demonstrations. If teachers get class printouts with students' responses to questions, as in Figure 9–1, but do not have access to the actual questions, they do not know the nature of the students' misconceptions. For example, looking at the printout, we know that the correct answer was *b* and that most of the class marked *c*, but we cannot determine the reason that students marked that particular distracter.

What the printout in Figure 9–1 does not show makes it similar to tests used at the end of the year. We know neither the actual questions posed to the students nor the correct answers and the alternate answer choices. While we might suspect that question 7 was not worded clearly because the entire class missed the question, the problem may have been an instructional issue rather than a poor item. Without knowing the specific questions, we are limited in the inferences we are able to make about the instruction and reteaching that we need to do.

Revisit Figures 9–1, 9–2, and 9–3 and look at them carefully. Then, turn to "Reflection 9–1: Inferences: Using Benchmark Tests Thoughtfully" (see pages 270–72). If you were the teacher in this class, what inferences might you make about your students that will help you determine next instructional steps? What questions do you have when studying the printouts? Complete Reflection 9–1 before continuing to read.

Some of the questions we might still ask but that are left unanswered include:

- In item 7, why were students drawn only to answer choices *b* and *d* and not to the correct response or even answer choice *a*? Was the question misleading?

- In item 8, why were students drawn only to *c* as an alternate answer choice, but not *a* or *d*? Is there a common misconception that answer *c* illustrates?

- In item 10, why did students choose only items *a* and *d* while ignoring *b* and *c*?

> **Reflection 9–1**
>
> Inferences: Using Benchmark Tests Thoughtfully
>
> Pages 270–72

- In item 15, what drew students to answer choices *b* and *d* and not to *a* and *c*? Since we know that objective 1.11 relates to numeration, was answer *b* a distracter that involved place value?

- In item 17, no student chose *b* or *d*. Why was that?

- In items 18 and 19, no students were drawn to answer choice *d*. What was it about this answer choice in each item that caused students to reject it?

- And, in item 20, no student answered choice *c*. What was the question and what were the answer choices?

Making Benchmark Tests More Helpful

The intent of our discussion is not to say that benchmark tests or other similar assessments are not useful. We just need to be aware of what we can and cannot learn from them; for instance, we can use testing data to:

- receive some feedback about student achievement;

- identify students who seem to be mastering the content we are teaching and those who are struggling; and

- identify individuals who need additional help and possibly need focused interventions.

In addition, if while reviewing global testing data, we notice that they indicate a student is struggling with almost all of the mathematics objectives, we have the opportunity to look carefully at our instructional programs. We can consider shaping preteaching lessons in which we give students *feedforward* information to give them a start on new content rather than waiting to provide feedback on what they have not mastered.

In many school districts, the implementation of benchmark tests is accompanied by an increase in grade-level discussions or the organization of more formal learning communities. In school districts where the actual benchmark test items are available to teachers, tests can be critical tools for formative purposes: groups of teachers work together to study the test results from their classrooms, discuss how each one taught the content that was tested, and then plan interventions and form student groups for specific lessons. In these situations, everyone benefits from benchmark tests. Implementing such strategies for making benchmark tests more helpful is within the reach of all schools.

Inferences Related to Interventions

The interpretations we make—our inferences—about students' accomplishments need to be as accurate as possible since our teaching decisions arise from these interpretations. This is especially critical as we devote additional time and energy to specific interventions for individual students. Usually teachers give assessments at the end of the grading period, though district pacing guides may not include time for reteaching and remediation. In other situations, multiple-choice pretests may guide placement of students into groups.

If we lack specific information about what students understand as well as what they do not understand, planning for interventions is very difficult. Relying solely on benchmark tests or standardized multiple-choice quizzes to give the information that is needed for developing specific interventions may not be a wise decision and may lead us toward one-size-fits-all lessons.

Our attentive day-to-day interactions with students are likely to be the best source for recognizing what students know and where they still need assistance. As we become better at listening to our students and probing their thinking, we will be able to provide feedback to the students and adjust our instruction. Through what we learn from our INFORMative assessments, our inferences will help us shorten the time between identifying problems and taking action to address them.

Actionable Feedback to Support Student Learning

Feedback is information designed to help students improve their performance. It is a critical component of INFORMative assessment and has the potential to impact students' achievement, metacognition and self-regulation, and self-confidence. Researchers tell us that feedback is one of the most powerful strategies for supporting student learning (Black and Wiliam 1998; Butler and Winne 1995; Hattie and Timperley 2007). Used in an environment in which ideas are valued, mistakes represent what students still need to learn. In such a climate, we encourage students to self-assess so that feedback supports increased learning and improves the quality of their work. Grade improvements are a by-product of feedback, not the primary goal.

Feedback is not a new idea. For many years, we have used stamps, smiley faces, or phrases such as "good work" to encourage our students. We have also been guilty of saying "messy" or "needs work." None of these phrases tell students what aspects of their work are good and which parts need improvement. Rather than merely giving praise, we need to give our students what we like to call *actionable* feedback.

Actionable feedback is information that is descriptive, telling students what is correct or incorrect and suggesting where students might go next. It gives students enough information so that they have an idea of what they need to rethink or how to improve, but not so much direction that the thinking is done for them. Our actionable feedback should guide students to help them close any gaps between their current performance and the expectations for quality work.

> Actionable feedback is information that is descriptive, telling students what is correct or incorrect and suggesting where students might go next.

The following task, *Jackson Hole's Annual Tug-of-War Contest*, clarifies what we mean by *actionable feedback*. Take a moment to solve the problems:

Jackson Hole's Annual Tug-of-War Contest

Round One: Introducing the Brown Packers . . . 4 equally strong donkeys who practice their skills by taking adventurers on 10-day trail rides. They competed in Round One. Also competing in Round One are the Friendly Five, a team of moose who really like people. The Friendly Five are also equal in strength. The contest in Round One between the two teams was a draw.

Round Two: Round Two was an interesting match. Tuffie (an elephant) thought he would win, but when he faced a team made of 2 moose and 1 donkey, the tug-of-war in Round Two was a draw.

Round Three: Round Three of the *Jackson Hole's Annual Tug-of-War Contest* matched Tuffie, 1 moose, and 2 donkeys on 1 team against the remaining moose and donkeys as the opposing team.
- Which team will win Round Three?
- How do you know?

Round Four: Four donkeys, 5 moose, and Tuffie decide to play Round Four.
- Can you make 2 teams using players so that the round ends in a draw?
- Explain.

To introduce the task to her fourth graders, the teacher asked, "What is a tug-of war between two teams? What does the word *draw* mean in a tug-of-war contest?" and then asked them to read through and solve the problem.

After reading, one student, Margaret, said that she didn't know what to do. "Tell us, in your own words, what happened in rounds one and two," replied the teacher. After Margaret explained, the teacher asked, "What does *equally strong* mean?"

Jackson Hole's Annual Tug-of-War Contest

Round One: Introducing the Brown Packers . . . 4 equally strong donkeys who practice their skills by taking adventurers on 10-day trail rides. They competed in Round One.

$$\partial \partial \partial \bar{\partial} = M^+ M^+ M^+ M^+ M^+$$

Also competing in Round One are the Friendly Five, a team of moose who really like people. The Friendly Five are also equal in strength. The contest in Round One between the two teams was a draw.

$$^{13}E = M^+ A^+ D5$$

Round Two: Round Two was an interesting match. Tuffie (an elephant) thought he would win, but when he faced a team made of 2 moose and 1 donkey, the tug-of-war in Round Two was a draw.

Round Three: Round Three of the *Jackson Hole's Annual Tug-of-War Contest* matched Tuffie, 1 moose, and 2 donkeys on 1 team against the remaining moose and donkeys as the opposing team.

• Which team will win Round Three?

Tuffies team

• How do you know?

$$E + M + DD = 27 \quad M_h M + M + M + D + D = 26$$
$$27 > 26$$

Round Four: Four donkeys, 5 moose, and Tuffie decide to play Round Four.
• Can you make 2 teams using players so that the round ends in a draw?
• Explain.

Mo 53 is not divisable by 2

$$\underset{13}{E}\ \underset{4}{M}\ \underset{4}{M}\ \underset{4}{M}\ \underset{4}{M}\ \underset{4}{M}\ \underset{5}{D}\ \underset{5}{D}\ \underset{5}{D}\ \underset{5}{D}$$
$$53$$

FIGURE 9–4. Margaret's Answers to *Jackson Hole's Annual Tug-of-War Contest*

"Each donkey has the same strength as the other donkeys and each moose is also equal to each other moose," Margaret answered.

"That is an important bit of information. I think you can figure these problems out now," the teacher replied.

Once you've solved *Jackson Hole's Annual Tug-of-War Contest*, study Margaret's answers (refer back to Figure 9–4). Are the strategies you used similar to or different from Margaret's approach?

Is Margaret's thinking clear to you? What questions do you want to ask her? What actionable feedback do you think would be appropriate? If we say "good job," we are letting Margaret know that we are pleased with her work, but we have not let her know what is pleasing about the work or how she might improve it; our feedback is not *actionable*.

> "The moment when a student brings up a novel idea or claim is a special opportunity to promote mathematical learning. . . . Positive comments alone do not suffice to promote significant mathematics learning and inquiry."
> —*Knowing and Teaching Elementary Mathematics*
> (Ma 1999, 5)

Examples of Actionable Feedback

- "Your answers are correct, but I don't think that everyone can follow your thinking. What could you do to communicate your ideas more clearly?"

- "You are doing a good job of using your knowledge of equality to solve these problems, but your ideas may not be clear to others. For example, you say that fifty-three is not divisible by two. How does this answer the question in round four?"

- "Good thinking. You need to explain how you got your answers. For example, what does fifty-three represent?"

Learn More About Actionable Feedback

How to Give Effective Feedback to Your Students
(Brookhart 2008)

We must be cautious not to unintentionally lessen the learning opportunities for struggling students by telling them exactly what to do—thereby thinking for them—or praising work that is far from the standard in order to give the student a boost. When we are aware of actions that might unintentionally lessen learning opportunities, we avoid some of the negative consequences that have been associated with feedback in the past.

We should give the same type of actionable feedback to the student who is moving along as expected as we do to the struggling student, only perhaps more scaffolded and with closer supervision for the struggling individual. We encourage struggling students by highlighting their efforts and growth toward the target, rather than praising them for their neat papers or nice use of colors. Both research and experience remind us of the self-fulfilling prophecy that students tend to perform as their teachers expect them to. The following table summarizes classroom actions that we take related to feedback that benefit students.

> "Feedback has been shown to be one of the most significant activities a teacher can engage in to improve student achievement."
> —"Towards a Model of Schooling: A Synthesis of Meta-Analyses." *Australian Journal of Education* 36: 5–13 (Hattie 1992)

Knowledge About Feedback Translates into Positive Actions

We know . . .	Therefore . . .
Feedback helps improve student achievement.	We make a concerted effort to provide frequent feedback to individuals and to the class.
Feedback is most beneficial when it describes what is correct or incorrect about work.	We comment on the work rather than just assigning a grade.
Feedback is most beneficial when it suggests actions students can take to improve.	We communicate what is most critical for students to address and identify how they can improve.
Feedback is most beneficial when it is timely and the student has an opportunity to address the problem sooner rather than later.	We constantly observe our students at work and intervene daily through questions or comments when they need assistance.
Feedback is most likely to support student self-assessment when students can compare their work to rubrics or models of quality.	We make learning targets, expectations, and criteria for success clear to all students and provide opportunities for peer evaluation.
Feedback is viewed by students through the lens of their own experiences and self-concept.	We are thoughtful about what we write or say and work to create environments in which mistakes are seen as opportunities for learning.

We know . . .	Therefore . . .
Feedback affects motivation and can reinforce high expectations.	We provide opportunities for students to judge where they are and provide time for them to improve their work.
Feedback that is not truthful (more positive than the work represents) may give false impressions and does not serve students in the long run.	We are respectful of students' ideas, provide actionable feedback, and expect students to work hard—but with our support—to make sense of the mathematics.

What Feedback Is Best: Individual, Group, or Both?

The nature of feedback is that it is context-dependent. The feedback we give *to* our students should be specific and targeted and should be informed by the feedback we get *from* their work or conversations with them. The time between when students do the work and when they get feedback that points them in more productive directions needs to be as short as possible. Likewise, if only one or two students are having difficulty with the mathematics, we need to work with them individually rather than slow the progress of the whole class to revisit content needed by only a few.

"Explicit feedback about performance not only helps students understand what they know and can do but also helps ascertain what they have yet to learn." —*Assessment Standards for School Mathematics* (NCTM 1995, 35)

As we check student work, suppose we observe that the class as a whole accomplished the learning target from the previous day's work. By giving brief feedback to the group, we provide an opportunity to reinforce that content, establish another problematic situation for students to begin considering, compliment the class on its achievement, and link previous lessons to a new one we are planning. Our feedback is both positive and descriptive, acknowledging the effort of our students and restating the concept or procedure that was the focus of yesterday's lesson.

On the other hand, we take a different approach to feedback if we notice that a number of students seem to be making the same mistakes, such as consistently solving only the first of two steps, making errors in computing that indicate lack of understanding of procedures, or adding both the numerator and denominator in their fractions. Depending on the nature of the misconception, we may summarize our observations or write examples of the mistakes on the board and pose a series of questions to discuss the misconceptions, facilitating a conversation with students about the implications. An alternative form of feedback is to revisit portions of the previous lesson or design a new lesson that focuses on the type of knowledge—conceptual, procedural, factual—that students appear to be missing or misinterpreting. (See Chapter 3 for a review of types of knowledge.)

In the following classroom scenario, the feedback Mr. Holt had gathered from his fourth-grade students' work indicated that many of them lacked a conceptual understanding of the relationship between parts and wholes. Mr. Holt decided to structure a targeted, hands-on activity with careful discussion and actionable feedback to address his students' incomplete understandings and misconceptions. In the activity, Mr. Holt used trains of six connecting cubes wrapped in foil to represent flavored pieces from a candy bar to model referent units. One "cherry" piece represented one-sixth of the whole bar.

Mr. Holt's Actionable Feedback: A Targeted Activity

Mr. Holt: *Yesterday you were very successful in shading areas of figures to model fractions, but many of you do not seem to have a clear understanding of what happens as you combine fractions. Some of you wrote $\frac{1}{6} + \frac{2}{6} = \frac{3}{6}$ and others wrote $\frac{1}{6} + \frac{2}{6} = \frac{3}{12}$. Last night I made connecting cube candy bars. There is one for each of you* (hands one foil-covered bar to each student).

Kia: *I think my bar has six cubes.*

Mr. Holt: *All of the bars have six cubes. If we describe the whole bars using fractions, how many sixths would there be in each one* (pauses while students take a moment to examine their bars and then start raising their hands). *Ricardo?*

Ricardo: *The whole bar is six sixths.*

(Discussion follows as students tell how they know Ricardo is correct. Mr. Holt asks one student to write the fraction on the board: $\frac{6}{6} = 1$ whole candy bar.)

(continued)

(continued from page 259)

Mr. Holt: *These candy bars have pretend pieces: some are cherry [red cubes], some are lime [green cubes], blueberry [blue cubes], orange [orange cubes], and lemon [yellow cubes]. Open your bar and compare your candies with your partner. Be sure to keep your cubes separate.* (After a few minutes) *Lucy, will you go up to the board and record your pieces using fraction notation?*

Lucy: *This is what I have:*

2 orange pieces $= \frac{2}{6}$ of the bar

3 blue pieces $= \frac{3}{6}$ of the bar

1 green piece $= \frac{1}{6}$ of the bar

Mr. Holt: *Would I be correct to write* 2 orange + 3 blue + 1 green = 1 whole candy bar = 6 pieces? *How could we write the same information using fractions? Talk to your partner and write an equation to show what is in Lucy's bar.* ($\frac{2}{6} + \frac{3}{6} + \frac{1}{6} = \frac{6}{6} = 1$ bar)

As the lesson continues, Mr. Holt asks other students to describe their bars in fraction terms. He then gives students problems to complete (blueberry + cherry and lemon + lime) that reflect the contents of their own bars. Every student's work is different, so students compare equations with their partners as they work. One student may represent blueberry + cherry with $\frac{1}{6} + \frac{3}{6} = \frac{4}{6}$, while another student might write $\frac{2}{6} + \frac{1}{6} = \frac{3}{6}$. Mr. Holt made sure to provide a scenario in this activity for discussing what to write if there were no blueberry pieces. He said to his students, "Could we write $0 + \frac{1}{6} = \frac{1}{6}$, or would it be clearer to write $\frac{0}{6} + \frac{1}{6} = \frac{1}{6}$? Does zero-sixths communicate mathematically? Is it appropriate mathematical notation? Suppose someone ate his two cherry candies. Could this story be told by writing $\frac{6}{6} - \frac{2}{6} = \frac{4}{6}$?"

Revisiting the same learning target rather than moving on is an instructional decision we make on an as-needed basis. It is different from the reviews of learning targets we plan prior to tests; we are responding to students' incomplete grasp of content or their misconceptions right away. In other words, student work is feedback for us. It can be diagnostic information that causes us to adjust our instruction. It informs us about students' current thinking and gives us clues about customizing our next lessons.

We began this section by asking, "What Feedback Is Best: Individual, Group, or Both?" Obviously, what is best depends on the situation. When we identify incomplete knowledge or misunderstanding of individuals, we make decisions about the best way to help the student. The help might be actionable feedback or specific interventions and reteaching. When our INFORMative assessments reveal similar problems among several students, we may pull them aside in a small group and provide feedback that is appropriate for all of them. There are times, however, when we discover that a large number of our students are making similar mistakes or seem to be missing a critical concept and we decide to revisit a task or introduce a similar problem to the class as a whole. Our actionable feedback for the group is likely to summarize the problem we observed. We may probe students' thinking for more information or use questions and a class discussion to address the misconception.

What Feedback Is Best: Oral, Written, or Both?

When we examine students' solutions to complex tasks or assessments, oral feedback to the whole class, targeted instructional groups, or individual students may be appropriate. Other times, written feedback for each student is more valuable. However, we all recognize that writing feedback to every student on each assignment is not realistic; there is simply not enough time, nor does every worksheet for every student require that effort. We do need to give oral or written feedback to individuals whenever we identify misconceptions. If in reviewing student work we notice specific problems or have questions about what the student has done, a conversation or written feedback for that student is the right course of action. Feedback is a way of helping students become aware of where they are, identifying where they need to go, and suggesting how they might get there. Because timeliness is an issue, often the most effective feedback is through brief classroom conversations—those three-minute interviews that take place with an individual while the class is working. For young students and those who are not proficient readers, oral feedback—whether in the form of comments or questions—is preferable. There are times when what we want to discuss is more than we can efficiently write, or we may need to model something. In these cases, oral feedback is logical.

"Research suggests that other types of feedback, such as when a teacher is assigning grades, granting or withholding special rewards, or fostering self-esteem (trying to make the student feel better, regardless of the quality of his or her work) may be ineffective or even harmful." —*Knowing What Students Know: The Science and Design of Educational Assessment* (NRC 2001b, 235)

At times when we are studying student work and the students are not with us, writing notes to our students is appropriate lest we forget what we wanted to address. This does not mean that we need to write lengthy messages to each student:

Examples of Writing Actionable Feedback

- The way you displayed your data is interesting. Please add labels so what your data represent is clear.

- You used a correct process for multiplying, but you have made several number fact errors. Work on the sevens table.

- You placed the decimal numbers on the number line correctly, but you missed several problems comparing decimals. Try writing both numbers you are comparing as hundredths before you compare: Is 0.2 greater than, less than, or equal to 0.13? Write three other examples to let me know if this helps you.

- You know the number facts, but the answers are incorrect because you forgot about order of operations. Do you need some help with this?

One way to judge the appropriateness of our feedback is to remember that it should be *actionable* and focus on improving learning.

Writing actionable feedback is not easy, especially when we have difficulty figuring out what a student has done in solving a problem. One way to judge the appropriateness of our feedback is to remember that it should be *actionable* and focus on improving learning. If the feedback we give to our students—oral or in writing, individually or in a group—helps them improve their performance, then we are doing it right!

Like so many things in life, we become better at giving feedback through practice. Turn to "Reflection 9–2: Giving Actionable Feedback" (see pages 273–74) and record what you might say or write to Carley and Jerome after reviewing their solutions to *The Printer's New Book* problem. (See Figures 9–5 and 9–6.) These fifth- and sixth-grade students' examples remind us that writing helpful feedback means an investment of time in studying students' responses very carefully as well as time for thinking about what to say. Talk with a colleague and compare ideas on appropriate feedback for these students.

Reflection 9–2

Giving Actionable Feedback

Pages 273–74

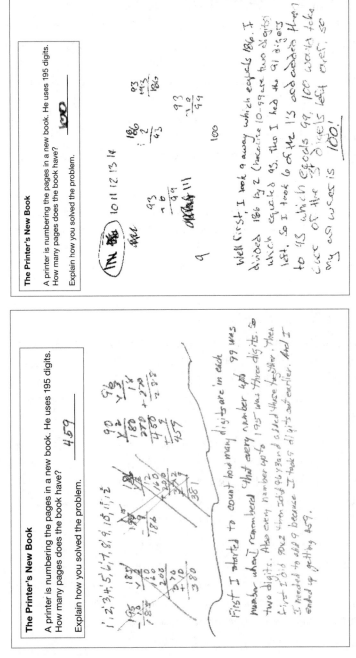

The Printer's New Book

A printer is numbering the pages in a new book. He uses 195 digits. How many pages does the book have? **459**

Explain how you solved the problem.

FIGURE 9-5. Carley's Solution to *The Printer's New Book* Problem

The Printer's New Book

A printer is numbering the pages in a new book. He uses 195 digits. How many pages does the book have? **100**

Explain how you solved the problem.

FIGURE 9-6. Jerome's Solution to *The Printer's New Book* Problem

The Feedback Potential of Rubrics

Rubrics are a feedback tool. We can use rubrics to give much more information to students than a letter or numerical grade because we create rubrics to list the criteria for what counts, describe levels of quality for each of these criteria, and communicate our expectations and help differentiate among work that ranges from poor to excellent. When students use rubrics to judge their own work or help their peers identify ways to improve, they recognize that they have control over the quality of the work they turn in. Parents, too, can better understand the evaluation of their student's performance when they have access to rubrics that describe expectations.

There are many ways to describe rubrics, including categorizing them as one of four basic types: *generic*, *holistic*, *analytic*, and *developmental*. All rubrics, in varying degrees of complexity, describe what knowledge teachers—and students, if they have assisted in the development of the rubrics—feel is important for students to know and be able to demonstrate.

Four Basic Types of Rubrics

- *Generic rubrics* are a starting point for creating task-specific rubrics and describe general expectations that are true across many tasks. Because generic rubrics have criteria that can be applied to a variety of tasks, they are helpful tools for students for self-assessment on a day-to-day basis.

- *Holistic rubrics* describe overall performance at different levels. Using a holistic rubric means that teachers will judge students' performance at the single level that best describes the work as a whole. These levels can be thought of as the work of a novice (level 1), apprentice (level 2), workman (level 3), and master (level 4).

- *Analytic rubrics* provide criteria and scores for specific aspects of the task or performance and enable teachers and students to evaluate different dimensions of the work separately. For example, using an analytic rubric, student work may be judged as strong in clarity of explanation but lower in computational accuracy.

- *Developmental rubrics* describe locations along a continuum of progress and characteristics of student work that are indicative of knowledge and skills at emerging, developing, and independent levels.

Many suggestions for designing and using rubrics are available in teacher resource books and online. For example, there are sample analytic rubrics for mathematics that identify criteria related to strategies and procedures, mathematical concepts, mathematics reasoning, clarity of explanation, and use of representations. There are rubrics that demonstrate multiple score points from simple scales of one to three to complex rubrics with ten to twelve performance levels. Numbers or descriptive phrases denote levels of proficiency.

Designing rubrics is more difficult than one might imagine. So that students are able to use the rubrics to judge their own and their peer's work, the language must be clear and appropriate for the age and experiences of the students. Each level must be sufficiently described so that everyone is clear about what distinguishes one from the other. Many times it is easiest to begin with a generic rubric, have students complete a task, and then use their work to help refine the descriptions for each level. Choose anchor papers and begin by describing characteristics of work that meet the expectations for quality, grade-level performance and then complete descriptions of work for the other levels below and above.

The table that follows is an example of a rubric that is both generic and holistic. Rather than numbers for the score points, we prefer rating descriptors that are positive even at the lowest performance level. We think there is a subtle difference in saying to students that their work is *not yet where it needs to be* rather than saying it is at *level 1*. Also, because our focus is on INFORMative assessment of student learning to make instructional decisions, provide feedback, and monitor students' progress, we suggest teacher actions for each level. As you read through the rubric, think about what you see as this rubric's strengths. Is there a way that you might use this rubric with your own students?

> **Learn More About Using Rubrics**
>
> Introduction to Rubrics: An Assessment Tool to Save Grading Time, Convey Effective Feedback and Promote Student Learning
> *(Stevens and Levi 2005)*
>
> Investigations, Tasks, and Rubrics to Teach and Assess Math, Grades 1–6
> *(Lilburn and Ciurak 2010)*

> Begin with a generic rubric and use student work to refine descriptions for each level.

A Generic, Holistic Mathematics Rubric

Rating	Description of Student Work	Teacher Actions
Wow!	Work demonstrates full understanding of underlying concepts and goes beyond expectations to make connections or give additional details in explanations. There is evidence of complex mathematical reasoning. Work exceeds grade-level expectations.	Provide extensions and enrichment that challenge student to dig deeper into the mathematics.
Right On	Work demonstrates understanding of the mathematics and use of mathematical reasoning. Work is accurate—though there may be minor errors—and complete, with all requirements of the task met. There is a clear explanation of the solution in words, pictures, and/or numbers. Representations are appropriate and properly labeled. Work is high quality and meets grade-level expectations.	Continue to provide specific models that clarify criteria for this level of work and provide opportunities for students to solidify knowledge and expand strategies.
Moving Along	Work demonstrates effort but is not yet at grade-level expectations and needs additional revision by the student. Work shows some understanding of the mathematics and some evidence of mathematical reasoning. There are computational or procedural errors and portions of the task may be missing. Representations may be difficult to understand.	Provide additional instruction and opportunities to explore the mathematics. Give specific feedback and assistance.
Not Yet	Work shows limited or no understanding of the mathematics and little evidence of reasoning. Work may show misconceptions and may not be appropriate for the task. Work may lack representations and explanations. Work is far below grade-level expectations.	Provide significant instruction and targeted interventions based on assessments. Seek additional adult assistance for student.

Reading through this rubric makes several issues immediately clear. First, for the rubric to be helpful to students, we need to modify it to be more specific in describing expectations for each particular grade level. For example, pairing the rubric with several anchor papers for the *Right On* level will clarify what the descriptors look like through examples of mathematics tasks. Second, the *Moving Along* score point is very broad. A wide range of student performances might be judged at this level. Some student work would be just above the *Not Yet* stage and other work would be almost at the level of quality work. Third, some rubrics do not designate a *Wow!* level; instead, the top level might be labeled *Right On* and describe the expectations for quality work and there would be a lower level of *Almost There*.

Choose a task that you will assign to your students in the next couple of weeks, then turn to "Reflection 9–3: Creating a Specific Rubric: Template" (see page 275). In this reflection, we have provided a reproducible chart with space for you to make the generic, holistic rubric on the previous page specific to your task. If a colleague is planning to use the same task, brainstorm what your expectations are for quality work. If the task proves to be one that gives students opportunities to reason mathematically and demonstrate their understanding of the mathematics involved in the task, you and your colleagues may want to refine the rubric for the next year. It may also become one of the models you provide for students to have them self- and peer-assess.

> **Reflection 9–3**
> Creating a
> Specific Rubric:
> Template
>
> Page 275
>
> REPRODUCIBLE

Intersections of Feedback and Rubrics

There are times when students are better able to judge and improve their work when we provide analytic rubrics or give specific feedback about the strategies they use, pointing them toward more sophisticated mathematics. With analytic rubrics, however, the correctness of computations and procedures, the clarity of explanations, and the level of sophistication and reasoning are often scored separately. We raise this issue not to advocate for a particular type of rubric but to reinforce the critical role of teacher guidance through feedback and the power of classroom discussions in conjunction with tools such as rubrics.

In one classroom, for example, Evan's response to *The Printer's New Book* problem meets the criteria for *Right On* because his answer is correct, we can follow the process he used, and he explained how he reasoned through the problem. (See Figure 9–7.) However, the strategy that Evan used was not

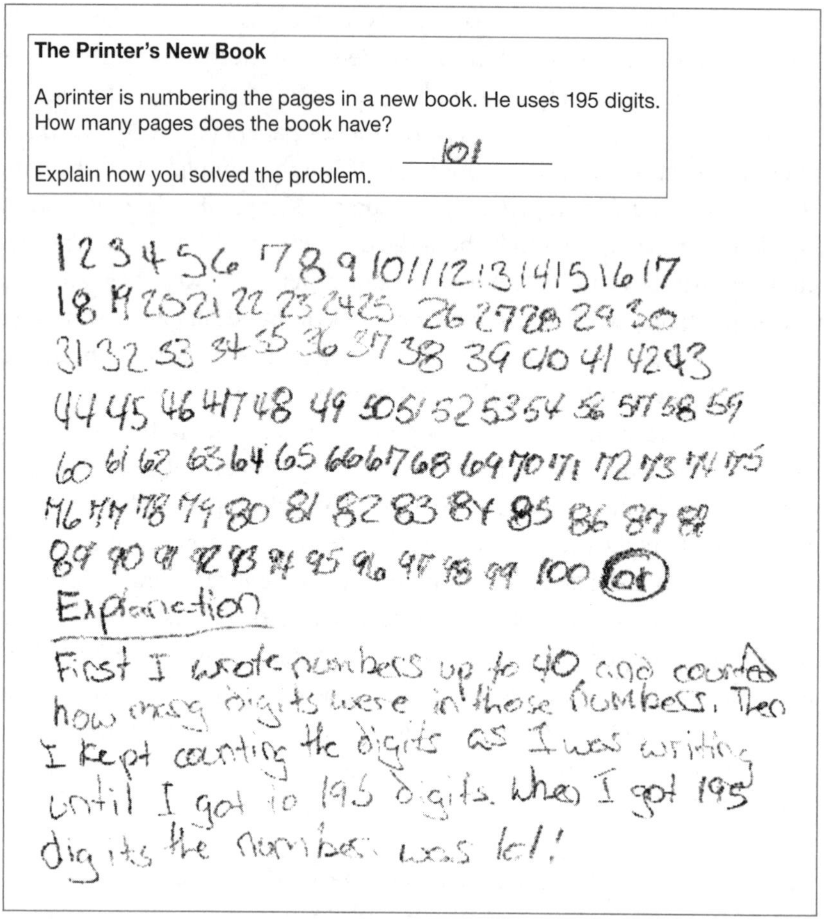

The Printer's New Book

A printer is numbering the pages in a new book. He uses 195 digits. How many pages does the book have?   ___101___

Explain how you solved the problem.

1 2 3 4 5 6 7 8 9 10 11 12 13 14 15 16 17 18 19 20 21 22 23 24 25 26 27 28 29 30 31 32 33 34 35 36 37 38 39 40 41 42 43 44 45 46 47 48 49 50 51 52 53 54 55 56 57 58 59 60 61 62 63 64 65 66 67 68 69 70 71 72 73 74 75 76 77 78 79 80 81 82 83 84 85 86 87 88 89 90 91 92 93 94 95 96 97 98 99 100 (101)

Explanation

First I wrote numbers up to 40, and counted how many digits were in those numbers. Then I kept counting the digits as I was writing until I got to 195 digits. When I got 195 digits the number was 101!

FIGURE 9–7. Evan's Solution to *The Printer's New Book* Problem

at all sophisticated. In this case, both the individual student and the class as a whole would benefit from a discussion of other possible approaches to solving the problem.

Feedback for Evan might include both comments and questions, such as "Your explanation told me how you solved this problem. Is there a way to group the numbers you wrote by the number of digits?" or "How might you organize the numbers in order to keep track of the digits?" What feedback might you give if you were Evan's teacher?

Inferences, Actionable Feedback, and Rubrics

We raise many issues in this chapter and leave many more untouched. Some decisions, such as whether a benchmark test will be used or not, are not left up to classroom teachers. How rubrics might be used to assign grades is another practice we have chosen not to address other than to plead for clarity and consistency among classrooms within the same school.

What we need to work toward in all of our classrooms is planning based on good information about what our students know and what they still need to learn. We need to question whether we have sufficient evidence for the inferences we make about our students' mistakes and misconceptions, and we need to provide our students with tools, such as rubrics, and actionable feedback so that they become more enthusiastic about their learning accomplishments and more responsible for their future work.

INFORMing My Practice

Throughout this book—especially in this chapter, where we focus specifically on making inferences—we stress that the inferences we make need to be as accurate as possible because they are the basis for decisions about teaching. In Chapter 2, we discuss the plethora of decisions we make each day, and subsequent chapters highlight INFORMative assessment strategies—all of which result in information about our students. Our inferences about what students know, what they misunderstand, and what they still need to learn influence what comes next in our teaching and what actionable feedback we provide to our students. Turn to "Reflection 9–4: INFORMing My Practice: Making Inferences, Giving Feedback" (see page 276). This reflection is an opportunity for you to think about inferences and feedback in your classroom.

> **Reflection 9–4**
>
> INFORMing My Practice: Making Inferences, Giving Feedback
>
> Page 276

Reflection 9–1: Inferences: Using Benchmark Tests Thoughtfully

Revisit Figures 9–1, 9–2, and 9–3 on pages 247–49 (see also the following pages). Think about the data and what you might infer about students' learning, then complete the following questions.

1. Suppose these data were from your class. What thoughts and questions might you have about your instructional program?

2. If you were the teacher in this class, what inferences might you make about your students that will help you determine next instructional steps?

3. What questions do you have when studying the printouts that seeing the actual test items would answer?

(continued)

Reflection 9-1: Inferences: Using Benchmark Tests Thoughtfully continued

Items	1	2	3	4	5	6	7	8	9	10	11	12	13	14	15	16	17	18	19	20	
Objective	1.8	1.8	1.9	1.9	1.9	2.1	2.1	2.1	2.2	2.2	1.1	1.1	1.1	1.11	1.11	3.1	3.1	3.2	3.2	3.2	
Response	a	d	b	c	a	a	c	b	d	d	a	c	b	a	d	c	c	b	a	d	% Mastery
Name																					
Alvarez, M.	a	d	b	c	a	a	d	b	d	d	a	c	a	a	b	d	a	b	a	d	75%
Bright, G.	a	d	b	c	a	a	b	b	d	d	a	c	b	a	d	c	c	b	a	d	95%
Byrn, S.	a	d	b	c	a	a	d	b	d	d	a	c	b	a	d	c	c	b	a	d	95%
Clima, R.	a	d	b	a	a	b	b	b	a	d	a	b	c	a	b	c	c	a	a	b	55%
Diaz, C.	a	d	b	c	a	b	b	b	d	d	a	c	b	a	d	c	c	b	a	d	90%
Dolan, Z.	a	d	b	a	a	a	d	b	d	a	a	c	b	a	d	d	a	b	a	b	65%
Gaerner, K.	c	d	a	a	a	a	d	c	d	a	a	c	b	d	d	a	a	b	b	a	55%
Giani, J.	a	a	b	c	a	c	d	b	d	d	b	c	b	a	b	c	a	b	b	a	65%
Gutirrez, J.	a	d	a	c	a	a	b	b	c	a	b	b	b	a	b	a	c	a	b	a	45%
Hendricks, L.	c	a	b	c	a	a	b	b	c	d	b	c	b	a	d	c	c	a	c	b	50%
Kelsey, C.	a	d	b	c	a	a	d	b	d	d	a	c	c	a	d	c	c	b	a	d	90%
Kosloski, S.	a	b	b	c	a	b	b	b	d	d	b	b	b	b	d	c	a	c	c	d	55%
Laesser, G.	a	d	c	c	a	c	b	b	a	d	a	c	d	d	d	c	c	b	a	d	70%
Langdon, O.	a	d	c	c	a	a	d	d	c	d	b	d	b	a	b	c	a	c	b	d	50%
Murdock, J.	a	d	a	c	a	a	d	d	d	a	b	c	b	b	d	d	c	a	a	b	60%
Quacchia, R.	b	c	b	a	a	c	b	b	a	d	a	c	c	a	b	a	a	c	c	b	40%
Sears, D.	a	d	c	c	a	c	b	b	a	d	a	c	d	d	d	c	a	b	a	d	70%
Torres, B.	a	b	b	c	a	b	d	b	d	a	a	b	b	a	d	c	a	b	b	a	70%
Warren, J.	a	d	b	c	a	b	d	c	d	a	a	d	b	a	d	d	c	b	c	a	60%
Waters, A.	a	d	b	c	a	a	d	b	d	d	c	d	c	a	d	c	c	b	a	d	80%
Weaver, B.	a	d	b	a	a	b	b	b	a	d	a	b	c	a	b	c	c	b	a	b	55%
Williams, G.	a	d	b	c	a	a	d	b	d	d	a	c	b	a	d	c	c	b	a	d	95%
% Mastery	86%	77%	73%	73%	100%	55%	0%	86%	64%	77%	73%	59%	64%	73%	68%	68%	68%	73%	64%	50%	

Benchmark Assessment: Class Roster — 2nd Quarter

Benchmark Test Results

(continued)

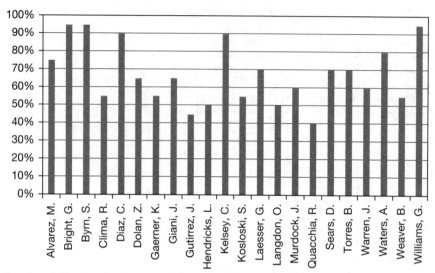

Benchmark Test Results: Percentage of Mastery of Individual Students

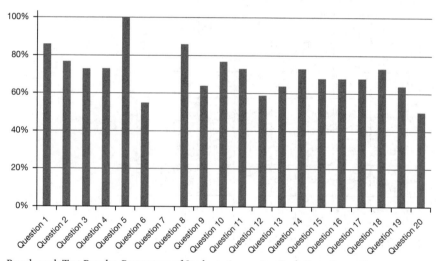

Benchmark Test Results: Percentage of Students Answering Each Item Correctly

Reflection 9-2: Giving Actionable Feedback

Examine each student's thinking in Figures 9–5 and 9–6 on page 263 (see also the following page). Record what you might say or write to Carley and Jerome about their work. Remember, actionable feedback lets the student know what is correct or what needs work and suggests positive action for the student.

Feedback for Carley:

Feedback for Jerome:

(continued)

The Printer's New Book

A printer is numbering the pages in a new book. He uses 195 digits.
How many pages does the book have?

Explain how you solved the problem.

Carley

1, 2, 3, 4, 5, 6, 7, 8, 9, 10, 11, 12

195   187   188
−18   −9
177   178   186

          140   200
          +40   +70
          186   380

459

90   270   98
×2   + 90   ×1
180   270   × 270
          450   2, 25

457

First I started to count how many digits are in each
number when I remembered that every number 4th   99 was
two digits. Also every number up to 195 was three digits. So
first I did 90×2 which is 98×93 and added these together. Then
I needed to add 9 because I took 9 digits out earlier. And I
ended up getting 459.

Jerome

10 11 12 13 14

          93   186   93
          ×6   −2   +93
          99   43   186

          99
9   ×9
          99

100   100

1000

Well first, I took 9 away which equals 186. I
divided 186 by 2 (because 10–99 are two digits)
which equals 93. Then I had the 93 digits
left. So I took 6 of the 93 which equals then
to 93 which equals 99. 100 words take
care of the 3 digits left over, so
my 93 words is 100!

Reflection 9-3: Creating a Specific Rubric: Template

Rating	General Description of Student Work	Specific to the Task
Wow!	Work demonstrates full understanding of underlying concepts and goes beyond expectations to make connections or give additional details in explanations. There is evidence of complex mathematical reasoning. Work exceeds grade-level expectations.	
Right On	Work demonstrates understanding of the mathematics and use of mathematical reasoning. Work is accurate—though there may be minor errors—and complete, with all requirements of the task met. There is a clear explanation of the solution in words, pictures, and/or numbers. Representations are appropriate and properly labeled. Work is high quality and meets grade-level expectations.	
Moving Along	Work demonstrates effort but is not yet at grade-level expectations and needs additional revision by the student. Work shows some understanding of the mathematics and some evidence of mathematical reasoning. There are computational or procedural errors and portions of the task may be missing. Representations may be difficult to understand.	
Not Yet	Work shows limited or no understanding of the mathematics and little evidence of reasoning. Work may show misconceptions and may not be appropriate for the task. Work may lack representations and explanations. Work is far below grade-level expectations.	

Reflection 9-4: INFORMing My Practice: Making Inferences, Giving Feedback

Look back to the opening paragraphs of this chapter (see page 246). Because what we infer about our students' understanding of mathematics influences how we plan lessons and how we interact with our students, it is critical that we have good information and provide helpful, actionable feedback to them.

- Examples of my use of INFORMative assessment to gather information (make inferences) about my students' understandings and misunderstandings:

- Ways I plan to focus on making certain my inferences about individual students are as accurate as possible as I plan for their mathematics instruction:

- Examples of how I will incorporate *actionable* feedback into my mathematics teaching—feedback to the class and to individuals:

Section VI

What Are the Next Steps in an INFORMative Assessment Journey?

10

INFORMative Assessment for Long-Term Success

In this final chapter, we come full circle on our INFORMative assessment journey, gathering together our ideas about INFORMative assessment, examining ways to communicate our students' progress to parents, and comparing grades with the richness of sharing student work. By highlighting the formativeness of teaching, we discuss what it means for teachers to be lifelong learners. We include reflections and suggestions of ways to put your beliefs into action for long-term teaching and learning success.

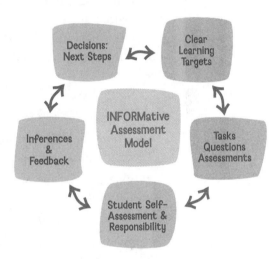

Overview

Communicating Students' Achievement to Parents

Beyond Grades

The Importance of Parent Conferences

The Formativeness of Teaching

Putting Our Beliefs into Action

Becoming Advocates of INFORMative Assessment

INFORMing My Practice

Developing expertise in formative assessment is a long-term investment of time and energy. Gathering data about students' thinking is only the first step. As teachers, we are motivated to develop skills that help us interpret the data as we plan lessons for individual students and the class. We know that to be successful in the long term our students must learn mathematics with understanding. Thus, we strive to become precise planners, flexible facilitators, and clear communicators.

Throughout *INFORMative Assessment: Formative Assessment to Improve Math Achievement*, we have talked about:

- beginning this INFORMative assessment journey together (Chapter 1);

- the many decisions we make as teachers (Chapter 2);

- the need for clear learning targets to guide mathematics teaching and learning (Chapter 3);

- gathering information, through oral and written assessments, about what students understand, misunderstand, and still need to learn (Chapters 4 and 5);

- providing opportunities for students to learn mathematics and to demonstrate that learning by choosing worthwhile tasks for both instruction and assessment (Chapter 6);

  - providing support for students to become self-assessors and to take greater responsibility for their learning—a component of INFORMative assessment that we must explicitly support (Chapter 7);

  - highlighting the critical role of questioning for different purposes (Chapter 8); and

  - synthesizing the importance of inferences and actionable feedback to students (Chapter 9).

"The star teachers of the twenty-first century will be teachers who work every day to improve teaching—not only their own but that of the whole profession."
—*The Teaching Gap: Best Ideas from the World's Teachers for Improving Education in the Classroom* (Stigler and Hiebert 1999, 179)

In this final chapter, we emphasize the formativeness of teaching as well as talk about the importance of communicating with parents and others who are involved in our students' education. We come full circle to reflect on our INFORMative assessment journey.

Communicating Students' Achievement to Parents

Clear and frequent communication with parents is essential for long-term success for both students and teachers. One of the positive outcomes of our efforts to implement INFORMative assessment is that we are better able to give actionable feedback to students, provide meaningful communications with their parents, and keep both parents and administrators apprised of students' progress.

Beyond Grades

For most schools, grades are a fact of life; parents, administrators, and the public hold widespread belief that grades accurately reflect students' accomplishments and can be compared across classrooms and schools. Grades are considered the primary vehicle by which we convey students' progress.

The following situation with Maia and Marissa illustrates the problem that sometimes arises when we focus primarily on grades as the main source of information in communicating with parents about students.

Scenario: What's in a Grade?

Maia and Marissa are twins who attend separate small elementary schools in the same district. The girls are in different schools because their parents did not want them to be in the same fourth-grade classroom. Both girls enjoy school, are strong readers, and complete their assignments. If we were to interview the girls, we would find they have similar levels of understanding of mathematics concepts and procedures. When report cards came home for the second grading period, Maia's grade in mathematics was a C+ and Marissa's grade was a B.

Turn to "Reflection 10–1: What's in a Grade? The Case of Maia and Marissa" (see page 294). Think about reasons why their understandings might be similar but their grades different. Use the reflection questions to support your thinking. Complete this reflection before reading further.

Reflection 10–1

What's in a Grade? The Case of Maia and Marissa

Page 294

What does the list you created in Reflection 10–1 suggest about the need for more evidence about the girls' understanding and use of mathematics beyond letter or numerical grades? With only a letter grade available, what do you know about Maia's and Marissa's mathematics understandings?

One reason similar performances may be evaluated differently relates to what "counts" in determining grades. Some teachers include effort, attitude, participation, and progress while others use strict averages of grades on written work. Some include homework scores and others only use scores from tests and quizzes. While educators know that an A in two different classes often does not represent the same level of understanding and achievement, many school districts continue to rely on grades as the primary means of communicating student learning.

All too often, student placements are made based primarily on grades. For some students, the As on their report cards represent illusions of learning rather than depth of understanding. For other students, the Ds on report cards cause them to be placed in less advanced groups, as if all poor performance is based on the exact same weakness. Because grades send powerful messages and influence how students feel about themselves as learners, we need to identify practices that communicate better what we learn through our INFORMative assessments. Using evidence from a variety of sources over time can make clearer what students have learned and what they still need to learn.

> **Because grades send powerful messages and influence how students feel about themselves as learners, we need to identify practices that communicate better what we learn through our INFORMative assessments.**

As we embrace assessment for the primary purpose of improving learning, assigning grades will become less important. We are not saying that we should abandon grades altogether; we are saying that we need to include multiple sources of information in our evaluation of student performance. There will continue to be a need for periodically evaluating student performance and, in most schools, assigning grades. However, with INFORMative assessment our ongoing focus becomes supporting learning—not grading or comparing students with one another.

The Importance of Parent Conferences

Back-to-school nights and PTA or PTO meetings are opportunities for us to tell parents about our expectations for their children. Usually we have only minimal time for questions or explanations of our mathematics program in detail; group discussions are most often about general goals rather than specific learning targets and the criteria for their accomplishment.

Parent conferences—either those between teachers and parents or those that are student-led—are better situations for sharing information about students' accomplishments and discussing students' progress based on achievement criteria. These conferences can be times of celebrations or meetings to brainstorm ways to help students who are temporarily off track. (Refer to Chapter 7, where we talk at length about student-led parent conferences.)

Daily or weekly work folders, telephone conversations, and notes provide some information for parents; however, formal conferences are necessary. These discussions allow parents to ask questions and teachers to be very specific about students' needs and challenges. When we share student work or portfolios—specific examples that support our comments—the conferences communicate even more information.

The Formativeness of Teaching

Although Stephen Covey was not specifically describing teachers who use INFORMative assessment in their classrooms in his book *The 7 Habits of Highly Effective People: Powerful Lessons in Personal Change* (1989), all of the habits he advocates do serve us well—especially being proactive, beginning with the end in mind, and seeking first to understand and then to be understood. Teachers continually search for ways to become better educators and to create environments in which all of our students will learn with understanding and confidence. This ongoing quest for excellence is the *formativeness of teaching*. Teachers are truly lifelong learners. Most of us are willing to examine our current practices and venture into new arenas that we may not be able to clearly envision. We are eager to become better at gathering information about our students' thinking, observing how close they are to achieving the learning targets we have established, and making adjustments in our instruction to intervene as needed.

Elementary teachers usually teach all content areas, and many factors contribute to our success as teachers. We need expertise related to many

> "Understanding is crucial because things learned with understanding can be used flexibly, adapted to new situations, and used to learn new things." —*Making Sense: Teaching and Learning Mathematics with Understanding* (Hiebert et al. 1997, 1)

disciplines, including mathematics. We continue to seek opportunities that help us delve more deeply into mathematics at an adult level. We also want professional development that improves our ability to think about mathematics through a student lens. Studying learning trajectories for mathematics topics, for example, will prove helpful in merging content knowledge and pedagogical knowledge.

With these thoughts in mind, we've proposed "Habits of Highly Effective Teachers of Mathematics":

Habits of Highly Effective Teachers of Mathematics

1. Seek mathematics content knowledge.

2. Hone classroom management skills.

3. Sharpen abilities to use questions and choose good tasks.

4. Develop knowledge of students.

5. Create environments that support student learning.

6. Use formative assessment to better plan and revise instruction.

7. Provide actionable feedback to students and clear communications to parents.

8. Reflect with colleagues on teaching experiences and practices.

Each habit is important in its own way, and increased expertise in any one of these areas contributes to our ability to help our students learn with greater understanding.

Putting Our Beliefs into Action

Every day in our classrooms some students appear to have mastered the learning targets, others are on the way but need more instruction, and still other students have misconceptions that need to be addressed specifically. Establishing an environment in which all students are willing to talk about their ideas and teaching students to self-assess takes time and energy. Our efforts to become better listeners and more attentive to students' work may mean that we are likely to have more, rather than fewer, decisions to make about future lessons. Becoming skilled at implementing INFORMative assessment does not mean our jobs will be easier—just more rewarding.

In the following table, "Where We've Been . . . Where We're Going" (see also pages xi–xii), we compare traditional classrooms with ones in which there is a focus on INFORMative assessment. On the left side of the chart, we list traditional classroom practices. The middle column identifies the corresponding chapters in this resource that address moving these practices toward INFORMative assessment. Classroom practices for long-term success in using INFORMative assessment are listed on the right side of the chart. These practices are not things we become expert at doing with two or three tries; they require planning and reflection and require us to be flexible and open to feedback on our teaching. In other words, we must be willing to engage in the formativeness of teaching.

> "According to Gerzon, research shows that students make dramatic achievement gains when their teachers break instructional units into a progression of clear, well-defined learning targets; involve students in setting learn goals and assessing their own progress; give students immediate and corrective feedback; and set up peer collaboration activities to build content mastery."
> —"Formative Assessment: Not Just Another Test." (WestEd 2010)

Where We've Been . . . Where We're Going

Moving from . . .	Chapter	Moving Toward . . .
Teaching primarily page-by-page from a textbook and covering everything in equal segments	Chapter 2	Using diagnostic assessments to determine what topics need more or less time and which students need extra assistance or additional challenges
Planning lessons based on general goals and the next topic in the textbook	Chapter 3	Clearly defining learning targets with criteria for their achievement and communicating these to students
Relying primarily on multiple-choice tests to measure achievement	Chapter 4 Chapter 5	Employing a variety of assessment strategies—personal conversations, constructed response, and open-ended questions—to identify achievement of learning targets
Assessing at the end of the week or the end of a unit and using the results primarily to assign grades	Chapter 4 Chapter 5 Chapter 6	Assessing daily throughout instruction to uncover student thinking and make decisions about instruction
Providing whole-class instruction with students working individually on the same tasks	Chapter 6	Having students work on tasks chosen to address identified strengths and needs with the whole class, alone, with partners, and in flexible groups

Expecting students to know how to improve their work	Chapter 7	Creating an environment that promotes reflection, self-assessment, and responsibility with rubrics, models, and class discussions that explain quality work
Showing and telling students the most efficient way to solve problems or to compute	Chapter 6 Chapter 7 Chapter 8	Encouraging students to share solution strategies and facilitating class discussions that move students to efficient algorithms
Calling on students who have raised their hands and accepting their answers	Chapter 6 Chapter 7 Chapter 8	Calling on a variety of students daily and asking them to justify their answers
Asking questions that are primarily recall or require yes-or-no responses	Chapter 8	Asking questions to engage students in the task or discussion and questions that probe students' thinking
Scoring student responses as *right* or *wrong* and giving feedback primarily in the form of grades	Chapter 9	Scoring student work for both the process and the answer and providing actionable feedback to inform the student on how to improve
Defining successful teaching as having a large percentage of the class score well on tests	Chapters 1–10	Defining successful teaching as having students who reason mathematically, exhibit perseverance in solving problems, communicate their ideas, and develop long-term knowledge and skills in using mathematics

Reflection 10-2

Moving Toward
INFORMative
Assessment
Practices

Page 295

In "Reflection 10–2: Moving Toward INFORMative Assessment Practices" (see page 295), we have placed the "Moving Toward . . . " column into a reflection chart for you to use as a self-assessment tool. Reflect on your own teaching; where do you feel you are in your INFORMative assessment journey?

Becoming Advocates of INFORMative Assessment

In the following story, a young teacher, Ms. Hanley, is thinking carefully about formative assessment with her fourth-grade students. Think back to the issues we have raised throughout this resource: In what ways would you help Ms. Hanley become better at using ongoing assessment to plan instruction and give feedback to her students? What questions would you ask her and what feedback might you give? Consider what you might learn if you took on the role of a mentor.

Ms. Hanley decided that the *Soccer Camp Problem* would be a good task to assign her fourth-grade students, along with one short textbook exercise. Her learning targets were for students to practice multidigit multiplication and to solve two-step problems. She wanted them to unpack the story problem as well as practice procedures. She knew many of her students liked to play soccer, so this problem would be of real-world interest to them.

Soccer Camp Problem

Carlo wants to go to a special soccer camp. The camp meets 3 afternoons a week for 16 weeks. The drive from his home to the camp and back is 29 miles. Carlo's mother says that the camp is too expensive because they would be driving so many miles. How many total miles would they drive if Carlo went to the soccer camp?

Many of the students in Ms. Hanley's class struggled whenever she assigned word problems; however, she had structured this particular problem to offer several ways that students could approach the task. In keeping with her goal of having students work cooperatively more frequently, she assigned groups of three with students of varying abilities in each group. Ms. Hanley encouraged students to talk with their groupmates about their answers to the exercises on the textbook page; for the *Soccer Camp Problem*, she suggested that students first discuss the situation as a group, ensure that everyone in the group understood the problem, and then work through the problem independently. If students had disagreements about the solution, they were to explain their ideas to each other and try to reach agreement on the correct answer.

As students worked, Ms. Hanley overheard this conversation:

Julianne: *I can do three times sixteen to get the number of trips. That would be, um, forty-eight trips. But I'm not sure how to multiply forty-eight times twenty-nine.*

Will: *You just make the numbers easier. Take one away from the forty-eight and give it to the twenty-nine. Then you can multiply thirty times forty-seven. My dad showed me how you just multiply by the three and add a zero at the end.*

Evan: *I don't think that is right.*

Julianne: (Addressing Will) *Show me.*

Will: (Writes on his paper) 47 × 3 = 141. *Then you just add a zero at the end* (writes *1,410*).

Evan: *No. Look, you do it like this* (multiplies 48 × 29 using a traditional algorithm). *The answer is one thousand, three hundred, and ninety-two* (writes *1,392*). (Julianne copies Evan's computation since he usually gets math problems correct.)

Will: *Well, whatever* (sits back from the group but eventually copies Evan's solution).

As she listened to the conversation among Will, Julianne, and Evan, Ms. Hanley gained some unexpected information about them. She learned that:

- Julianne grasped the problem and recognized that there were two steps; she knew how to multiply two digits by one digit, but did not know how to proceed when both factors were two-digit numbers.

- Will was confusing a strategy that would have worked well for addition, but not for multiplication. Ms. Hanley also suspected that Will had no idea what *adding zero to the end* meant mathematically.

- Evan applied a traditional algorithm, but did not give any explanation that would help his fellow students.

Ms. Hanley recognized that if she had not overheard this conversation, she might have thought that all three students understood multiplication of two two-digit numbers, since they had correct answers on their worksheets. This made her look more closely at the group interactions; she discovered that in several groups a number of students appeared to be hesitant and were allowing one student in the group to do most of the work.

Following are several possible courses of action that Ms. Hanley considered. Would you choose one of these paths or approach the situation differently? Read the scenarios and then take a moment to respond to the questions in "Reflection 10–3: Mentoring Ms. Hanley" (see pages 296–97).

Reflection 10–3

Mentoring
Ms. Hanley

Pages 296–97

Scenario 1: Context to Provide Meaning

Ms. Hanley decided not to address the incomplete understandings with Julianne and Will explicitly but first to reteach to the whole class a lesson on multiplication when both factors are two-digit numbers. She planned to have students model and describe what multiplication means and give specific examples of real-world contexts. Second, she wanted to ask students to describe situations involving two-digit numbers. Third, she planned to provide word problems for students to discuss how they would solve them, but not do the computation. Last, she planned to use the same word problems and have student volunteers explain how they would multiply two two-digit numbers.

Scenario 2: Estimates and the Meaning of Operations

Ms. Hanley considered a number sense approach as a first step in solving multidigit problems. She planned to begin by having students suggest and justify a range of possible answers for a set of problems. By identifying that the answer should be *between this and that*, she wanted students to think about what the operations mean and distinguish between the results of adding two two-digit numbers and multiplying them. She was aware that some students correctly used strategies such as *breaking apart* or *multiplying with friendly numbers* (using associative and distributive properties) and wanted them to model their thinking along with those who used a traditional algorithm. Ms. Hanley planned to talk with Will before the class lesson. She felt that he needed individual feedback and hoped that a discussion before the lesson would encourage him to listen carefully to his peers.

Scenario 3: Properties and Number Sense

The conversation Ms. Hanley overheard caused her to wonder if other students would benefit from a discussion of properties and operations. She decided to use Carlos and the *Soccer Camp Problem* as a basis for the discussion and also to review the process for two-digit multiplication. She planned to have students work in new groups of three or four to talk about the flaw in thinking that strategies that work for addition and subtraction will automatically work for multiplication. She suggested they consider specific examples of ways that students mistakenly changed 48×29 to new problems of 49×30 (adding one to each factor) and 47×30 (taking one from one factor and giving to the other). After students talked in their groups, she planned to have volunteers explain again what multiplication means. She also planned to ask students several questions: "Did you notice what the digit in the ones place would be in each of the three multiplication problems?" and "If the numbers in the ones place are not the same, what kind of clue does that give you about the different products and whether the three problems are equivalent when multiplied?"

We offer these three scenarios only as possibilities; you may have different ideas, especially since we do not know how other students in the class responded to the task. For example, if you decide to give feedback to just Will, Julianne, and Evan, what beneficial comments and next steps would you give to each of them? Remember to take a moment to respond to the questions in "Reflection 10–3: Mentoring Ms. Hanley" (see pages 296–97).

Situations such as the one described in Ms. Hanley's class reveal a lack of understanding among specific students. These situations occur in all of our classrooms. They serve as reminders that we are likely to learn the most about students' thinking by listening to their conversations or asking them directly to explain how they arrive at answers. While we may not know one best strategy to use in situations like this, we know that doing nothing to address the incomplete knowledge and the misconceptions in hopes that students will eventually get it does not work.

It is important that we listen for, watch for, and address students' misunderstandings and incomplete ideas. From experience we all know that even with clear lessons and discussions, many students need multiple opportunities to learn the same content and to sort out what they currently believe with new information. We also know that sometimes students apply multiple misconceptions in a single situation. In the case of Ms. Hanley's fourth graders, when a student says "just multiply by three and add a zero to the end," it means that the teacher needs to address additional mathematics through discussion, modeling, and practice.

INFORMing My Practice

Reflecting the research from the work of Paul Black, Dylan Wiliam, and other researchers, the National Council of Teachers of Mathematics (NCTM) has stated that effective formative assessment can be based on the following five key strategies:

Effective Formative Assessment: Five Key Strategies

1. Clarifying, sharing, and understanding what students are expected to know.

2. Creating effective classroom discussions, questions, activities, and tasks that offer the evidence of how students are progressing to the learning goals.

3. Providing feedback that moves learning forward.

4. Encouraging students to take ownership of their own learning.

5. Using students as learning resources for one another. (NCTM 2007)

If you and your colleagues are building a community of educators in your school with similar goals related to classroom assessment, the five aforementioned strategies are a good conversation starter. Equally powerful in starting conversations is the *National Council of Teachers of Mathematics Assessment Research Brief: Five "Key Strategies" for Effective Formative Assessment* (see page 299). Reflecting on your practices and communicating your thoughts and successes with others will enhance your community.

As we come to the end of our conversations in *INFORMative Assessment: Formative Assessment to Improve Math Achievement, Grades K–6*, consider all that we have discussed and how your ideas have changed. Make sure you have taken time to reflect on where you are in your INFORMative assessment journey (see Reflection 10–2). Now is also the time to set new goals for yourself. "Reflection 10–4: INFORMing My Practice: Final Reflections and Goals" (see page 298) is similar to the chart you completed in Chapter 1, with an additional column for your goals.

Thoughtfully implementing INFORMative assessment means taking seriously the notion of reflecting more frequently on what our students understand and do not understand and the logic behind students' wrong answers. This is how all of us begin to change the culture of our teaching. At the beginning of this journey in the first chapter, we noted our belief that formative assessment is not a one-time event. It is not the product or end result of a set of well-defined steps. Rather, it is a process—a collection of strategies that engage teachers and students in becoming partners to support students' learning. We are confident that your journey will lead you to richer interactions with your students. Allowing them to INFORM your instructional decisions will allow you to lead your students to more powerful learning experiences and long-term success in mathematics.

Reflection 10-4

INFORMing My Practice: Final Reflections and Goals

Page 298

> For teaching to have the greatest impact on the learner, teachers must be thoughtful in their planning, flexible in their delivery, and relentless in their focus on what students are understanding. The formativeness of teaching means that teachers are constantly planning, implementing, and revising their lessons and instruction. Teachers choose lesson goals and plan activities; they anticipate student responses and possible misconceptions. When they implement lessons, teachers look for evidence that students are making sense of the mathematics. The formativeness of teaching occurs within the classroom as teachers immediately react to their students' needs and outside the classroom as they reflect upon what they might do differently to strengthen future lessons. —Katherine Mawhinney, Appalachian State University, email message to author, August 26, 2010

Reflection 10–1: What's in a Grade? The Case of Maia and Marissa

Read the scenario on page 281. Think about reasons why Maia's and Marissa's grades may be different. Use the following questions to help guide your thinking.

1. List reasons why Maia's and Marissa's understandings might be similar even if their grades are different.

2. From your list put a ✓ before items that are reflections of the way grades are determined by different teachers and a ☆ before items that might point to the girls' different understandings of the mathematics.

3. If you were one of the twins' parents, what would you think about each girl's mathematics understandings based on their report card grades?

4. If your school uses a different grading system, how do your report cards communicate information to parents?

Reflection 10-2: Moving Toward INFORMative Assessment Practices

Rate yourself: 1 = Not yet   2 = Sometimes   3 = Usually   4 = I do this!

Moving Toward These Classroom Practices	Self-Assessment
Clearly defining learning targets with criteria for their achievement and communicating these to students	1 2 3 4
Using diagnostic assessments to determine what topics need more or less instructional time and which students need extra assistance or additional challenges	1 2 3 4
Employing a variety of assessment strategies—personal conversations, constructed response, and open-ended questions to identify achievement of learning targets	1 2 3 4
Having students work on tasks chosen to address identified strengths and needs with the whole class, alone, with partners, and in flexible groups	1 2 3 4
Assessing daily throughout instruction to uncover student thinking and make decisions about instruction	1 2 3 4
Asking questions to engage students in the task or discussion and questions that probe students' thinking	1 2 3 4
Scoring student work for both the process and the answer and providing actionable feedback to inform the student on how to improve	1 2 3 4
Encouraging students to share solution strategies and facilitating class discussions that move students to efficient algorithms	1 2 3 4
Calling on a variety of students daily and asking them to justify their answers	1 2 3 4
Creating an environment that promotes reflection, self-assessment, and responsibility with rubrics, models, and class discussions that explain quality work	1 2 3 4
Defining successful teaching as having students who reason mathematically, exhibit perseverance in solving problems, communicate their ideas, and develop long-term skills in using mathematics	1 2 3 4

Reflection 10-3: Mentoring Ms. Hanley

Read Ms. Hanley's experience on pages 288–90. Answer questions 1–4. Then read the three scenarios regarding Ms. Hanley's decisions on pages 290–91 and answer questions 5–6.

1. Are there any questions you would like to ask Ms. Hanley about her class or her lesson?

2. What foundational ideas (conceptual, factual, and procedural knowledge) do Ms. Hanley's students need to be successful in multiplying multidigit numbers?

3. Ms. Hanley chose not to intervene when she overheard the three students' discussion but decided to respond during the next day's lesson so she could think carefully about what to do. Would you have made a similar decision? Why or why not?

(continued)

4. When multiplying a number by thirty, what does it mean to "just multiply by three and add a zero to the end"?

5. Would you choose one of the three scenarios Ms. Hanley considered or would you approach the situation differently? Explain how you think Ms. Hanley (or you) should proceed.

6. What overall feedback might you give Ms. Hanley?

Reflection 10–4: INFORMing My Practice: Final Reflections and Goals

My beliefs . . .	are reflected in my actions . . .	that support student learning . . .	and my goals are . . .

Compare with the draft you completed in Chapter 1, page 11.

National Council of Teachers of Mathematics Assessment Research Brief: Five "Key Strategies" for Effective Formative Assessment

In order to build a comprehensive framework for formative assessment, Wiliam and Thompson (2007) proposed that three processes were central:

1. Establishing where learners are in their learning

2. Establishing where they are going

3. Establishing how to get there

By considering separately the roles of the teacher and the students themselves, they proposed that formative assessment could be built up from five "key strategies."

1. Clarifying, Sharing, and Understanding Goals for Learning and Criteria for Success with Learners

There are a number of ways teachers can begin the process of clarifying and sharing learning goals and success criteria. Many teachers specify the learning goals for the lesson at the beginning of the lesson, but in doing so, many teachers fail to distinguish between the learning goals and the activities that will lead to the required learning. *When teachers start from what it is they want students to know and design their instruction backward from that goal, then instruction is far more likely to be effective (Wiggins and McTighe 2000).*

Wiggins and McTighe also advocate a two-stage process of first clarifying the learning goals themselves (what is worthy and requiring understanding?), which is then followed by establishing success criteria (what would count as evidence of understanding?). Only then should the teacher move on to exploring activities that will lead to the required understanding.

However, it is important that students also come to understand these goals and success criteria, as Royce Sadler (1989, p. 121) notes:

> The indispensable conditions for improvement are that the student comes to hold a concept of quality roughly similar to that held by the teacher, is continuously able to monitor the quality of what is being produced during the act of production itself, and has a repertoire of alternative moves or strategies from which to draw at any given point.

Indeed, there is evidence that discrepancies in beliefs about what it is that counts as learning in mathematics classrooms may be a significant factor in the achievement gaps observed in mathematics classrooms. In a study of 72 students between the ages of seven and thirteen, Gray and Tall (1994) found that the reasoning of the higher-achieving students was qualitatively different from that of the lower-achieving students. In particular, the higher-achieving students were able to work successfully despite unresolved ambiguities about whether mathematical entities were concepts or procedures. Lower-achieving students were unable to accept such ambiguities and could not work past them. By refusing to accept the ambiguities inherent in mathematics, the lower-achieving students were, in fact, attempting a far more difficult form of mathematics, with a far greater cognitive demand.

A simple example may be illustrative here. When we write $6\frac{1}{2}$, the mathematical operation between the 6 and the $\frac{1}{2}$ is actually addition, but when we write $6x$, the implied operation between the 6 and the x is multiplication, and the relationship between the 6 and the 1 in 61 is different again. And yet, very few people who are successful in mathematics are aware of these inconsistencies or differences in mathematical notation. In a very real sense, being successful in mathematics requires knowing what to worry about and what not to worry about. *Students who do not understand what is important and what is not important will be at a very real disadvantage.*

In a study of twelve seventh-grade science classrooms, White and Frederiksen (1998) found that giving students time to talk about what would count as quality work, and how their work was likely to be evaluated, reduced the achievement gap between the highest- and lowest-achieving students in half and increased the average performance of the classes to such an extent that the weakest students in the experimental group were outperforming all but the very strongest students in the control group.

This is why using a variety of examples of students' work from other classes can be extremely powerful in helping students come to understand what counts as quality work. Many teachers have found that students are better at spotting errors in the work of other students than they are at seeing them in their own work. By giving students examples of work at different standards, students can begin to explore the differences between superior and inferior work, and these emergent understandings can be discussed with the whole class. As a result of such processes, students will develop a "nose for quality" (Claxton 1995) that they will then be able to use in monitoring the quality of their own work.

2. Engineering Effective Classroom Discussions, Questions, Activities, and Tasks that Elicit Evidence of Students' Learning

Once we know what it is that we want our students to learn, then it is important to collect the right sort of evidence about the extent of students' progress toward these goals, but few teachers plan the kinds of tasks, activities, and questions that they use with their students specifically to elicit the right kind of evidence of students' learning. As an example, consider the question shown in figure 1 below.

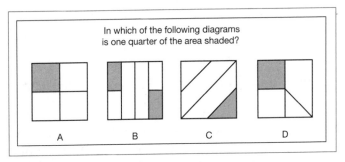

FIGURE 1. Diagnostic Item on Elementary Fractions

Diagram A is the obvious answer, but B is also correct. However, some students do not believe that one-quarter of B is shaded because of a belief that the shaded parts have to be adjoining. Students who believe that one-quarter of C is shaded have not understood that one region shaded out of four is not necessarily a quarter. Diagram D is perhaps the most interesting here. One-quarter of this diagram is shaded, although the pieces are not all equal; students who rely too literally on the "equal areas" definition of fractions will say that D is not a correct response. *By crafting questions that explicitly build in the undergeneralizations and overgeneralizations that students are known to make (Bransford, Brown, and Cocking 2000), we can get far more useful information about what to do next.* Furthermore, by equipping each student in the class with a set of four cards bearing the letters A, B, C, and D and by requiring all students to respond simultaneously with their answers, the teacher can generate a very solid evidence base for deciding whether the class is ready to move on (Leahy et al. 2005). If every student responds with A, B, and D, then the teacher can move on with confidence that the students have understood. If everyone simply responds with A, then the teacher may choose to reteach some part of the topic. The most likely response, however, is for some students to respond correctly and for others to respond incorrectly, or incompletely. This provides the teacher with an opportunity to conduct a classroom discussion in which students with different views can be asked to justify their selections.

Of course planning such questions takes time, but by investing the time before the lesson, the teacher is able to address students' confusion during the lesson, with the students still in front of him or her. Teachers who do not plan such questions are forced to put children's thinking back on track through grading, thus dealing with the students one at a time, after they have gone away.

3. Providing Feedback that Moves Learning Forward

The research on feedback shows that much of the feedback that students receive has, at best, no impact on learning and can actually be counterproductive. Kluger and DeNisi (1996) reviewed more than three thousand research reports on the effects of feedback in schools, colleges, and workplaces and found that only 131 studies were scientifically rigorous. In 50 of these studies, feedback actually made people's performance worse than it would have been without feedback. The principal feature of these studies was that feedback was, in the psychological jargon, "ego-involving." In other words, the feedback focused attention on the person rather than on the quality of the work _____ for example, by giving scores, grades, or other forms of report that encouraged comparison with others. The studies where feedback was most effective were those in which the feedback told participants not just what to do to improve but also how to go about it.

Given the emphasis on grading in U.S. schools, teachers may be tempted to offer comments alongside scores or grades. However, a number of studies (e.g., Butler 1987, 1988) have shown that when comments are accompanied by grades or scores, students focus first on their own grade or score and then on those of their neighbors, so that grades with comments are no more effective than grades alone, and much less effective than comments alone. The crucial requirement of feedback is that it should force the student to engage cognitively in the work.

Such feedback could be given orally, as in this example from Saphier (2005, p. 92):

Teacher: *What part don't you understand?*

Student: *I just don't get it.*

Teacher: *Well, the first part is just like the last problem you did. Then we add one more variable. See if you can find out what it is, and I'll come back in a few minutes.*

Written feedback can support students in finding errors for themselves:

- There are 5 answers here that are incorrect. Find them and fix them.
- The answer to this question is … Can you find away to work it out?

It can also identify where students might use and extend their existing knowledge:

- You've used substitution to solve all these simultaneous equations. Can you use elimination?

Other approaches (Hodgen and Wiliam 2006) include encouraging pupils to reflect:

- You used two different methods to solve these problems. What are the advantages and disadvantages of each?

- You have understood … well. Can you make up your own more difficult problems?

Another suggestion is to have students discuss their ideas with others:

- You seem to be confusing sine and cosine. Talk to Katie about how to work out the difference.

- Compare your work with Ali and write some advice to another student tackling this topic for the first time.

The important point in all this is that as well as "putting the ball back in the students' court," the teacher also needs to set aside time for students to read, respond to, and act on feedback.

4. Activating Students as Owners of Their Own Learning

When teachers are told they are responsible for making sure that their students do well, the quality of their teaching deteriorates, as does their students' learning (Deci et al. 1982). In contrast, when students take an active part in monitoring and regulating their learning, then the rate of their learning is dramatically increased. Indeed, it is common to find studies in which the rate of students' learning is doubled, so that students learn in six months what students in control groups take a year to learn (Fontana and Fernandes 1994; Mevarech and Kramarski 1997).

In an attempt to integrate research on motivation, metacognition, self-esteem, self-efficacy, and attribution theory, Monique Boekaerts has proposed a dual-processing theory of student motivation and engagement (Boekaerts

2006). When presented with a task, the student evaluates the task according to its interest, difficulty, cost of engagement, and so on. If the evaluation is positive, the student is likely to seek to increase competence by engaging in the task. If the evaluation is negative, a range of possible outcomes is possible. The student may engage in the task but focus on getting a good grade from the teacher instead of mastering the relevant material (e.g., by cheating) or the student may disengage from the task on the grounds that "it is better to be thought lazy than dumb." *The important point for teachers is that to maximize learning, the focus needs to be on personal growth rather than on a comparison with others.*

Practical techniques for getting students started include "traffic lights," where students flash green, yellow, or red cards to indicate their level of understanding of a concept. Many teachers have reported that initially, students who are focusing on well-being, rather than growth, display green, indicating full understanding, even though they know they are confused. However, when the teacher asks students who have shown green cards to explain concepts to those who have shown yellow or red, students have a strong incentive to be honest!

5. Activating Students as Learning Resources for One Another

Slavin, Hurley, and Chamberlain (2003) have shown that activating students as learning resources for one another produces some of the largest gains seen in any educational interventions, provided two conditions are met. The first is that the learning environment must provide for group goals, so that students are working as a group instead of just working in a group. The second condition is individual accountability, so that each student is responsible for his or her contribution to the group, so there can be no "passengers."

With regard to assessment, then, a crucial feature is that the assessment encourages collaboration among students while they are learning. To achieve this collaboration, the learning goals and success criteria must be accessible to the students (see above), and the teacher must support the students as they learn how to help one another improve their work. One particularly successful format for doing this has been the idea of "two stars and a wish." The idea is that when students are commenting on the work of one another, they do not give evaluative feedback but instead have to identify two positive features of the work (two "stars") and one feature that they believe merits further attention (the "wish"). Teachers who have used this technique with students as young as five years old have been astonished to see how appropriate the comments are, and because the feedback comes from a peer rather than someone in authority over them, the recipient of the feedback appears to be more able to accept the feedback (in other words, they focus on growth rather than on preserving their well-being). In fact, teachers have told us that the feedback that students give to one another, although accurate, is far more hard-hitting and direct than they themselves would have given. Furthermore, the research shows that the person providing the feedback benefits just as much as the recipient because she or he is forced to internalize the learning intentions and success criteria in the context of someone else's work, which is less emotionally charged than doing it in the context of one's own work.

Conclusion

The available research evidence suggests that considerable enhancements in student achievement are possible when teachers use assessment, minute-by-minute and day-by-day, to adjust their instruction to meet their students' learning needs. However, it is also clear that making such changes is much more than just adding a few routines to one's normal practice. It involves a change of focus from what the teacher is putting into the process and to what the learner is getting out of it, and the radical nature of the changes means that the support of colleagues is essential. Nevertheless, our experiences to date suggest that the investment of effort in these changes is amply rewarded. Students are more engaged in class, achieve higher standards, and teachers find their work more professionally fulfilling. As one teacher said, "I'm not babysitting any more."

By Dylan Wiliam
Judith Reed, Series Editor

REFERENCES

Boekaerts, Monique. "Self-Regulation and Effort Investment." In *Handbook of Child Psychology*, Vol. 4: *Child Psychology in Practice*, 6th ed., edited by K. Ann Renninger and Irving E. Sigel, pp. 345–77). Hoboken, N.J.: John Wiley & Sons, 2006.

Bransford, John D., Ann L. Brown, and Rodney R. Cocking. *How People Learn: Brain, Mind, Experience, and School.* Washington, D.C.: National Academies Press, 2000.

Butler, Ruth. "Task-Involving and Ego-Involving Properties of Evaluation: Effects of Different Feedback Conditions on Motivational Perceptions, Interest and Performance." *Journal of Educational Psychology* 79, no. 4 (1987): 474–82.

———. "Enhancing and Undermining Intrinsic Motivation: The Effects of Task-Involving and Ego-Involving Evaluation on Interest and Performance." *British Journal of Educational Psychology* 58 (1988): 1–14.

Claxton, G. L. "What Kind of Learning Does Self-Assessment Drive? Developing a 'Nose' for Quality: Comments on Klenowski." *Assessment in Education: Principles, Policy and Practice* 2, no. 3 (1995): 339–43.

Deci, Edward L., N. H. Speigel, R. M. Ryan, R. Koestner, and M. Kauffman. "The Effects of Performance Standards on Teaching Styles: The Behavior of Controlling Teachers." *Journal of Educational Psychology* 74 (1982): 852–59.

Fontana, David., and M. Fernandes. "Improvements in Mathematics Performance as a Consequence of Self-Assessment in Portuguese Primary School Pupils." *British Journal of Educational Psychology* 64, no. 4 (1994): 407–17.

Gray, Eddie M., and David O. Tall. "Duality, Ambiguity, and Flexibility: A 'Proceptual' View of Simple Arithmetic." *Journal for Research in Mathematics Education* 25 (March 1994): 116–40.

Hodgen, Jeremy, and Dylan Wiliam. *Mathematics inside the Black Box: Assessment for Learning in the Mathematics Classroom.* London: NFER-Nelson, 2006.

Kluger, Avraham N., and Angelo DeNisi. "The Effects of Feedback Interventions on Performance: A Historical Review, a Meta-analysis, and a Preliminary Feedback Intervention Theory." *Psychological Bulletin* 119, no. 2 (1996): 254–84.

Leahy, Siobhan, Christine Lyon, Marnie Thompson, and Dylan Wiliam. (2005). "Classroom Assessment: Minute-by-Minute and Day-by-Day." *Educational Leadership* 63, no. 3 (2005): 18–24.

Mevarech, Zemira R., and Bracha Kramarski. "IMPROVE: A Multidimensional Method for Teaching Mathematics in Heterogeneous Classrooms." *American Educational Research Journal* 34, no. 2 (1997): 365–94.

Sadler, D. Royce. "Formative Assessment and the Design of Instructional Systems." *Instructional Science* 18, no. 2 (1989): 119–44.

Saphier, Jonathon. "Masters of Motivation." In *On Common Ground: The Power of Professional Learning Communities,* edited by Richard DuFour, Robert Eaker, and Rebecca DuFour, pp. 85–113. Bloomington, Ill.: National Education Service, 2005.

Slavin, Robert E., Eric A. Hurley, and Anne M. Chamberlain. "Cooperative Learning and Achievement." In *Handbook of Psychology,* Vol. 7: *Educational Psychology,* edited by W. M. Reynolds and G. J. Miller, pp. 177–98. Hoboken, N.J.: John Wiley & Sons, 2003.

White, Barbara Y. , and John R. Frederiksen. "Inquiry, Modeling, and Metacognition: Making Science Accessible to All Students." *Cognition and Instruction* 16, no. 1 (1998): 3–118.

Wiggins, Grant, and Jay McTighe. *Understanding by Design.* New York: Prentice Hall, 2000.

Wiliam, Dylan, and Marnie Thompson. "Integrating Assessment with Instruction: What Will It Take to Make It Work?" In *The Future of Assessment: Shaping Teaching and Learning,* edited by C. A. Dwyer. Mahwah, N.J.: Lawrence Erlbaum Associates, 2007.

References

Ainsworth, Larry, and Donald Viegut. 2006. *Common Formative Assessments: How to Connect Standards-Based Instruction and Assessment.* Thousand Oaks, CA: Corwin Press.

Anderson, Lorin W., and David R. Krathwohl, eds. 2001. *A Taxonomy for Learning, Teaching, and Assessing: A Revision of Bloom's Taxonomy of Educational Objectives.* 2d ed. Boston: Allyn & Bacon.

Anderson, Nancy C., Suzanne H. Chapin, and Catherine O'Connor. 2011. *Classroom Discussions: Seeing Math Discourse in Action, Grades K–6: A Multimedia Professional Learning Resource.* Sausalito, CA: Math Solutions.

Assessment Standards Working Group. 1995. *Assessment Standards for School Mathematics.* Reston, VA: National Council of Teachers of Mathematics.

Austin, Terri. 1994. *Changing the View: Student-Led Parent Conferences.* Teacher to Teacher Series. Portsmouth, NH: Heinemann.

Barton, Mary Lee, and Clare Heidema. 2002. *Teaching Reading in Mathematics: A Supplement to* Teaching Reading in the Content Areas Teacher's Manual. 2d ed. Aurora, CO: Mid-Continent Research for Education and Learning.

Becker, Jerry P., and Shigeru Shimada, eds. 1997. *The Open-Ended Approach: A New Proposal for Teaching Mathematics.* Reston, VA: National Council of Teachers of Mathematics.

Bender, William N. 2009. *Differentiating Math Instruction: Strategies That Work for K–8 Classrooms.* 2d ed. Thousand Oaks, CA: Corwin Press.

Black, Paul, and Dylan Wiliam. 1998. "Inside the Black Box: Raising Standards Through Classroom Assessment." *Phi Delta Kappan* 80 (2): 139–44, 146–48.

———. 2009. "Developing the Theory of Formative Assessment." *Educational Assessment, Evaluation and Accountability* 21 (1): 5–31.

Black, Paul, Christine Harrison, Clare Lee, Bethan Marshall, and Dylan Wiliam. 2003. *Assessment for Learning: Putting It into Practice.* Berkshire, England: Open University Press; New York: McGraw-Hill Education.

———. 2004. *Working Inside the Black Box: Assessment for Learning in the Classroom.* London: King's College Department of Education and Professional Studies.

Bloom, Benjamin S., ed. 1956. *Taxonomy of Educational Objectives: The Classification of Educational Goals; Handbook I: Cognitive Domain.* New York: David McKay.

Bright, George W., and Jeane M. Joyner, eds. 1998. *Classroom Assessment in Mathematics: Views from a National Science Foundation Conference.* Lanham, MD: University Press of America.

———. 2004. *Dynamic Classroom Assessment: Linking Mathematical Understanding to Instruction in Middle Grades and High School (Participant's Guide).* Vernon Hills: ETA Cuisenaire.

———. 2005. *Dynamic Classroom Assessment: Linking Assessment with Instruction in Elementary School Mathematics (Participant's Guide).* Vernon Hills: ETA Cuisenaire.

Brockhoff, Beverly, et al. 1992. *The Maharajas' Tasks: A Problem Solving Unit to Develop Division Concepts.* Beyond Activities Project: Mathematics Replacement Curriculum. Sharon Ross, Project Director. Chico: Department of Mathematics and Statistics, California State University, Chico.

Brookhart, Susan M. 2008. *How to Give Effective Feedback to Your Students.* Alexandria, VA: Association for Supervision and Curriculum Development.

Burns, Marilyn. 1987. *A Collection of Math Lessons from Grades 3–6.* Sausalito, CA: Math Solutions.

———. 1996. *50 Problem-Solving Lessons: The Best from 10 Years of Math Solutions Newsletters.* Sausalito, CA: Math Solutions.

——. 2007. *About Teaching Mathematics: A K–8 Resource.* 3d ed. Sausalito, CA: Math Solutions.

Burns, Marilyn, and Robyn Silbey. 2000. *So You Have to Teach Math? Sound Advice for K–6 Teachers.* Sausalito: Math Solutions.

Burns, Marilyn, and Bonnie Tank. 1987. *A Collection of Math Lessons from Grades 1–3.* Sausalito, CA: Math Solutions.

Butler, Deborah L., and Philip H. Winne. 1995. "Feedback and Self-Regulated Learning: A Theoretical Synthesis." *Review of Educational Research* 65 (3): 245–81.

Butler, Susan M., and Nancy D. McMunn. 2006. *A Teacher's Guide to Classroom Assessment: Understanding and Using Assessment to Improve Student Learning, Grades K–12.* Jossey-Bass Teacher Series. San Francisco, CA: Jossey-Bass.

Carpenter, Thomas P., Elizabeth Fennema, Megan Loef Franke, Linda Levi, and Susan B. Empson. 1999. *Children's Mathematics: Cognitively Guided Instruction.* Portsmouth, NH: Heinemann.

Chapin, Suzanne H., and Art Johnson. 2006. *Math Matters: Understanding the Math You Teach, Grades K–8.* 2d ed. Sausalito, CA: Math Solutions.

Chapin, Suzanne H., Catherine O'Connor, and Nancy C. Anderson. 2003. *Classroom Discussions: Using Math Talk to Help Students Learn, Grades 1–6.* 1st ed. Sausalito, CA: Math Solutions.

——. 2009. *Classroom Discussions: Using Math Talk to Help Students Learn, Grades K–6.* 2d ed. Sausalito, CA: Math Solutions.

Chappuis, Steve, Jan Chappuis, and Rick Stiggins. 2009. "The Quest for Quality." *Educational Leadership* 67 (3): 14–19.

Clarke, David. 1997. *Constructive Assessment in Mathematics: Practical Steps for Classroom Teachers.* Emeryville, CA: Key Curriculum Press.

Clarke, Shirley. 2008. *Active Learning Through Formative Assessment.* London: Hodder Education.

Clements, Douglas H., and Julie Sarama, eds. 2003. *Engaging Young Children in Mathematics: Standards for Early Childhood Mathematics Education.* Mahwah, NJ: Lawrence Erlbaum.

Cohen, Elizabeth G. 1994. *Designing Groupwork: Strategies for the Heterogeneous Classroom.* 2d ed. New York: Teachers College Press.

Cole, Ardith Davis. 2002. *Better Answers: Written Performance That Looks Good and Sounds Smart.* Portland, ME: Stenhouse.

Commission on Standards for School Mathematics, National Council of Teachers of Mathematics. 1989. *Curriculum and Evaluation Standards for School Mathematics.* Reston, VA: National Council of Teachers of Mathematics.

Conklin, Melissa. 2010. *It Makes Sense! Using Ten-Frames to Build Number Sense, Grades K–2.* Sausalito, CA: Math Solutions.

Conklin, Wendy. 2006. *Instructional Strategies for Differentiated Learning.* Huntington Beach, CA: Shell Educational Publishing.

Corwin, Rebecca B., with Judith Storeygard and Sabra L. Price. 1996. *Talking Mathematics: Supporting Children's Voices.* Portsmouth, NH: Heinemann.

Covey, Stephen R. 1989. *The 7 Habits of Highly Effective People: Powerful Lessons in Personal Change.* New York: Simon & Schuster.

Dacey, Linda, and Rebeka Eston. 2002. *Show and Tell: Representing and Communicating Mathematical Ideas in K–2 Classrooms.* Sausalito, CA: Math Solutions.

Dacey, Linda, and Karen Gartland. 2009. *Math for All: Differentiating Instruction, Grades 6–8.* Sausalito, CA: Math Solutions.

Dacey, Linda, and Jayne Bamford Lynch. 2007. *Math for All: Differentiating Instruction, Grades 3–5.* Sausalito, CA: Math Solutions.

Dacey, Linda, and Rebeka Eston Salemi. 2007. *Math for All: Differentiating Instruction, Grades K–2.* Sausalito, CA: Math Solutions.

Depka, Eileen M. 2001. *Designing Rubrics for Mathematics.* Thousand Oaks, CA: Corwin Press.

Developmental Studies Center. 1997. *Blueprints for a Collaborative Classroom.* Oakland, CA: Developmental Studies Center.

Diller, Debbie. 2007. *Making the Most of Small Groups: Differentiation for All.* Portland, ME: Stenhouse; Markham, Ontario: Pembroke Publishers Limited.

Driscoll, Mark, and Jere Confrey. 1986. *Teaching Mathematics: Strategies That Work K–12.* Teachers Writing to Teachers Series. Portsmouth, NH: Heinemann.

Eisenmann, Beth Herbel, and Michelle Cirillo. 2009. *Promoting Purposeful Discourse: Teacher Research in Secondary Math Classrooms.* Reston, VA: National Council of Teachers of Mathematics.

Fisher, Douglas, and Nancy Frey. 2007. *Checking for Understanding: Formative Assessment Techniques for Your Classroom.* Alexandria, VA: Association for Supervision and Curriculum Development.

———. 2009. "Feed Up, Back, Forward." *Educational Leadership* 67 (3): 20–25.

Forsten, Char, Jim Grant, and Betty Hollas. 2002. *Differentiated Instruction: Different Strategies for Different Learners.* Peterborough, NH: Crystal Springs Books.

Frey, Nancy, Douglas Fisher, and Sandi Everlove. 2009. *Productive Group Work: How to Engage Students, Build Teamwork, and Promote Understanding.* Alexandria, VA: Association for Supervision and Curriculum Development.

Fuson, Karen, Douglas Clements, and Sybilla Beckmann. 2010. *Focus in Grade 1: Teaching with Curriculum Focal Points.* Reston, VA: National Council of Teachers of Mathematics.

Gardner, Howard. 1983. *Frames of Mind: The Theory of Multiple Intelligences.* 10th anniversary ed. New York: Basic Books.

Gawronski, Jane D., Anne Collins, Marthe Craig, Mary Eich, Kim Morris, and Karen Aguilar. 2005. *Mathematics Assessment Sampler: Items Aligned with NCTM's Principles and Standards for School Mathematics,* Grades 3–5. Reston, VA: National Council of Teachers of Mathematics.

Gersten, Russell, Sybilla Beckman, Benjamin Clarke, Anne Foegen, Laurel Marsh, Jon R. Star, and Bradley Witzel. 2009. "Assisting Students Struggling with Mathematics: Response to Intervention (RtI) for Elementary and Middle School." Washington, DC: U.S. Department of Education. http://ies.ed.gov/ncee/wwc/publications/practiceguides/.

Glanfield, Florence, William S. Bush, and Jean K. Stenmark. 2003. *Mathematics Assessment: A Practical Handbook for Grades K–2.* Reston, VA: National Council of Teachers of Mathematics.

Graves, Donald H., and Bonnie S. Sunstein, eds. 1992. *Portfolio Portraits.* Portsmouth, NH: Heinemann.

Guskey, Thomas R., ed. 2009a. *Practical Solutions for Serious Problems in Standards-Based Grading.* Thousand Oaks, CA: Corwin Press.

———. 2009b. *The Principal as Assessment Leader.* Bloomington, IN: Solution Tree.

———. 2009c. *The Teacher as Assessment Leader.* Bloomington, IN: Solution Tree.

Hansen, Pia M. 2009. *Mathematics Coaching Handbook: Working with Teachers to Improve Instruction.* Larchmont, NY: Eye on Education.

Hattie, J. A. 1992. "Towards a Model of Schooling: A Synthesis of Meta-Analyses." *Australian Journal of Education* 36: 5–13.

Hattie, John, and Helen Timperley. 2007. "The Power of Feedback." *Review of Educational Research* 77 (1): 81–112.

Heacox, Diane. 2002. *Differentiating Instruction in the Regular Classroom: How to Reach and Teach All Learners, Grades 3–12.* Minneapolis, MN: Free Spirit.

Hiebert, James, Thomas P. Carpenter, Elizabeth Fennema, Karen C. Fuson, Diana Wearne, Hanlie Murray, Alwyn Olivier, and Piet Human. 1997. *Making Sense: Teaching and Learning Mathematics with Understanding.* Portsmouth, NH: Heinemann.

Huinker, DeAnn, Anne Collins, Lynn McGarvey, Gladis Kersaint, and Linda Landin. 2006. *Mathematics Assessment Sampler: Items Aligned with*

NCTM's Principles and Standards for School Mathematics, Pre-K–Grade 2. Reston, VA: National Council of Teachers of Mathematics.

Islas, Dana. 2011. *How to Assess While You Teach Math: Formative Assessment Practices and Lessons, Grades K–2: A Multimedia Professional Learning Resource.* Sausalito, CA: Math Solutions.

Jacobs, Heidi Hayes. 2010. *Curriculum 21: Essential Education for a Changing World.* Alexandria, VA: Association for Supervision and Curriculum Development.

Johnson, David R. 1994. *Motivation Counts: Teaching Techniques That Work, Grades 5–12.* Palo Alto, CA: Dale Seymour.

Joyner, Jeane M. 2002a. *Thinking Algebraically with Numbers and Shapes, Level A: Student Activity Book.* New York: Dale Seymour.

——. 2002b. *Thinking Algebraically with Numbers and Shapes, Level B: Student Activity Book.* New York: Dale Seymour.

Joyner, Jeane M., and Wade H. Sherard III. 2003. *Thinking Algebraically with Numbers and Shapes, Level C: Student Activity Book.* New York: Dale Seymour.

Kenney, Joan M., and Judah L. Schwartz. 2007. *Tasks and Rubrics for Balanced Mathematics Assessment in Primary and Elementary Grades.* Thousand Oaks, CA: Corwin Press.

Krasa, Nancy, and Sara Shunkwiler. 2009. *Number Sense and Number Nonsense: Understanding the Challenges of Learning Math.* Baltimore: Paul H. Brookes Publication Co.

Krathwohl, D. R., B. S. Bloom, and B. B. Masia. 1970. *Taxonomy of Educational Objectives: The Classification of Educational Goals (Handbook II: Affective Domain).* New York: David McKay.

Krulik, Stephen, and Jesse A. Rudnick. 2002. *Roads to Reasoning: Grades 2, 3, 4, 5.* Chicago: Wright Group.

Leahy, Siobhan, Christine Lyon, Marnie Thompson, and Dylan Wiliam. 2005. "Classroom Assessment: Minute by Minute, Day by Day." *Educational Leadership* 63 (3): 18–24.

Leinwand, Steven. 2009. *Accessible Mathematics: Ten Instructional Shifts That Raise Student Achievement.* Portsmouth, NH: Heinemann.

Lilburn, Pat, and Alex Ciurak. 2010. *Investigations, Tasks, and Rubrics to Teach and Assess Math, Grades 1–6.* Sausalito, CA: Math Solutions.

Lilburn, Pat, and Pam Rawson. 1994. *Let's Talk Math: Encouraging Children to Explore Ideas.* Portsmouth, NH: Heinemann.

Ma, Liping. 1999. *Knowing and Teaching Elementary Mathematics.* Mahwah, NJ: Lawrence Erlbaum.

Mager, R. F. 1962. *Preparing Instructional Objectives.* Palo Alto, CA: Fearon Publishers.

Marzano, Robert J. 2009. *Formative Assessment and Standards-Based Grading.* The Classroom Strategies Series. Bloomington, IN: Solution Tree and Marzano Research Laboratory.

Mathematical Sciences Education Board and National Research Council. 1993. *Measuring Up: Prototypes for Mathematics Assessment.* Washington, DC: The National Academies Press.

McNamara, Julie, and Meghan M. Shaughnessy. 2010. *Beyond Pizzas and Pies: 10 Essential Strategies for Supporting Fraction Sense, Grades 3–5.* Sausalito, CA: Math Solutions.

Myren, Christina. 1995. *Posing Open-Ended Questions in the Primary Classroom.* San Leandro, CA: Watten/Poe Teaching Resource Center.

National Council of Teachers of Mathematics. 1991. *Professional Standards for Teaching Mathematics.* Reston, VA: National Council of Teachers of Mathematics.

———. 1995. *Assessment Standards for School Mathematics.* Reston, VA: National Council of Teachers of Mathematics.

———. 2000. *Principles and Standards for School Mathematics.* Reston, VA: National Council of Teachers of Mathematics.

———. 2007a. Assessment *Research Brief: Five "Key Strategies" for Effective Formative Assessment.* Reston, VA: National Council of Teachers of Mathematics.

———. 2007b. *Research Brief: Formative Assessment Benefits* and *Research Clip: Formative Assessment Key Strategies.* Reston, VA: National Council of Teachers of Mathematics.

National Research Council. 2001a. *Adding It Up: Helping Children Learn Mathematics,* edited by Jeremy Kilpatrick, Jane Swafford, and Bradford Findell. Mathematics Learning Study Committee, Center for Education, Division of Behavioral and Social Sciences and Education. Washington, DC: The National Academies Press.

———. 2001b. *Knowing What Students Know: The Science and Design of Educational Assessment.* Committee on the Foundations of Assessment, edited by James W. Pellegrino, Naomi Chudowsky, and Robert Glaser. Board on Testing and Assessment, Center for Education. Division of Behavioral and Social Sciences and Education. Washington, DC: The National Academies Press.

———. 2005. *How Students Learn: Mathematics in the Classroom.* Committee on *How People Learn, A Targeted Report for Teachers,* edited by M. Suzanne Donovan and John D. Bransford. Division of Behavioral and Social Sciences and Education. Washington, DC: The National Academies Press.

Nichols, Beverly, Sue Shidaker, Gene Johnson, and Kevin Singer. 2006. *Managing Curriculum and Assessment: A Practitioner's Guide.* Santa Barbara, CA: Linworth Books.

Ogle, Donna M. 1986. "K-W-L: A Teaching Model That Develops Active Reading of Expository Text." *Reading Teacher* 39 (6): 564–70.

Parker, Ruth E. 1993. *Mathematical Power: Lessons from a Classroom.* Portsmouth, NH: Heinemann.

Parrish, Sherry. 2010. *Number Talks: Helping Children Build Mental Math and Computation Strategies, Grades K–5: A Multimedia Professional Learning Resource.* Sausalito, CA: Math Solutions.

Popham, W. James. 2008. *Transformative Assessment*. Alexandria, VA: Association for Supervision and Curriculum Development.

Reeves, Douglas B. 2004. *Accountability for Learning: How Teachers and School Leaders Can Take Charge*. Alexandria, VA: Association for Supervision and Curriculum Development.

——, ed. 2007. *Ahead of the Curve: The Power of Assessment to Transform Teaching and Learning*. Bloomington, IN: Solution Tree.

——. 2010. *Transforming Professional Development into Student Results*. Alexandria, VA: Association for Supervision and Curriculum Development.

Reys, Robert E., Mary M. Lindquist, Diana V. Lambdin, and Nancy L. Smith. 2009. *Helping Children Learn Mathematics*. 9th ed. Hoboken, NJ: John Wiley & Sons.

Richardson, Kathy. 2003a. *Assessing Math Concepts, Book 2: Changing Numbers*. Bellingham, WA: Math Perspectives.

——. 2003b. *Assessing Math Concepts, Book 9: Two-Digit Addition and Subtraction*. Bellingham, WA: Math Perspectives.

Romberg, Thomas A., John G. Harvey, and the Wisconsin Research and Development Center for Cognitive Learning, University of Wisconsin. 1974. *Developing Mathematical Processes: Resource Manual, Topics 1–40*. Chicago: Rand McNally.

Rose, Cheryl M., Leslie Minton, and Carolyn Arline. 2007. *Uncovering Student Thinking in Mathematics: 25 Formative Assessment Probes*. Thousand Oaks, CA: Corwin Press.

Shulman, Judith H., Rachel A. Lotan, and Jennifer A. Whitcomb, eds. 1998. *Facilitator's Guide to Groupwork in Diverse Classrooms: A Casebook for Educators*. New York: Teachers College Press.

Silver, Harvey F., Richard W. Strong, and Matthew J. Perini. 2000. *So Each May Learn: Integrating Learning Styles and Multiple Intelligences*. Alexandria, VA: Association for Supervision and Curriculum Development.

Skinner, Penny. 1999. *It All Adds Up! Engaging 8-to-12-Year-Olds in Math Investigations*. Sausalito, CA: Math Solutions.

Small, Marian. 2009. *Good Questions: Great Ways to Differentiate Mathematics Instruction*. New York: Teachers College Press.

———. 2010. "Beyond One Right Answer." *Educational Leadership* 68 (1): 28–32.

Stake, Robert E. 2004. *Standards-Based and Responsive Evaluation*. Thousand Oaks, CA: Sage Publications.

Steen, Lynn Arthur, ed. 1990. *On the Shoulders of Giants: New Approaches to Numeracy*. Washington, DC: The National Academies Press.

Stenmark, Jean Kerr. 1991. *Mathematics Assessment: Myths, Models, Good Questions, and Practical Suggestions*. Reston, VA: National Council of Teachers of Mathematics.

———. 1994. *Assessment Alternatives in Mathematics: An Overview of Assessment Techniques That Promote Learning*. Prepared by EQUALS and the Assessment Committee of the California Mathematics Council. Berkeley: University of California, Lawrence Hall of Science.

Stenmark, Jean Kerr, and William S. Bush. 2001. *Mathematics Assessment: A Practical Handbook for Grades 3–5*. Reston, VA: National Council of Teachers of Mathematics.

Stevens, Dannelle D., and Antonia Levi. 2005. *Introduction to Rubrics: An Assessment Tool to Save Grading Time, Convey Effective Feedback and Promote Student Learning*. Sterling, VA: Stylus Publishing.

Stiggins, Richard J., Judith A. Arter, Jan Chappuis, and Stephen Chappuis. 2006. *Classroom Assessment for Student Learning: Doing It Right—Using It Well*. Boston, MA: Allyn & Bacon.

Stigler, James W., and James Hiebert. 1999. *The Teaching Gap: Best Ideas from the World's Teachers for Improving Education in the Classroom*. New York: Free Press.

Sullivan, Peter, and Pat Lilburn. 2002. *Good Questions for Math Teaching: Why Ask Them and What to Ask, Grades K–6*. Sausalito, CA: Math Solutions.

Sutton, John, and Alice Krueger, eds. 2002. *EDThoughts: What We Know About Mathematics Teaching and Learning*. Aurora, CO: Mid-Continent Research for Education and Learning.

Taylor-Cox, Jennifer. 2009. *Math Intervention: Building Number Power with Formative Assessments, Differentiation, and Games, Grades 3–5*. Larchmont, NY: Eye On Education.

Tomlinson, Carol Ann. 2001. *How to Differentiate Instruction in Mixed-Ability Classrooms*. 2d ed. Alexandria, VA: Association for Supervision and Curriculum Development.

———. 2003. *Fulfilling the Promise of the Differentiated Classroom: Strategies and Tools for Responsive Teaching*. Alexandria, VA: Association for Supervision and Curriculum Development.

———. 2004. *The Differentiated Classroom: Responding to the Needs of All Learners*. Alexandria, VA: Association for Supervision and Curriculum Development.

Tomlinson, Carol Ann, and Jay McTighe. 2006. *Integrating Differentiated Instruction and Understanding by Design: Connecting Content and Kids*. Alexandria, VA: Association for Supervision and Curriculum Development.

Tough, Paul. 2010. "Bill Gates: The Parade Interview: What I've Learned About Great Teachers." *Parade Magazine* (October 24). www.parade.com/news/2010/10/24-bill-gates-what-ive-learned-about-great-teachers.html.

Van de Walle, John A., and Lou Ann H. Lovin. 2006a. *Teaching Student-Centered Mathematics: Grades K–3*. Boston, MA: Allyn & Bacon.

———. 2006b. *Teaching Student-Centered Mathematics: Grades 5–8*. Boston, MA: Allyn & Bacon.

Weiss, Iris R., Joan D. Pasley, P. Sean Smith, Eric R. Banilower, and Daniel J. Heck. 2003. *Looking Inside the Classroom: A Study of K–12 Mathematics and Science Education in the United States*. Chapel Hill, NC: Horizon Research, Inc.

West, Lucy, and Fritz C. Staub. 2003. *Content-Focused Coaching: Transforming Mathematics Lessons.* Portsmouth, NH: Heinemann.

WestEd. 2010. "Formative Assessment: Not Just Another Test." *R&D Alert* 11 (2): 18–21.

Wheatley, Grayson. 1992. "The Role of Reflection in Mathematics Learning." *Educational Studies in Mathematics* 23 (5): 529–41.

Wiggins, Grant P., and Jay McTighe. 2000. *Understanding by Design.* 2d expanded ed. Alexandria, VA: Association for Supervision and Curriculum Development.

Wiliam, Dylan, and Marnie Thompson. 2007. "Integrating Assessment with Instruction: What Will It Take to Make It Work?" In *The Future of Assessment: Shaping, Teaching, and Learning,* edited by Carol Ann Dwyer, pp. 53–84. Mahwah, NJ: Lawrence Erlbaum.

Wilkins, Michelle M., Jesse L. M. Wilkins, and Tamra Oliver. 2006. "Differentiating the Curriculum for Elementary Gifted Mathematics Students." *Teaching Children Mathematics* 13 (1): 6–13.

Yagi, Seanyelle, and Melfried Olson. 2007. "Math by the Month: Supermarket Math." *Teaching Children Mathematics* 13 (7): 376–77.

Index

About the Authors

Jeane M. Joyner (right) has taught preschool through college courses. Before retiring from the North Carolina Department of Public Instruction, she was the elementary mathematics consultant and a classroom assessment consultant. Jeane served as the Co-Principal Investigator for a number of National Science Foundation projects and Mathematics–Science Partnership projects. Jeane is currently a Research Associate in the Department of Mathematics and Computer Science at Meredith College and is a past president of the North Carolina Council of Teachers of Mathematics.

Mari Muri (left) was an elementary classroom teacher before becoming the math instructional consultant in her Killingly, Connecticut, district. She then served as mathematics curriculum consultant for fifteen years at the Connecticut Department of Education. For many years she taught university-level elementary math courses and has provided professional develop for elementary teachers for over twenty-five years. Mari has served on the Board of Directors of the National Council of Teachers of Mathematics, National Council of Supervisors of Mathematics, and U.S. Math Recovery.

Continued from page iv

The publisher would like to thank those who gave permission to reprint borrowed material:

Pages 229–32: "Asking Questions" reprinted with permission. *Assessment Alternatives in Mathematics: An Overview of Assessment Techniques That Promote Learning.* Berkeley: University of California, Berkeley, Lawrence Hall of Science, 1994.

Page 299: "Research Brief: Formative Assessment: Benefits" and "Research Clip: Formative Assessment: Key Strategies" are reprinted with permission by the National Council of Teachers of Mathematics, copyright 2007. All rights reserved.

The publisher would like to acknowledge adapted material:

Pages 21, 22, and 44: Fifth-grade problem is adapted from the Hawaii Algebra Learning Project.

Pages 218 and 235: *The Kings' Melons Problem* is adapted from *The Maharajas' Tasks: A Problem Solving Unit to Develop Division Concepts* by Beverly Brockhoff et al., Beyond Activities Project: Mathematics Replacement Curriculum. Sharon Ross, Project Director. Chico: Department of Mathematics and Statistics, California State University, Chico, 1992.

Pages 227 and 240: Problem 2 is adapted from "Math by the Month: Supermarket Math" by Seanyelle Yagi and Melfried Olson. © 2007 *Teaching Children Mathematics* 13 (7): 376–377.

Pages 229–32: "Questions for Many Mathematical Purposes" table is adapted from *Assessment Alternatives in Mathematics*, a booklet by Jean Kerr Stenmark and prepared by the California Mathematics Council and EQUALS, 1994.